DARKER
SHADES
of BLUE

Other McGraw-Hill Aviation Titles

Lewis Bjork
PILOTING FOR MAXIMUM PERFORMANCE

Robert N. Buck
WEATHER FLYING, 4TH EDITION

Jerry A. Eichenberger
YOUR PILOT'S LICENSE

Tony Kern
REDEFINING AIRMANSHIP
FLIGHT DISCIPLINE

Shari Stamford Krause
AIRCRAFT SAFETY: ACCIDENT INVESTIGATIONS, ANALYSES, AND APPLICATIONS

Wolfgang Lanewiesche
STICK AND RUDDER: AN EXPLANATION OF THE ART OF FLYING

Michael C. Love
BETTER TAKEOFFS AND LANDINGS

John F. Welch, Editor
VAN SICKLE'S MODERN AIRMANSHIP, 7TH EDITION

Richard L. Taylor
INSTRUMENT FLYING, 4TH EDITION

DARKER SHADES
of BLUE

The Rogue Pilot

TONY KERN

McGraw-Hill

New York   San Francisco   Washington, D.C.   Auckland   Bogatá
Caracas   Lisbon   London   Madrid   Mexico City   Milan
Montreal   New Delhi   San Juan   Singapore
Sidney   Tokyo   Toronto

Library of Congress Cataloging-in-Publication Data

Kern, Anthony T.
    Darker shades of blue : the rogue pilot / Anthony T. Kern.
      p.   cm.
    Includes index.
    ISBN 0-07-034927-4
    1. Air pilots—Psychology.   2. Airplanes—Piloting—Human factors.
  3. Self-control. I. Title.
  TL555.K4697   1999
  629.132'52'019—dc21   98-43508
                                     CIP

McGraw-Hill

A Division of The McGraw·Hill Companies

1 2 3 4 5 6 7 8 9 0 DOC/DOC 9 0 4 3 2 1 0 9

ISBN 0-07-034927-4

Printed and bound by R. R. Donnelley & Sons Company.

McGraw-Hill books are available at special quantity discounts to use as premiums and sales promotions, or for use in corporate training programs. For more information, please write to the Director of Special Sales, McGraw-Hill, 11 West 19th Street, New York, NY 10011. Or contact your local bookstore.

This book is printed on recycled, acid-free paper containing a minimum of 50% recycled de-inked fiber.

To Dr. Alan Diehl,
a great American and
pursuer of truth.

Contents

Foreword

Hi. My name is Skip, and I am a rogue pilot. If that sounds a bit like the start of a 12-step program called "Rogue Pilots Anonymous," maybe it should. When Tony approached me to write this, I was a little taken back. Me—a rogue? No way! I've never broken a jet or injured anybody. And besides, who was he to judge me? I'm twice the pilot Kern ever though of being! But as I read through his manuscript, and saw the definition of a rogue, I began to ask myself a few questions. If, as the author suggests, "a pilot is as a pilot does," and if flying unnecessarily low to impress friends and challenge your own limits is a rogue act—then I am—or at least have been on several occasions—a rogue.

Flying has always been an adventure to me, but I get bored quickly with the mundane. As I read through Chapter 1, the part about the perceived need to expand our personal envelopes by chasing fictitious characters like *Top Gun*'s legendary Maverick, I saw that the way I have tried to expand my personal envelope may have been inappropriate. But I had no other ideas at the time. Tighter formations, lower passes, more aggressive traffic patterns—that's what pilots brag about. I thought it must be what was important. Lately, however, I've begun to have second thoughts. I'm getting past my denial.

I guess my recovery began when I read Tony's first book, *Redefining Airmanship*. For the first time in my 16-year aviation career, I had standards to shoot for beyond the ridiculously easy numerical standards and examinations required for my annual flight evals. If you haven't read *Airmanship*, you need to, although there is a nice synopsis of it in the last chapter of this book. Understanding what airmanship is came easy for me. I'm a bright guy. But *practicing* it, now that was a horse of a different color.

I found the disciplined approach to flying difficult, if not impossible, for me. I had 16 years of apathy working against me and I had given up on the idea of studying about 15 years ago. I saw myself as way past the "education and training" stage. I have been flying commercially for a major carrier and with the Air Force Reserve—two pretty professional organizations—for some time. I haul in a pretty hefty paycheck. Whey should I go back and study? What was in it for me?

My conversion began in earnest when I lost a close friend in a mishap that should not have happened. Kirk was an experienced instructor pilot who somehow forgot an elementary procedure and flew a very expensive multiengine aircraft into the ground, killing himself and three other crewmembers. We were all shocked, and it caused me to review how I approached this whole game. I have always separated my flying into business and pleasure. When I'm flying for the company or Uncle Sam, I play it pretty much by the rules, but when I'm out in my private aircraft, I often cut loose. But after Kirk died, I took a hard look at all of my flying preparation—and found myself lacking in several areas. I also started to recognize my own rogue attitudes and behaviors.

Darker Shades of Blue is an insightful look into flyers like me, or at least like I used to be. It has some great stories, but perhaps more important are the lessons behind the stories. The author is a professor of history at one of the nation's elite military academies, and his expertise in this area shows. His analysis of the early barnstormers ("When Rogues Were Required," Chapter 3) makes it clear that what we now call rogue behavior was a prerequisite at one time to nudge aviation into the next era. He also points out that this era has long since passed, but the siren song for rogue behavior still plays in the heads of many modern day aviators. Modern aviators, Kern says, look correctly to the courageous aviators of yesteryear as role models, but fail to account for the changing situation—a point that it takes a practiced historian to bring into perspective.

I think there are more pilots like me (rogues) than most people care to know about. Stories abound about pilots who step over the line, most told by the pilots themselves. I understand from talking to Tony that many in the academic community think this rogue issue is overplayed, that there are so few as to make a discussion of them meaningless. I disagree. Not only are there numerous rogues in every arena of flight operations, but the damage—to innocent lives as well as to the reputation and bottom line of a business or organization—that can be done by a single rogue makes the issue a front-burner challenge for the entire aviation community.

Having bared my soul to the group, I return to the cockpit—perhaps not cured of my rogue behaviors, but recovering one day at a time, thanks in large part to having read *Darker Shades of Blue*. Enjoy the book. It's a good read and an insightful look into the minds of some wild dudes.

Skip
A recovering rogue

Preface

In the winter of 1981, I graduated from U.S. Air Force Undergraduate Pilot Training. It climaxed a year of intensive study of everything associated with aviation. I thought I had been exposed to everything there could possibly be. I was sadly mistaken. Throughout my career I have bumped up against rogue pilots who, for one reason or another, could not take a disciplined approach to my chosen profession. This group has always deeply offended me for their lack of professionalism and their disregard for the safety of others. I will make no attempt to hide that bias here.

In love to fly airplanes. In fact, as I look back on my life, the decision I made to become a pilot was one of the most significant things I have ever done. I'd probably put it third on my list of great decisions, right behind accepting the Lord and choosing my lovely wife. I have pursued excellence in aviation for nearly 20 years now, and I have *never* lost my respect for the sky. I always keep in mind the thousands of ways I can screw up, and I want to keep my takeoffs-and-landings total to an even number. Let me share a quick story about that equation that has always kept it fresh in my mind.

When I was younger, I had an occasion to go into a lieutenant colonel's office, at a base I had been newly assigned to, on some issues pertaining to new taxi routes for the squadron. I think he was in charge of airfield management or something like that. I knocked at his outer door, requested permission to enter, and was invited in to sit down.

As I walked in I noticed a handsome but weathered gray-haired gentleman in his late forties sitting behind a large government-style desk.

The first thing I noticed when I entered was the command pilot wings on his chest, meaning he had spent most of his career behind a stick and a throttle, not a desk. I made a mental note that I did not want to end my Air Force career pushing paper instead of burning jet fuel. The second thing I noticed was a couple of color photographs on the wall behind his desk. The first was a picture of an F-15 taking off in full afterburner. It appeared to have been taken out of some European base on a foggy morning, the sun just coming up in the background and vapor trails streaming off the wingtips. It was really a beautiful shot.

As we spoke about the changes in the taxi procedures, I couldn't help but keep glancing past the man at the pictures behind him. He noticed but didn't say anything, so I pressed on with our business.

The second picture was odd. It appeared to be a big patch of burned grass next to a lake—no—it was more than that, it was a big crater with an extensive charred area around it, and what looked like shards of glass and metal.

"The proverbial smokin' hole, son."

"Sir?" I responded, now completely embarrassed to be caught gazing at the wall in the middle of a military discussion. I hadn't noticed, but there were two small wooden plaques sharing the wall, one just below each picture. They appeared to be blank. The colonel leaned back in his chair and tapped the cover of each of the small plaques, which immediately fell down on small hinges to reveal the simple inscriptions behind them. On the left, beneath the beautiful photo of the Eagle, it read, *My Last Takeoff.* Underneath the picture of the charred hole, it said—you guessed it—*My Last Landing.*

The colonel must have known that I would be too embarrassed to ask, so he went right into the story. It seems that he and his archrival buddy in the fighter squadron, both of whom were high-time instructor pilots, had a few minutes to spare on the way home from a short deployment and decided to "mix it up" a bit in the local military operating area (MOA). Because the MOA was small and because they were low on fuel, they agreed not to use afterburner during any of the manuevering. The first one to "tap the burner" was the loser. "Fight's on!" After about 90 seconds of mock dogfighting, the colonel related they both went "into the vertical," and airspeed was dropping fast. The first to fall out of the climb would be at the mercy of the other. Pressing well past common sense, the pilot pushed the Eagle past its aerodynamic limits, snapped out of controlled flight and into a spin. The afterburner would likely have saved him at the top, but that would be admitting defeat. After several unsuccessful recovery attempts, he ejected just barely in time to get a full chute. He said he experienced "a few leg and back injuries."

I thanked him for his candor and we completed our business on the taxi routes. As I stood to let myself out of the office, the final lesson of the day was delivered. As the senior officer got up to shake my hand, he stood with the assistance of a stout cane that he kept behind his desk. As he walked me to the door, I saw that he moved with a significant limp and apparently a great deal of pain, judging from the controlled grimace on his face.

"How long ago did this happen, Sir?" I inquired.

"Let's see, I think it was seven years ago this spring."

This man hadn't chosen to end his career pushing a desk, a bad decision in the air had made it the only option left. I've never forgotten that moment, and I suspect that's why he kept the pictures and the captions where he did, to pass the lesson on to young guys like me who thought they were bulletproof.

Nope. I've never lost my respect for flying, but I have lost respect for some flyers, and that is what this book is about. I know that not everyone is cut out to be a pilot. I doubted myself on this concern for quite some time, and although my instructors never told me, I'm dead certain they had to wonder about my suitability to drive government jets. My learning curve was—and is—a bit flatter than most pilots'. I know my strengths. I know my weaknesses. Most important, though, I know my limitations.

One of these limitations is my competitive spirit. Throughout my career in sports, flying, and in life in general—I play to win. Just enjoying the game has never been enough for me. If someone is keeping score, I want to finish first, and even when no one is keeping score, I usually have a running tally in the back of my head. It's a character flaw I hope to conquer someday, but I haven't yet. What does this have to do with flying? I think many of you already know.

If I am ever to drift over the line into rogue behavior, I think it will be a result of trying to outperform someone else, just like the colonel. I'm not a show-off or a daredevil. Adrenaline rushes scare me—they certainly don't excite me. I harbor no secret ambitions to be a Blue Angel. But put me in a competitive situation, and . . . it could be me with the cane, or worse.

I hope that this book helps all pilots who read it to accomplish the same sort of self-analysis. I say this because I truly believe that a rogue lurks inside many—if not all—of us. In some cases it lies just beneath the surface, like with me. In other cases, I suspect that it will come forward slowly, through progressive deviations or poor role models. The collections of essays and case studies that follow are all true, down to the last detail. They are designed to introduce the concept of rogue behavior and rogue pilots, the first defining the latter.

I have striven mightily to keep the analysis and footnoting to a minimum, but those who know me or have read my previous books know that at the core of my soul I am a teacher. For this I make no apologies. My greatest fear when writing this book was that it would come off as a collection of stories about dumb aviators, and that I would be accused of wagging a condescending finger of blame at dead pilots, most of whom I did not know. That was certainly not my purpose, and to protect their memories and their families, I have chosen to use pseudonyms throughout.

In point of fact, I have now lost 14 friends and acquaintances to aviation fatalities. Most were my equal or better in terms of flying skill. Although we don't like to admit it, pilots all tend to second-guess the actions of a peer who drove one in. It's in our very nature to do so, and I think it is healthy as long as we learn from others' mistakes and retain that respect for flying that I spoke of in the first paragraph.

This book contains a good amount of anecdotal material. I did this for two reasons. First, I hope it makes for more effective and entertaining reading. The second—and more important—reason is to use these stories to provide clues to the nature of the rogue pilot. The ultimate aim of this book is not to provide the definitive definition or description of the rogue, although I offer both in the pages that follow. If it stirs a debate between a few pilots, or challenges some researchers to look closer at the phenomena, I will have succeeded in what I have set out to do. Most of all, I ask the reader not to overreact to the stories within. Most pilots exercise sound judgment, but you will never get that impression from the stories here! You are about to be introduced to some of the wildest guys and gals who ever strapped an airplane to their butt, and some—like the good colonel—who may have just been a rogue once for a few fleeting seconds. After reading this book, you may be tempted to look at all pilots with more suspicion. Don't. Respect the flight environment, but don't fear it. The greater risk is within.

Tony Kern

Contributors

Alan Diehl
Doug Edwards
Noel Fulton
"Skip"

Introduction

"CAN YOU DO THAT in your airplane, Daddy?" my son asked as Thunderbird #3 pointed his F-16 toward the sky and did a series of aileron rolls, trailing smoke. The air show crowd oohed and ahed their approval. "No," I replied simply, not yet prepared to go into the multiple aspects of flight and flyers that his simple question begged answers for. To my six-year-old son, the pilot of that Falcon was a superman. To me, as a fellow military tactical aviator, he was a precise machine operator, rapidly scanning and adjusting multiple flight parameters. To the high school Civil Air Patrol member beside us, who was proudly dressed in his military-style uniform, the Thunderbird pilot was an inspiration for the future.

But for many pilots in attendance, I knew that the breathtaking maneuver they had just witnessed had somehow impinged on their self-images as pilots. To this group of flyers, the marvelous precision of the military demonstration pilot issued a challenge to their egos. They would have answered my son's simple question—*"Can you do that in your airplane, Daddy?"*—much differently. They would have replied, *"Not yet."* They are the rogues, and although most of us don't like to think about it, we share the sky with this breed of misfit pilot every day. On occasion, *we are the rogues.*

Most pilots are safe most of the time. They understand risk management far better than the public at large does. A host of statistical evidence suggests that flying is safer than many other modes of transportation. But lost in the mass of numbers that generate these statistics is the story of a splinter group of pilots who cannot—or will not—control their unsafe practices and impulses. These undisciplined men and women account for a disproportionate number of accidents and incidents. If they killed only themselves with their antics, most of us would see it as an improvement in the gene pool, one through which the survival of the fittest would eventually purge our ranks of this undisciplined subspecies of pilot. But these pilots don't just hurt themselves. Far too often the result of an act of poor flight discipline results in the death of innocents, and for this reason alone we cannot rely on natural selection to rid us of the rogue pilot.

The Last Trip up the Mountain

The skies were clear and the winds were light—a great day for skiing at Dolomite Mountain in central Italy. It was a cool but not bitterly cold February morning, and many European tourists and even a few locals had decided to try their luck on the snow-covered slopes. A group of 20 waited their turn to catch a lift on the gondola for another crack at the excellent powder. As they climbed aboard, they had no way of knowing that this was to be their last trip, for they were about to cross paths with a pilot who decided that today he did not feel like following the rules. As the lift approached the halfway point on the mountain, a military EA-6B electronic warfare plane screamed into view, flying at less than half of the legally required altitude.

The intent of the pilot may never be known, but some local residents say it was not unusual for military aircraft to fly *under* the cables that supported and moved the gondola. As the aircraft sped across the ski area, its tail ripped through the two-inch cable—and 20 innocent skiers spent the last five seconds of their lives in abject terror as they plunged to their deaths on the rocks below. Less than 48 hours later a defense department spokesperson stated, "It's going to take several days to sort this out . . . but we cannot dispute that tragic recklessness may have caused the disaster."[1] We will look into this tragedy in more detail later in the book.

Rogue Pilots or Rogue Behavior?

Even good pilots go bad. In my research for this book, I found numerous examples of ordinarily disciplined pilots stepping over the line into undisciplined and dangerous rogue behaviors. This led me to ask the question, "Are there really such creatures as rogue pilots, or are we all capable of these types of behaviors, given the right set of circumstances?" The answer I uncovered was frightening. Simply stated, both are true. There are certainly a few aviators who routinely violate rules, procedures, air traffic control (ATC) instructions, and common sense without necessity. Their motivations for doing so are varied. Perhaps more frequently, I found aviators who suffered from what the literature describes as "sudden losses of judgment," during which these pilots would, without warning, do the most bizarre things. In one example, an instructor pilot at a small firm in Texas was flying with his boss, a Federal Aviation Administration (FAA) flight examiner—a situation commonly referred to as a "brother-in-law check"—on a recurrent evaluation. During the last traffic pattern, he suddenly accelerated on base leg, and instead of making a left turn to final, he pulled the nose up 70 degrees, rolled to the right *and did a cloverleaf to final approach!* The close connection to the check pilot hurt more than helped, as our would-be Blue Angel was looking for a new job the next morning. When his former boss asked him why he had attempted such a foolish stunt, his only reply was, "I don't know, I guess I always wanted to do that." Go figure.

Perhaps the most frightening finding of this research was the discovery that there are actually *rogue organizations* that encourage undisciplined behaviors. In some cases the motivation is profit or mission-oriented. In other cases, it is just a culture of noncompliance that develops over time. We will look at each of these phenomena in detail later in the book.

This book delivers a powerful historical description of rogues in aviation, individuals who are capable—and willing—to risk their own personal safety, as well as the safety of the general public at large, for personal gain. Often peer pressure is not sufficient to curb the rogue. The English philosopher C. S. Lewis points out that, once the advanced stage of pride and ego are reached, little can be done. He calls this "the real black, diabolical pride [that] comes when you look down on others so much that you no longer care what they think of you."[2] So how are we to deal with the rogue?

This book proposes to contribute to personal and organizational health and development in four ways. The first purpose is to provide a holistic description of rogue aviators, in order that we might recognize them (us?) when we see them. Only then can we take action. The second purpose is to describe the particular hazards posed by the rogue in aviation, whereby lapses of judgment and discipline often play out in the most tragic ways, as we have already seen in the example. Unfortunately, there are more examples like this in the pages that follow. Third, the book looks at organizational implications and hazards posed by these individuals in terms of safety, lost profit, and organizational survival. The final role of this book is to describe strategies to *prevent* the dangers posed by rogue aviators, while simultaneously managing intellectual and creative resources in a positive manner. Mostly, though, it's just to read. I've tried to tell the stories in an entertaining way, while still grappling with the inevitable tragedy that aircraft mishaps invariably involve.

In short, the goal of this book is to help individuals and organizations create safeguards without stifling creativity or innovation in the process. Flying is fun. We want to keep it that way. But it can be fun and safe at the same time. In point of fact, flying must be safe to be fun. It is hoped that after reading this book, you will help reduce unnecessary risk in aviation by putting the vital information in the hands of those who have their hands on the controls—pilots and organizational leaders.

The Organization of This Book

The first half of this book details the results of a historical research project, which identified common traits of rogue aviators. This analysis scrutinized the personality characteristics, habit patterns, and actions of individuals who, for personal reasons, caused disproportionate damage to themselves, others, or their organizations. Using historical case studies, this section details the common behavioral patterns of the typical rogue inside and outside of aviation and presents the findings in an analytical summary of common characteristics. Common characteristics are described, illustrating that aviators are not alone in this challenge and that tools for addressing the problem of the rogue can be brought in from disciplines outside of aviation.

The book's final section details preventative and corrective actions available to individuals and organizations in assessing the danger of falling victim to a rogue pilot. It outlines strategies for developing healthy organizational culture and climate, and looks at the role of pilot attitudes. Special attention is given to sensing the state of the institutional climate, with an emphasis on highlighting high-risk individuals and areas of the organization as a whole.

This book is grounded in established organizational psychology and management methods, as well as a small dose of educational theory. In spite of this solid theoretical grounding, this book is meant for the lay reader and aviation enthusiast.

Chapter Summaries

Chapter 1, "The Rogue Unmasked," identifies the concept of the rogue aviator and whom it affects, (student pilots, certified pilots, aviation managers, aviation CEOs/culture creators). Additionally, it defines what a rogue is, as opposed to merely an unconventional aviator. Case studies from other fields bring together a set of common rogue characteristics.

Chapter 2, "The Quintessential Rogue," uses an actual case study from military aviation to bring the rogue to life. A brief analysis of leadership and followership issues fleshes out the identification features and definitions from Chapter 1.

Chapter 3, "When Rogues Were Required," discusses the period in aviation history when rogues were necessary to push aviation to the next level. The chapter looks at several of these early rogues in detail and then is careful to point out that the situation that at the time required rogue behavior no long exists today.

Chapter 4, "Discovering a Rogue: An Accident Investigator's Sobering Journey," looks at the rogue through the eyes and mind of an Australian accident investigator, who uncovers a classic rogue during the investigation of a fatal mishap. A tragic and ironic twist at the end of the chapter reminds us all of the power of a role model—especially a bad one.

Chapter 5, "Valery Chkalov: Russian Rogue," continues the international theme from Chapter 4 with this gripping story of the life of a communist rogue before and during the Cold War. It illustrates that, even when their political ideologies are diametrically opposed, rogues share very common tendencies.

Chapter 6, "Special Mission Rogues," posits that there are some types of flying that are inherently dangerous, and that agricultural pilots and firefighters are prime candidates for rogue behaviors. It concludes with a far less likely scenario from the normally conservative Civil Air Patrol.

Chapter 7, "The Failing Aviator," provides an in-depth look at everyday factors that can build up to create a rogue out of anyone. Once again several interesting case studies—including the story of a commercial airline pilot described as a "rage-a-holic"—tie the theoretical to the practical world of flight. This chapter shows the danger that any one of us can become a rogue, given enough stress and the wrong set of circumstances.

Chapter 8, "One-Act Rogues," may be the most controversial chapter in the book. The author makes his case that good pilots go bad with all-too-frequent regularity. Case studies of model airmen who suddenly and without warning slip into rogue behaviors warn us all of the ever present danger of poor judgment.

Chapter 9, "Bad Attitudes," looks at the hazards posed by bad attitudes in the cockpit. Real-world examples illustrate the classic hazardous attitudes of *pressing, mission hacking, the take-a-look syndrome, macho attitudes*, and *complacency*. Cues for recognition and corrective actions are also provided.

Chapter 10, "The Rogue Organization," shows how an entire organization can go bad. Two case studies illustrate two different causes for organizational ineptitude. Additionally, this chapter demonstrates to the average aviator how he or she can personally impact flight discipline within an organization in several ways. The first step is to be knowledgeable about rogue behaviors. After this is accomplished, individual aviators can impact others through peer pressure or simply by "voting with their feet"—or by refusing to fly with or near known rogues. This is surprisingly effective with small and large organizations alike, as it forces the organization to take notice of a hazardous situation.

Chapter 11, "What to Do About the Rogue?," summarizes the book by putting the problem of the rogue aviator in the larger perspective of good airmanship. Using historical case studies juxtaposed with modern failures, we see that roguism and its antithesis, solid airmanship, have coexisted since the dawn of flight. This book's analysis provides the tools to finally rid ourselves of the dark side of airmanship, represented by the rogue aviator.

How to Read This Book

This book can be read from front to back, from back to front, or from the inside out. The only prerequisite is to read and understand Chapter 1, so that you have a grasp of the author's definition of the rogue. But even without the definition, the messages come through loud and clear, so sit back, open it up, and enjoy.

CHAPTER ONE

The Rogue Unmasked

ROGUE AVIATORS KILL, and they often kill innocent folks who just happen to get into the way. If for no other reason, this fact makes understanding and identifying rogue aviators critically important. As professional aviators and enthusiasts, we have a moral responsibility to rid them from our midst. Professional flying organizations have another important reason to want to identify potential rogues. In addition to killing or injuring individuals, rogues can also, in some extreme cases, destroy an entire organization. It has happened.

What Is a Rogue Aviator?

Historical research into the nature of rogue behavior has revealed certain common traits that can help us identify rogue practitioners by typical patterns of behavior. Additionally, these character traits manifest themselves in recognizable patterns, which can also be of great assistance in identifying a rogue before it is too late and the damage is done. But first we must deal with the dangerous issue of labeling. During my research, this contentious issue was raised time and again. Was the great English pilot Douglas Bader a rogue? How about Billy Mitchell or Chuck Yeager? Does a single rogue act make an individual a rogue? Is being a rogue always a bad thing? These are important points—ones we must deal with up front in this discussion.

Many pilots like to think of themselves as rogues. The romantic mystique of the white-scarved daredevil of an earlier time holds firm in our collective pilot psyche. Certainly there are times, especially in combat, when courage and audacity are keys to overcoming difficult odds. The feats of our greatest combat heroes became our inspiration for flying, so we naturally tend to emulate their actions, at least in our imaginations. The Hollywood version of flight also feeds this fire, with *Top Gun*'s Maverick and Iceman always pushing the edge of the performance envelope. This is not just a recent phenomenon. Steve McQueen in *The War Lover* and John Wayne in *The High and the Mighty* were typical of earlier Hollywood rogue aviators. There are dozens of other examples. A personal example from my own career in the U.S. Air Force also lends credence to this idea. In 1988 I had become the most recent addition to a new B-1B bomber squadron at McConnell Air Force Base in Wichita, Kansas. Since I had previously been stationed there flying the KC-135,[1] a newspaper reporter asked me to compare the two aircraft. I responded, "The B-1 is much easier to fly. In fact, it is so sophisticated, it nearly flies itself to the target. All the pilots have to do is take off, air refuel, and land; the autopilot does the rest." This was a tactical error of the highest magnitude on my part. Upon hearing of my comment, my new squadron commander called me into his office and informed me in no uncertain terms that I had stained the reputation of the squadron as a group of elite, handpicked, stick-and-rudder experts (which they truly were) and I was to refrain from making any further comments of this sort. The 28th Bomb Squadron enjoyed basking in the mystique of the high-speed, low-drag, hair-on-fire combat pilot, and they weren't about to have some "tanker toad"[2] spoiling their image.

While it may be fun to think of oneself as a rogue pilot, and advantageous at the bar to have others think of you as one (the opposite sex is often attracted to the rogue type), the fact is that the vast majority of situations in the air do not call for rogue behavior. Yet we have difficulty leaving the image on the ground. Before I leave this idea of the rogue advantage with the opposite sex, let me relate a true story that demonstrates that it is not always the rogue that gets the date.

Several years ago on a return trip from the United Kingdom, I found myself fetched up on a stool in the Officer's Club bar at Lajes Air Force Base in the Azores. I was waiting for a hurricane to move out of the way so that my crew and I could navigate our KC-135 back through the Canadian Maritimes to our home base in Michigan. Aviators of all sorts found themselves in the same boat, and as the evening wore on, the club began to resemble the bar scene in *Star Wars*, where Obi-Wan Kenobi goes to hire Han Solo. Every pilot crossing the Atlantic that night—from both the commercial and military sectors—came in decked out in their respective uniforms. None of us had planned on diverting in to Lajes, so we wore what was on our backs.

As the evening progressed I watched a competition develop between two SR-71 Blackbird crewmembers and two middle-aged major airline pilots for the attention of two young ladies. The Air Force boys appeared to have all the advantages—youth, green nomex flight suits with sleeves rolled up and cool-looking navigational charts hanging out of their leg pockets, and great stories about flying at Mach 3 and 70,000 feet. But the age and wisdom of the airline pilots kept them in the game for most of the evening. As the evening wore down to last call it became obvious that this game was drawing to a close and the ladies were giving no indication who the winners would be. In a direct attack at the masculinity of a commercial airline operation, the Blackbird pilot challenged his older and slightly paunchy foe. "You airline guys never get above six-zero-zero [referring to flight level 600—60,000 feet] where we fly, do ya?" The older and wiser commercial captain smiled at his foe like a chess master who has just seen the final piece of his well-designed trap fall into place and replied, "Only in salary, son. But then again I don't suppose you get much above one-three-zero, zero-zero-zero (referring to his $130,000 annual salary) where I'm at, do ya?" I'll let the reader decide who got the date with the ladies.

A Rogue Is as a Rogue Does

To handle this question of labeling, I would like to draw on a recent sermon I heard at church. The chaplain was discussing the notion of identity and stated, "You are not who you think you are. You are not who others think you are. You are not what you—or others—say you are. You are what *you do*—pure and simple." So it is with the rogue pilot. Of course, there are those who consistently exhibit rogue behavior, which I will define simply as *willingly and unnecessarily failing to comply with existing guidance or taking unwarranted risks*. These pilots, one of whom is described in detail in Chapter 2, have earned the disreputable title of "rogue." But what about the rest of us?

Rogue behaviors are often found in the best of pilots, who for one reason or another, let their guard down and succumb to undisciplined acts in an aircraft. There are many reasons that this occurs, and we will discuss them in detail as the book progresses. But for our purposes, when a pilot intentionally and unnecessarily strays from the path of compliance, he or she is a rogue. This may not sit well with many pilots, who do not want to admit to this failing of character—and that is exactly what it is. This is a critical point: you are what you do. Perhaps this is better stated in the present tense: you are what you *are doing*. This is the central theme of our definition of a rogue and will be repeated often in the pages that follow. This is true even if an aviator strays only a single time from the proven path of compliance. Let's expand on this theme with an example of one outstanding pilot, who perished ingloriously with a single undisciplined act.

The Best Pilot in the Squadron[3]

Many years ago, as an unproductive happy hour wound to a close, several military flyers were gathered around the dregs of the last pitcher of beer, which was rapidly becoming too flat to drink. As is often the case when pilots and other crew members stand to their glasses, the conversation drifted from war stories through "where is ol' so-and-so," to memories of those no longer with us. If there is a special eulogy for pilots, it is not delivered by a chaplain from a pulpit—it is spoken by fellow pilots in the bar as the happy-hour crowd thins out and the beer gets warm. No congregation could be more sad-faced. No higher praise can be given. The ceremony is as predictable as any formal funeral. Sometimes there are even hymns of a sort. Unfortunately, the scene described is a familiar one to most of us who have been around for a few years. Inevitably, someone will say, "Ya know, he was the best pilot in the squadron." All who knew him will typically nod their heads in silent accord. Such was the case with John.

John was known as the best pilot in the squadron. He was a graduate of one of the nation's finest military academies and had distinguished himself in pilot training. In an early tour of duty he had won one of the nation's highest medals for heroism during a rescue operation overseas. He was known as a stickler for details and was considered one of the most knowledgeable and gifted pilots most of his friends had ever seen or known. He was always chosen to lead the tough missions and earned the total respect of his superiors at all levels. His exploits were legendary. He was the one who was sent to the development conferences and who flew the test program. His physical appearance was striking. He was always available when the schedule changed at the last minute, and he more than pulled his weight in other areas as well. Besides that, he was a damn nice guy and no one was surprised when he was selected for early promotion to the next rank. Everyone knew John was the best pilot in the squadron.

But wait a minute! If he was so good, why is he dead? And how about all those other well-remembered colleagues who have been honored with the posthumous title of "best pilot in the squadron?" Is there something about being the best that is fatal? What good is being the best if it kills you? What good is having the best we know end up in a box when he is needed in the cockpit? Let's take another look at this paragon of pilot virtues.

A Second Look at the Definition of "the Best"

John was aggressive, ambitious, and confident. These are admirable qualities—in fact, they are requirements for flying high-performance aircraft in combat. Many would say these are also requirements to be a top-notch general aviation or commercial instructor pilot. There is, however, a fine line between confidence and overconfidence, an important distinction between aggressiveness and overaggressiveness, a critical difference between the quest for achievement and rogue behavior. This is the lesson of this case study: that even the best of us can go bad in a moment of lost judgment or overaggressiveness. In short, we are what we do and it takes only one moment of rogue behavior to buy the proverbial farm.

Because of his demonstrated expertise early in his flying career, John was given an upgrade to a higher-performance aircraft. Although he mastered the aircraft, systems knowledge, and regulations almost immediately, his gunnery scores were not equal to his normally high standards. As a result of John's relentless pursuit of perfection, he willingly pushed himself beyond a reasonable margin of safety in order to improve his scores for low-level gunnery.

The accident investigators found nothing wrong with the aircraft. It appears as if John simply flew into the ground after pulling off the target. This was an in-flight evaluation, and the evaluator pilot in the other aircraft saw the hazardous situation developing and made a "knock it off" call. John either didn't hear the call or chose to disregard it. In any case, John—the best pilot in the squadron—had flown his last mission.

A closer look at this outstanding aviator reveals some tendencies and trends that are disturbing but common among aggressive, ambitious, and confident aviators. John felt he was good enough, and he was ambition-oriented enough, to take an airplane with minor maintenance discrepancies. He was able to work around small problems to get the job done, even if it meant bending—or breaking—a few rules along the way. In short, John was a mission hacker—a flyer who is willing to take small but often unnecessary risks to get the job done. "You gotta be tough," John used to say on more than one occasion.

It Only Takes Once

In the final analysis, the accident report concluded that the cause of the mishap was distraction or disorientation—pilot error. But the source of this error is what interests us. Of course, we will never know what was in John's mind in the final minutes and seconds prior to impact. But we do know that his drive for perfection had caused him on many other occasions to take unnecessary risks. Although John was not known as a reckless flyer, there were several small indicators available for diagnosis. It only takes once, a single moment of suspended judgment when delayed reaction is often fueled by overaggressiveness or ambition. The diagnosis of latent rogue behavior—that which lies just below the surface—must come before it's too late.

The distinction between a spirited pilot and a dangerous lack of caution is not always readily apparent. What passes for aggressiveness may be found to be—or at least labeled as—recklessness after a mishap has occurred. The fighting spirit, however, is a prerequisite for action in all types of aviation. No one is suggesting that the spirit should in any way be diminished. Excessive caution can lead to a debilitating lack of action at the moment of truth. This is certainly not what we're looking for in pilots. Timid pilots, reluctant to take any risks, are not good aviators. But neither is a force of kamikazes with disdain for death.

Rogue behavior—not rogue pilots—is the key to understanding and correcting this problem. What is required to turn the tide are pilots with a will to accomplish the task and the common sense to recognize that a given result is not worth the loss of an aircraft or a single human life. This delicate balance is reached by staying inside regulatory, procedural, and policy guidelines. The best pilot in the squadron is still flying. The pilots who met their demise as a result of exiting the proven path of compliance are by definition bad pilots. They died due to rogue behavior.

The pilot's epitaph, unfortunately, will occasionally be intoned in the bar while the ice melts and the happy-hour crowd drifts out the door with the smoke. It's a traditional way to honor our dead. In the meantime, let's be honest. Here's to the *real* best pilots in our midst— the ones who live to fly another day by staying within the rules.

We can see from this example that even the best of us can fall victim to occasional rogue behavior with disastrous and often tragic results. Ironically, there are flyers who routinely practice undisciplined behavior, and yet they often survive hundreds of such undisciplined acts before the law of averages catches up with them. The distinction between an average or even a highly skilled pilot who occasionally strays from disciplined behavior and the chronic rogue who rarely stays within the confines of regulatory compliance is an important one for our analysis.

Lords of Undiscipline

Pilots are a microcosm of society as a whole. As such, our ranks include both men and women, and people of all races, creeds, and colors. Unfortunately, they also number among them criminals, psychopaths, drug users, alcoholics, thrill seekers, and adrenaline junkies. For some, the freedom provided by the sky is too much to handle. This group is incapable of containing their own urges, tendencies which are often present in their ground-based lives as well as in their in-flight activities, but are magnified by the relatively unregulated environment of flight. This group of flyers may take off, planning to maintain a disciplined approach to flight, but at the first opportunity to deviate they cannot control their actions. Much like an alcoholic who after the first drink is incapable of controlling his or her cravings, this brand of undisciplined flyer sees a single deviation as a gateway to completely undisciplined flight. The baby goes out with the bathwater.

There are others who do not simply succumb to temptation, but who actually plan to execute undisciplined behavior by design. These are rogues in the truest sense of the word. These aviators are usually well known for their ability to get away with it, and they appear to be able to slip through the cracks of regulatory oversight. This is the group we will examine first in our analysis of behavioral characteristics, trends, and attitudes. It must be emphasized that the presence of these qualities does not guarantee rogue behavior. In fact, many of these qualities are present in some of the finest aviators. However, my research reveals that rogue practitioners from all fields demonstrate some or most of these common traits. The purpose of this discussion is not to label individuals who manifest these tendencies as rogues, but rather to identify tendencies which may indicate the potential for rogue behavior in time to take preventative measures. You should not be surprised to find out that rogue practitioners can be found in nearly every professional discipline, and that the character traits in the rogue pilot are also manifested in nonpilot rogues. This adds considerable credibility to the discussion at the end of this chapter of common character traits found in rogues.

Typical Patterns: Rogues Cross All Disciplines

Rogue practitioners are certainly not limited to aviation. In fact they can be found in any field. In aviation, however, the exploits of the rogue often have immediate and highly visible results. A brief look at rogues from other fields can help aviators to realize that the danger represented by rogue pilots is not entirely unique to our profession or hobby, or even to our century. It can also help us to see common threads which may be useful in identifying these men and women before their aberrant behaviors take a toll in human lives.

Rogues on the Rails

On April 25, 1853, one of the worst train wrecks in history occurred as a result of the incompetence and ego of a well-known rogue engineer. Robert Reed, a historian who specializes in the history of train accidents, describes what occurred that fateful night at 10 o'clock in the outskirts of Chicago at a place called Grand Crossing.

An eastbound Michigan Central express, headed for Toledo, rammed a Michigan Southern emigrant train broadside, killing twenty-one German emigrants. According to an eyewitness, the wrecked cars lay piled up in a swamp that flanked the tracks. The scene was "an immense heap of iron, splinters, doors, and baggage with the crushed locomotive of the express train hissing steam from its ruptured boiler . . . cries assailed the ears . . . mingled in strong discord with the deeper groans of the dying."

The cause of the accident was "gross carelessness and ignorant rivalry between the crews of both trains." Singled out as particularly responsible was one Mr. Buckman, the engineer of the Michigan Central train, who had a reputation as a "me first" engineer with an ego to match the size of his locomotive. Reed maintains that Buckman could have easily avoided the accident, "either by stopping or going on, but as he had the right of way, he took his time in passing through the intersection. His petty attitude of 'me first' took twenty-one lives." Like many rogues, Buckman also apparently felt that the rules did not necessarily apply to him or his operation. At the time of this disaster, he was running at night without a headlight.

From an organizational standpoint, it is understandable how this could have occurred in the mid-1850s. Railways had been extremely safe for their first 20 years of operation. In fact, between 1829 and 1853, no more than a half a dozen people had perished in any single wreck. But the 1850s brought night travel and expansion. Competition was fierce and was becoming tied to profit margins, and hard-driving engineers like Buckman were likely seen as an asset rather than a liability to their company. At least until April 25.

Our next look into the mind of a rogue and the organizational response occurs a century later and half a world away, in an even larger vehicle—a U.S. Navy ship-of-the-line.

Rogues at Sea

In the mid-1960s, the U.S. Navy removed Marcus Aurelius Arnheiter from command of the *U.S.S. Vance*, a small escort destroyer, after a series of self-serving—and quite bizarre—actions at sea. In an effort to gain fame and perhaps the command of a larger warship, Captain Arnheiter issued false position reports so he could leave his assigned area of responsibility, several miles off the coast of Vietnam. He did this so he could get to "where the action is," which in his mind was in the shallows along the Vietnamese coastline. On several occasions, he steamed his vessel in front of firing U.S. Navy destroyers, which had to cease their combat missions when the *Vance* fouled their firing line. The commander of one of these destroyers even began to tape-record the outlandish requests and radio transmissions from Arnheiter, to send to higher headquarters as evidence of this unprofessional and dangerous behavior.

The *Vance* was a picket ship, designed with small, three-inch guns to intercept any smugglers attempting to bring contraband or war materials to the Vietcong in South Vietnam, especially along the Mekong Delta area, as part of a 1965 operation called "Market Time." This patrol duty was routine but important to stop the resupply of Vietcong guerrillas operating against American and ARVN (Army of the Republic of Vietnam) troops in the south. However, it wasn't the kind of mission that would bring great opportunity for glory. In fact, while under command of the previous captain, the *Vance* had never fired a hostile shot. That was all about to change.

To fulfill his lifetime ambition as a naval combat commander, Arnheiter called a "war council" of his ship's officers almost immediately after taking command. He explained—behind a locked door with an armed sentry—that the *Vance* was to become a fighting ship. In short order, he forced his sailors to train as a Marine assault force and used ship recreation funds to purchase a small speedboat, upon which he painted shark's teeth and mounted a machine gun to be used on a "hot Vietcong target." He assumed that he could draw fire from the coastline so the *Vance* could manipulate the rules of engagement and enter the close-in battle. When this bait did not work as expected, Arnheiter had the *Vance* fire into empty sand dunes and desolate cliffs, following fictitious "urgent fire" requests and grand victories, and then wrote bogus press releases that he mailed to senior officers. To add insult to injury, he coerced junior officers, by threatening their careers, to put him in for the Silver Star after apparently stalking a Chinese submarine. All of these actions were an attempt to make a name for himself as the next Admiral Nelson, his lifelong idol who had died at Trafalgar.

The Navy was better equipped (at least in this case) to deal with the presence of a rogue than were the railroad companies of the 1850s. Through communication with a visiting chaplain and the testimony of other ship captains, the Navy decided enough was enough and removed Arnheiter from command after 99 days at sea. A long and bitter public battle followed, and only Neil Sheehan's well-researched book, *The Arnheiter Affair*, finally convinced the public and the media that the Navy was not on a witch-hunt.

The military is certainly not the only home for rogues. Sometimes they can be found as close as your nearest doctor's office or local hospital.

Medical Rogues

The medical field, and likely other professions where individual contractors can move from place to place where their services are in demand, is ideally suited for rogues. Perhaps one of the best examples comes from a city in Ohio, where a well-known gynecologist, whom we will call Dr. B, performed reconstructive surgery on the genitalia of dozens of women without their consent or knowledge. This practice was well known to other doctors in the area who had to "undo" what Dr. B had done. Yet none of his colleagues reported him, and the practice was allowed to continue for years. Finally, several of Dr. B's patients got together and surmised what had happened to them under anesthesia. A huge lawsuit and trial soon followed.

Dr. B was a rogue in the classic sense. He was highly skilled and intelligent, and he thought that the rules and regulations were for those of lesser ability. We will see this refrain repeated many times in the pages that follow. The medical field is perfect for rogues for another reason as well.

State and federal bureaucracy and jurisdictions limit the information flow and oversight capability. The information age has allowed some citizen action groups to tackle this problem, and the results are startling. In a reference text called *Questionable Doctors: Disciplined by States or the Federal Government*, the Public Citizen Health Research Group has compiled over 13,000 entries of doctors who have been disciplined for various infractions or incompetence. This is not to say that all of these entries constitute rogue doctors—certainly most do not. But you don't have to turn too many pages to find multiple entries under the same name, indicating a prolonged period of recurring infractions.

Dr. Larry Konhut (a pseudonym) was first disciplined in September 1980 by the state of Michigan. The 42-year-old doctor had his medical license revoked for causes which are not stated in the short report. We cannot be certain when he began to practice medicine again, but in August 1990 he had a restriction placed on his controlled-substance license and his medical license suspended in Michigan "due to an administrative complaint involving sexual misconduct . . . Medicaid fraud . . . and contributing to the delinquency of a minor."

The trail is next found in Kansas, where in 1992 Dr. Konhut was forced to surrender his license again. The reason stemmed from a Michigan conviction of Medicaid fraud and "allegations that he traded drugs, alcohol, and other gifts for sexual favors with a minor male patient." Although the state of Kansas was clear that Konhut "shall not apply for reinstatement of licensure in Kansas," he simply moved west to Colorado and began again. The final entry for Dr. Konhut is listed on May 21, 1993, when the Colorado authorities ordered that he surrender his license again. There is no indication of where Dr. Konhut might be practicing today.

The medical community faces difficult organizational challenges when dealing with rogue practitioners. Although there is the loosely aligned American Medical Association, which is attempting to deal with the issue of negligence and incompetence among its own ranks, the job of rooting out rogues really falls into the hands of the licensing authorities at the state and federal governments—two groups which are notorious for bureaucratic constrictions of information flow. But information flow does seem to be key in identifying and dealing with rogue practitioners from all walks of life, including the business community. Consider the case of Barings Bank in identifying the reckless activities of the most well-known rogue of our time, futures trader Nick Leeson.

Rogues in Business: Nick Leeson

Barings Bank was more than two centuries old when a single individual—Nick Leeson—destroyed it. It had been used to finance the Louisiana Purchase for the fledgling United States and had funded the Napoleonic Wars. The cover flap of Judith Rawnsley's *Total Risk: Nick Leeson and the Fall of Barings Bank* contains the following quote from Duc Le Richelieu in 1818: "There are six great powers in Europe: England,

France, Prussia, Austria, Russia, and Barings Brothers." The notion that one man could manipulate the system and bring down such a durable and powerful financial institution is reason enough to learn more about the nature of rogues, regardless of your particular profession.

Nick Leeson worked for Barings's most profitable subsidiary in Singapore, a freewheeling, entrepreneurial securities operation. To make an exceedingly complex story short and to-the-point, Leeson overextended Barings by several hundred million pounds through the invention of a fictitious client and by defrauding bank officials with bogus reports. He had been operating in this manner for over two years. He had been a corporate hero—Barings's finest. He was called "the Michael Jordan of the trading floor" by others and "Superman" by himself. But it was all a lie. By the time anyone found out about the scam, the powerful blue-blooded bank was financial history. In relatively short order, the bank was placed into "administration," the British equivalent of U.S. Chapter 11 bankruptcy proceedings.

Back in London, chairman Peter Baring apologized to his fellow bankers and blamed the entire mess on a "rogue trader." At the corporate headquarters research department, panic broke out when it was announced that a bailout of the bank had fallen through. After one employee made a joke by saying, "Grab what you can and run," many employees took him to heart and began to copy files and load boxes into the backs of their cars. For Barings, things had hit rock bottom. On March 6, 1995, a Dutch financial corporation bought out all interests and liabilities from Barings Bank for *one pound*.

In the aftermath of the Leeson affair, financial analysts, management and business gurus, and CEOs from around the world asked themselves the same question: how could this have happened? By their own admission, officials at Barings were aware that the "systems and control culture are distinctly flaky," as a memo to Barings CEO Peter Norris stated fully three months before the collapse. But there was a more fundamental issue at hand. The organization had been unable to identify or control a rogue.

Common Characteristics

Rogues from all disciplines appear to share similar characteristics and patterns of behavior, and these can be very helpful in trying to identify rogue pilots—or rogue tendencies in ourselves. If these patterns can be recognized before a problem arises, the possibility for effective intervention is increased. This is not to say that all who fall into these behavior patterns will become rogues or damage an organization. On the contrary, many who exhibit these same qualities do extremely well. The point is simply that organizations—just like pilots—need to have situational awareness, and the following characteristics can help to focus some attention on potentially hazardous patterns of behavior.

1. *Rogues are socially adept.* They communicate effectively and often are accomplished at corporate politics. They seem to have the ability to play off of hot-button issues to impress superiors, while simultaneously sensing the strengths and weaknesses of peers and subordinates, and utilizing them for personal leverage. This typically results in social strata where the individual is perceived much differently by superiors than by peers or subordinates, and where there is very little ambivalence. People tend to take sides when a rogue is around and are either groupies who believe the rogue can do no wrong or enemies who sense the impending disaster.

2. *Rogues are often untruthful.* Information is power, and rogues seem to be able to use fact and fiction for personal gain. By rationalizing that their cause is worth any means of accomplishment, lying becomes simply another tool in their bag of tricks.

3. *Rogues and potential rogues often feel that they are trapped in a system that was designed for "lesser people."* They see themselves as superior to others in the organization, even those above them on the career ladder. They often seem to believe that circumstance, and not talent, loyalty, or hard work, is what has made them subordinate to others. As such, they believe that the rules of the organization should not apply to them, because these rules were designed to protect against the lowest common denominator, not superior beings such as themselves.

4. *Rogues are driven, but often by different motivations.* Some seek fame and glory; others seek only to gratify their egos, which are typically quite large. Many seek to fulfill a childhood dream or quest to be the best . . . something. For others it is simply money. But whatever the motivation, the ambition is strong enough to overcome the normal and healthy inhibitions that govern behavior. These characteristics are often bolstered by some early success, which rogues see as validating their personal superiority.

5. *Even when identified, rogues can be extremely difficult to deal with.* Keep in mind that they are often quite popular in the organization, and in some cases their exploits may have been used as a positive example by senior leadership or management earlier in their careers. They can, and often do, become organizational cult heroes. Rogues have learned what rules they can break, when, and with whom. Because of their perceived skill and expertise, some younger members of the organization see rogues as role models and begin to copy their style and actions. When this occurs, the negative impact can expand exponentially.

6. *Progressive deviations.* One of the most telling characteristics of the rogue is the pattern of progressive deviations which characterizes their undisciplined behavior. Although early deviations may be seemingly insignificant, follow-on acts are likely to become much more severe.

One of the most difficult challenges in unmasking rogues is to get them to reveal their true ambitions and agendas at a time and place where harm is not done and help can be forthcoming. Far too often, the events that unmask rogues are the same ones that kill them.

A Chance to Shine: A Rogue Unmasked

Until recently, the U.S. Air Force practiced a unique and rather challenging mission to off-load cargo from an extremely low flying (5 to 7 feet above the ground) aircraft. These missions were called the low-altitude parachute extraction system (LAPES). A "LAPES drop" was executed by the aircraft flying just barely above the ground with the rear cargo door open. As the crew approached the extraction zone (EZ), a drogue parachute, attached to the cargo, was inflated out the rear of the aircraft and the cargo was "skidded" into the landing zone (Figure 1-1). The idea was to deliver cargo into a hostile area that needed precise airdrop but was too "hot" to land at. The perfect example of an effective LAPES operation was at the battle of Khe Sahn in Vietnam, where C-130 deliveries were the lifeblood for trapped U.S. Army forces surrounded by North Vietnamese regulars. LAPES deliveries require exact discipline and effective crew coordination. Occasionally, pilots see the LAPES mission as an opportunity to strut their stuff. When the same pilots have convinced the rest of the crew that they can do no wrong, the stage is set for disaster.

Figure 1-1. High-risk maneuver. A C-130 flies only a few feet off the ground to perform a low-altitude parachute extraction system (LAPES) delivery. *(U.S. Air Force photo)*

During a practice LAPES mission for a demonstration the following day, the mishap pilot executed a steep approach, a two-step flare, and a very aggressive climbout that was outside established regulatory standards. Wing and squadron supervisors observed the entire practice sequence, but they did not take any action against the mission commander. The aggressiveness of the practice maneuver frightened the copilot and the flight engineer, and after the mission the copilot confronted the pilot about the lack of discipline on the practice LAPES delivery. The pilot agreed to "shallow out" the maneuver the next day.

Although the copilot's assertiveness was a step in the right direction toward restoring discipline, the squadron commander later praised the aircrews for an outstanding performance on the practice flight, thereby inappropriately reinforcing the undisciplined behavior. This phenomenon of supervisors praising an undisciplined act has become such a frequent aspect in my study of rogue flyers that I now refer to it as "rogue-building."

Prior to the actual LAPES demonstration flight the following day, a copilot change was made, thereby negating the previous agreement to "shallow it out" and significantly reducing the pilot crew experience level. The accident chain was building and a rogue was about to emerge.

On the day of the demonstration, the pilot was intent on making a steep approach to enhance the entertainment value of the event. He established an excessive nose-low attitude and a vertical velocity of 2900 feet per minute within 100 feet of the ground, a flight condition from which a safe recovery is simply not possible. The aircraft impacted the ground with sufficient force to fracture the aircraft structure. The rogue had made an impression all right—on the ground, on the aircraft, and in the minds of all who witnessed the undisciplined act.

As the aircraft skidded out of the extraction zone, it passed over a crest, and at approximately 1680 feet from touchdown, the engines and propellers departed the aircraft. At approximately 1800 feet, the right wing tip contacted a parked vehicle, which was propelled down track about 35 feet, where it exploded. At approximately 1850 feet, the left external fuel tank struck a jeep, and an Army soldier in the passenger seat of the jeep was killed instantly. At approximately 1900 feet, the aircraft flipped over and fell to the ground 2040 feet from the initial impact. During the rotation, the empennage separated and came to rest vertically 160 feet beyond the center wing section. There were many sources of ignition: hot engines and components, hot electrical components, and possible sparking. All four main fuel tanks, oil, and fuel vapors ignited, resulting in a fireball and flash fire.

Both loadmasters sustained fatal injuries during the mishap sequence. The pilot and the navigator survived the crash but received horrific facial burn injuries in the postcrash fire. The copilot and flight engineer were found outside the flight deck area but within the perimeter of fire and received serious burn injuries. The aircraft was completely destroyed.

Air Force regulations stated, "It is permissible to use an approach altitude higher than 200 feet if operational requirements dictate; however, in all cases, base the descent point on gross weight, ground speed, and pilot judgment. . . . The descent rate should normally be 1000 to 1500 feet per minute." This pilot had nearly doubled the recommended descent rate to put on a good show.

The mishap chain of events began with the mission briefing for the Monday practice. Significant emphasis to provide a "big show" was directed at all aircrews from the airborne division commanding general—more rogue-building. Although the wing commander stressed that it was just another training exercise and to perform the mission safely, the Hercules pilot intended to put on a good show. After Monday's practice mission, he made certain conscious decisions regarding the manner in which he would perform the next day. In short, he had a hidden agenda. At the onset of the mishap the pilot intentionally delayed drogue chute deployment and descent in order to steepen the approach to the extraction zone. His overconfidence was writing checks his hands could not cash. The mishap pilot's confidence level can best be exemplified by the comments he made to the originally scheduled copilot, after the copilot expressed his concerns about the aggressive nose-high climb that exceeded 20 degrees, accompanied by a significant loss of airspeed. The mishap pilot explained that he had a lot of experience flying LAPES that way, that he was very comfortable with the maneuver, and that it made for a good show. However, he relented, stating that if the maneuver really bothered the copilot he would "shallow all that stuff out." *Later Monday afternoon, the mishap pilot was overheard to say to another crewmember that he would make the next run-in a little steeper.*

Other squadron members confirmed the mishap pilot to be compulsive, devoted, and a perfectionist. These traits were important in determining how the pilot became internally motivated. The underlying factor was self-motivation, a desire to magnify his self-image, reputation, or career. The role of outside motivating factors can be illustrated by the pre-mission briefing. The commanding general underscored the need to "fill the sky with parachutes" and to put on a "big show." Although the mishap pilot's aberrant behavior on the previous day's demonstration caused concern for the wing director of operations (DO) and the squadron commander, they applauded his effort at the post-mission debrief.

The skill and experience of the pilot were well known by all crewmembers on the aircraft, and this could have resulted in overconfidence in his abilities. A no drop/go-around was not suggested by the mishap copilot or any other crewmembers, in spite of the fact that they certainly recognized the abnormality of the situation. The mishap pilot was perceived by the other crewmembers as being highly experienced and skilled—their attitude is referred to as *excessive deference*, and is common among those who fly with a highly experienced rogue. The copilot on the mishap flight had only 200.1 hours of C-130 flying time; he was a dedicated, highly motivated individual, but lacked knowledge and experience not only in LAPES and the C-130 in general, but, more important, in dealing with overconfident aircraft commanders. He was out of his league.

During the mishap sequence, the crew relied entirely on the mishap pilot's ability to conduct the approach. What developed was a copilot syndrome whereby the copilot and possibly other crewmembers were satisfied to have the pilot in complete control of the final approach. Their trust was poorly placed in a rogue and many paid the price with their lives.

A Final Word on Unmasking the Rogue

Rogue pilots kill innocent people—remember that. This fact alone makes the effort to unmask them worthwhile. Because rogues are often very popular, it takes considerable moral courage to take on this challenge. It can be even more difficult to tackle rogue behavior in ourselves, as the denial factor is often powerful in those of us who follow the rules *most of the time.* Rogue pilots are often high-energy people who make good things happen, but for good or evil, high-energy people who display the profile of the rogue bear close watching to protect the lives of innocents and the reputations of all pilots who follow the rules.

In Chapter 2, we will look at the rogue of all rogue pilots, the quintessential picture of a pilot who was able to routinely violate flight discipline for over three years in spite of numerous efforts to stop him at various levels. Perhaps scariest of all, he was a B-52 nuclear bomber pilot.

CHAPTER TWO

The Quintessential Rogue

ROGUE INDIVIDUALS have always enjoyed a certain mystique in our western culture. This is especially true in America, where the idea of mastering a frontier by any and all available means is seen as an important part of our heritage. We remember images of John Wayne in *True Grit* or James Arness as Marshall Matt Dillon throwing caution (and often common sense) to the wind and stepping into the fray in the nick of time to save the day. We admire these fictional characters not only for their courage, but also for the sheer audacity in abandoning conventional wisdom to get the job done. The connotation of the term "rogue" in America is usually considered to be positive. Unfortunately, this admiration for the Hollywood qualities of fictional characters often plays out tragically in the real world, which is not governed by special effects and retakes, but by facts and physics.

This chapter takes a look at a real-life rogue in action and the real-life consequences of his reckless behavior. This case study has become the quintessential example of rogue behavior. It is now used in human factors courses on five continents and has been reprinted in at least four languages. It is the story of a military aviator gone out of control and the inability of the organization to stop him before it was too late. In it you will see that the negative impact of a rogue aviator extends well beyond the individual pilot and aircraft—or even those he or she may injure or kill in an undisciplined act. A rogue infects the soul of an organization like a festering wound that won't heal. The actions and attitudes of a single individual can create an atmosphere of confusion, frustration, and distrust. The negative impact of this individual reverberates to this day, as his influence on developing aviators with whom we continue to share the skies was lasting and profound.

Prologue to a Tragedy

"What's the deal with *this* guy?" Captain Bill Kramer[1] asked, indicating a car conspicuously parked in the center of the red-curbed no parking zone adjacent to the military base wing headquarters building. It was a short walk from the HQ building, commonly referred to as "The White House," to the parking lot where they had left their own vehicles while attending the briefing on the upcoming air show. As they passed the illegally parked car and then the various spaces reserved for the wing and operations group commanders, Lieutenant Colonel Winslow turned to Captain Kramer and replied, "That's Bob's car. He always parks there." After a few more steps the captain inquired, "How does he get away with that?" The lieutenant colonel reflected for a moment and responded, "I don't know—he just does."

Leaders and Rogues

Failed leadership can have tragic consequences. In the words of Major General Perry Smith, a career military aviator and former commandant of the National War College, "Leaders make a difference, and large and complex organizations make special demands on the men and women who run them." This is the story of a group of leaders who did not meet all the demands required to establish a healthy organizational climate and, when confronted with evidence of a rogue pilot, did not take appropriate disciplinary actions. There were several manifestations of these failings. Only the most tragic and dramatic is addressed here—the crash of *Czar 52*, an eight-engine B-52 bomber.

An examination of evidence from three years preceding the crash reveals several examples of failed leadership relating to a prolonged series of breaches of air discipline on the part of a senior pilot, Lieutenant Colonel Arthur "Bob" Hammond, the pilot in command of *Czar 52* at the time of the crash. The reasons why the organization failed to deal effectively with this rogue pilot may never be completely understood, but they hint strongly at the unique ability of an individual to bend the will of a large organization to further his personal agenda.

The Final Ride

On June 24, 1994, *Czar 52*, a B-52 H-model bomber assigned to a military base in the western United States, launched at approximately 1:58 P.M. Pacific Daylight Time, to practice maneuvers for an upcoming air show. The pilot had planned and briefed a profile that grossly exceeded aircraft and regulatory limitations. Upon preparing to land at the end of the practice air show profile, the control tower directed *Czar 52* to execute a go-around because of another aircraft on the runway. At midfield, the lumbering B-52 began an extremely tight, 360-degree, slow-speed turn with full flaps. It attempted a left turn around the control tower at only 250 feet of altitude above ground level (AGL), in the process violating bank angle and altitude restrictions. Approximately three-quarters of the way through the turn, the aircraft banked past 90 degrees, stalled, clipped a power line with the left wing, and crashed. There were no survivors out of a crew of four field-grade officers.

Killed in the crash were Lieutenant Colonel Hammond, the chief of the bomb wing standardization and evaluation branch. Hammond, an instructor pilot, was designated as the aircraft commander and was undoubtedly flying the aircraft at the time of the accident. The copilot was Lieutenant Colonel Mark McCloud, also an instructor pilot and the bomb squadron (BMS) commander. There is a great deal of evidence that suggests considerable animosity existed between the two pilots who were at the controls of *Czar 52*. This was a result of McCloud's unsuccessful efforts to have Bob Hammond grounded for what he perceived as numerous and flagrant violations of air discipline while flying with squadron aircrews. Colonel Robert Moulton was the vice wing commander and was added to the flying schedule as a safety observer on the morning of the mishap.

This was to be Moulton's "finis-flight," an Air Force tradition whereby an aviator is hosed down following his last flight in an aircraft. As the aircraft made its final approach to landing, the colonel's wife and friends waited on the flight line to congratulate him with a champagne toast to a successful flying career. Lieutenant Colonel Ken Wilson, the BMS operations officer, and a husband and father, filled the radar navigator position. While all aircraft accidents that result in loss of life are tragic, those that could have been prevented are especially so.

The crash of *Czar 52* was primarily the result of actions taken by a singularly outstanding stick-and-rudder pilot, but one who, ironically, practiced incredibly poor airmanship. The distinction between these two similar-sounding roles will be made clear as we progress in this analysis. Of equal or greater significance was the fact that supervision and leadership facilitated the accident through failed policies of selective enforcement of regulations, as well as failing to heed the desperate warning signals raised by peers and subordinates over a prolonged period prior to the accident. At the time of the accident, there was considerable evidence of Hammond's poor airmanship spanning a period of over three years.

This example is worth our contemplation, not because it was a unique aberration from what occurs in other flying organizations, but rather because it is a compilation of tendencies that are seen throughout the spectrum of flying organizations. Many aviators report that rules and regulations are bent on occasion, and some individuals seem to be "Teflon-coated" because their mistakes are ignored or overlooked by their supervisors. This case study presents examples of a pilot who felt that the rules were different for him—one of the most easily recognizable characteristics of a rogue pilot.

Even more important, this case study shows the personal power of the rogue as an individual who can impose his or her will on an entire organization. The results of this manipulation are numerous, as the rogue behaviors chip away at the spirit of teamwork and camaraderie that earmark a healthy flying organization.

Key Concepts: Airmanship, Rogue Aviators, and the Culture of Compliance

At a gut level, most aviators can determine reasonable from unreasonable courses of action. This quality is referred to as *judgment* or *airmanship*. From the beginning of an aviator's training, he or she is taught that *flexibility is the key to airpower* and is given considerable latitude in employing methods for accomplishing flight objectives. This is one of the major advantages for pilots with sound judgment and should not be changed. But there are also those aviators, usually of a high level of experience, skill, and confidence, who see this built-in flexibility as a chaotic environment which may be manipulated for their own egos—often with tragic results. These rogue aviators are usually popular and respected, possess considerable social skills, and have learned what rules they can break, when, and with whom. As Chapter 1 pointed out, superiors usually perceive rogues much differently than they do the rogue's peers or subordinates. This level of sophistication makes the direct oversight role of the supervisor more difficult and the role of effective *organizational climate* more important. What the leader may not recognize as an individual must be identified for him by the organization. Further, upon this recognition, the leader must act. Failure to act after the organization has fulfilled its role in identifying a problem leads to a deterioration of faith in the system by subordinates, who now feel that their input is of little value. A culture of compliance must be inculcated and constantly nurtured to prevent the downward spiral into disaster, such as occurred at this military base in June 1994.

The culture of compliance was certainly not in place in the three years preceding the crash of *Czar 52*, and this allowed a rogue pilot to flourish in the midst of the normally strict military environment. In this case study, the signs of trouble were present early and often. A pattern of negative activity could be found in complaints from other crewmembers, maintenance problems from overstressing or exceeding aircraft limitations, and stories of Hammond's grand accomplishments and plans that circulated throughout the crew force. Fully two years before this event, one instructor pilot who was flying in formation with Hammond reported that he had flown so low over the desert floor that he had "kicked up a 200-foot rooster tail" behind the aircraft. What is worse, the vice wing commander, who was on this instructor's aircraft, had encouraged the instructor to descend and do the same thing.

After reviewing the history contained in the testimonies, one suspects that an energetic historian could find earlier signs of Hammond's departure from the aviators' proven path of regulatory compliance. For our purposes, we will limit the analysis to the period between 1991 and June 1994.

By the summer of 1994, the entire organization was caught up in the activities of a single B-52 pilot. Red flags of warning were abundant—and yet those who could act did not do so, in spite of multiple recommendations to ground Hammond. As one B-52 crewmember said about the accident, "You could see it, hear it, feel it, and smell it coming. We were all just trying to be somewhere else when it happened."

The Rogue

As the chief of the wing standardization and evaluation section at the air force base, Hammond was responsible for the knowledge and enforcement of academic and in-flight standards for the wing's flying operations. By nearly any measuring stick, Hammond was a gifted stick-and-rudder pilot. With over 5200 hours of flying time and a perfect 31-0 record on checkrides, Hammond had flown the B-52G and H models since the beginning of his flying career. He was regarded by many as an outstanding pilot, perhaps the best in the entire B-52 fleet. He was an experienced instructor pilot and had served with the Strategic Air Command's 1st Combat Evaluation Group (CEVG), considered by many aviators to be the "top of the pyramid." But between 1991 and June 1994, a pattern of poor airmanship began to surface. Perhaps his reputation as a gifted pilot influenced his superiors, who allowed this pattern of behavior to continue. The following were typical comments from Hammond's superiors:

> "Bob is as good a B-52 aviator as I have seen."

> "Bob was . . . very at ease in the airplane . . . a situational awareness type of guy . . . among the most knowledgeable guys I've flown with in the B-52."

> "Bob was probably the best B-52 pilot that I know in the wing and probably one of the best, if not *the* best within the command. He also has a lot of experience in the CEVG which was the Command Stan Eval . . . *and he was very well aware of the regulations and the capabilities of the airplane*" (emphasis added).

A far different perspective on Hammond's flying is seen in statements by more junior crewmembers, who were required to fly with him on a regular basis.

> "There was already some talk of maybe trying some other ridiculous maneuvers . . . his lifetime goal was to roll the B-52."

> "I was thinking that he was going to try something again, ridiculous maybe, at this air show and possibly kill thousands of people."

"I'm not going to fly with him, I think he's dangerous. He's going to kill somebody some day and it's not going to be me."

"[Lieutenant] Colonel Hammond made a joke out of it when I said I would not fly with him. He came to me repeatedly after that and said, 'Hey, we're going flying, Mikie, you want to come with us?' And every time I would just smile and say, 'No. I'm not going to fly with you.'"

"Lieutenant Colonel Hammond broke the regulations or exceeded the limits . . . virtually every time he flew."

The reasons for these conflicting views may never be entirely known, but they hint at a sophisticated approach to breaking the rules that became a pattern in Hammond's flying activities. But Hammond himself had no illusions about what kind of aviator he was. An instructor stationed with Hammond reports that just after the 1994 air show planning briefing, Hammond told him, "I can't believe that the Air Force is so stupid that they are going to let me fly my last mission of my career at an air show."

The Events

Each of the events leading up to the crash of *Czar 52* on June 24, 1994, provides insights into rogue personality and behavior. Let's look at each event by providing a synopsis of what occurred as determined from eyewitness testimony. It is important to understand that a historical case study cannot provide definitive guidance for all other situations. All situations are unique and must be defined in terms of their own circumstances. It is hoped however, that this discussion will provide some general lessons that may carry over into other environments.

As the analysis develops, it will be important to understand the flight manual and regulatory restrictions and limitations of the aircraft and the flying environment, all of which were blatantly disregarded by Bob Hammond. The aging B-52 was limited to 30 degrees of bank and 15 degrees of pitch in the traffic pattern area. Federal Aviation Regulations (FAR) prohibit overflight of buildings or people at altitudes lower than 500 feet above the ground. Air Force regulations prohibit formation flying in B-52s and require multiple clearances and approvals for flyover-type demonstrations. None of these restrictions would influence this rogue pilot's actions in the slightest.

Situation One: Base Air Show, May 19, 1991

Hammond was the pilot and aircraft commander for the B-52 exhibition in the 1991 base air show. During this exhibition, Hammond violated several regulations and flight manual limits, exceeding bank and pitch limits and flying directly over the air show crowd in violation of FAR. In addition, a review of videotape of the maneuvers leaves one with the distinct impression that the aircraft may have violated FAR altitude restrictions as well. Although the maneuvers themselves are indicative of rogue behavior, what occurred after the event is crucial to understanding how his rogue behavior escalated.

Many B-52 aviators who observed the air show testified that no large public or private outcry resulted from the 1991 B-52 exhibition. However, some aircrew members had already began to lose faith in the system. When asked why more crewmembers didn't speak up about the violations, one B-52 pilot said, "The entire wing staff sat by and watched him do it [violate regulations] in the '91 air show. What was the sense in saying anything? *They had already given him a license to steal"* (emphasis added). There is no evidence to indicate that commanders at any level took disciplinary action as a result of Hammond's flight activities at the 1991 air show. This would *not* be the only lost teaching opportunity.

Situation Two: 325th BMS Change of Command Flyover, July 12, 1991

Hammond was the aircraft commander and pilot for a flyover for a bomb squadron change of command ceremony. During the practice and actual flyover, Hammond accomplished passes that were clearly well below 100 feet above ground level (AGL). Additionally, he flew steep bank turns and extremely high pitch angles, in violation of the flight manual and FAR. He completed his impromptu air show with a *wingover,* a maneuver in which the pilot rolls the aircraft 90 degrees onto its side and allows the nose of the aircraft to fall "through the horizon" to regain airspeed. The flight manual specifically recommends against wingover-type maneuvers because the sideslip may cause damage to the aircraft.

Clearly, this rogue behavior was facilitated by Hammond's "success" at the 1991 base air show. This time, however, many thought that he would surely be reprimanded. One officer stated that the huge B-52 flew so low it blew his hat off as he stood at attention for the ceremony.

Because the vast majority of the other B-52 aircrew members were standing at attention in ranks for the change of command ceremony, they did not personally see the violations as they occurred. Most had to rely on descriptions from family and friends. The followers were acutely aware, however, that the wing leadership had a ringside seat and therefore may not have felt the need to report or complain about a situation that their leaders had witnessed directly.

This time the leadership was forced to take action, or at least project the appearance of taking action. One supervisor remarked, "We can't have that, we can't tolerate things like that, we need to take action for two reasons—it's unsafe and we have a perception problem with the young aircrews." Evidence indicates that Hammond may have been debriefed and possibly verbally reprimanded. However, the outgoing bomb squadron commander stated, "No overt punishment that I know of ever occurred from that [the change of command flyover]."

As in the previous situation, the flyover plan was developed, briefed, and executed without intervention. The flyover for a change of command required approval by the USAF vice chief of staff. No such approval was requested or granted. Although the senior staff was spurred to action by the magnitude of the violations, the response appeared to be little more than a slap on the wrist, a point certainly not missed by other flyers in the wing.

Situation Three: Base Air Show, May 17, 1992

Once again, Hammond was selected to fly the B-52 exhibition at the base air show. The profile flown included several low-altitude steep turns in excess of 45 degrees of bank and a high-speed pass down the runway. At the completion of the high-speed pass, Hammond accomplished a high pitch angle climb, estimated at over 60 degrees nose high. At the top of the climb, the B-52 leveled off, using a wingover maneuver. Although these maneuvers were not much different from the ones performed at the 1991 air show, they were slightly more dramatic and were accomplished at lower altitudes. In addition, they occurred under a different set of leaders. Although the leadership had changed, the response did not, and further degradation of flight discipline was certain to follow. Rogues feed on acceptance and approval.

As in the 1991 air show, most junior crewmembers kept their opinions on the flyby to themselves. One B-52 pilot remarked, "I was amazed that they [the senior staff] let him keep doing that. Getting away with it *once* you could understand, you know—forgiveness is easier to get than permission. But this was the *third* time in less than a year. I was appalled, but not surprised." Further deterioration of airmanship should not have come as a surprise. After all, Bob Hammond was a rogue (Figure 2-1).

Situation Four: Global Power Mission, April 14–15, 1993

While most of the folks on the ground were trying to meet their income tax deadlines, Hammond was winging his way toward Guam. He had

Figure 2-1. The huge, eight-engine B-52 doesn't look much like an aerobatic aircraft, but many were convinced Bob Hammond was planning to attempt a full 360-degree roll at the 1994 air show.

been selected as the mission commander of a two-ship formation of B-52s on a Global Power mission to the bombing range in the Medina de Farallons, a small island chain off the coast of Guam in the Pacific Ocean. While in command of this mission, Hammond broke numerous well-known regulations, including flying a close visual formation with another B-52 in order to take close-up pictures. This type of maneuver was strictly prohibited by Air Combat Command (ACC) regulations. Later in the mission, Hammond requested a member of his crew to leave the main crew compartment and work his way back to the bomb bay to take a video of live munitions being released from the open bay of the aircraft. This was not only illegal but ridiculously dangerous. Hammond's power of suggestion worked again, and the young captain navigator climbed back into the open bomb bay, like Slim Pickens in *Dr. Strangelove*, to comply with his commander's wishes. The pictures and videos that were taken were clear and unequivocal evidence that regulations had been broken once again.

After the mission, the crewmember who took the illegal video began to have second thoughts about his participation in the undisciplined behavior. He took the video to his mentor, a senior officer in the aviation hierarchy on the base and was told, "I would not show any of this," relating to certain sequences of the videotape which the leader felt were in violation of regulations. When the next officer in the chain of command was made aware of the presence of the potentially incriminating video, he allegedly responded, "Okay, I don't want to know anything about that video—I don't care." The entire episode began with Hammond's impression that he was given "some orders [presumably from a senior officer] to basically freestyle to get good photographs and video . . . to make the video presentation more spectacular." It is hard to imagine anyone at the base giving Hammond an order to "freestyle." If it did occur, it was like giving a pyromaniac a book of matches and some lighter fluid. If not, it is merely another example of a rogue twisting the truth for his own ends.

For the first time, the wing leadership was confronted with hard-copy evidence of wrongdoing on the part of Hammond in a setting other than a base air show or special-occasion flyover. Yet there was no attempt at any level to interview the crewmembers or to reprimand the guilty parties. Integrity, the cornerstone of military professionalism, had been sacrificed at the altar of the rogue.

Situation Five: Base Air Show, August 8, 1993

By now it should come as no surprise that Hammond was able to get himself selected to fly the B-52 exhibition at the 1993 base air show. It will also not surprise you that he flew aggressive steep turns over the crowd in violation of multiple regulations, accomplished extremely low altitude passes, and a high-pitch maneuver which one crewmember estimated to be *80 degrees* nose high—10 degrees shy of completely vertical. Keep in mind, this is not the space shuttle or an F-16 we are talking about here, but a 30-year-old B-52 with a wingspan of over 150 feet!

The Ripple Effect of a Rogue Pilot

The crewmembers of the local bomb squadron had grown accustomed to Hammond's air show routine. But a more insidious effect of his ability to consistently break the rules with apparent impunity was starting to take shape in younger, less skilled pilots. In one example, a young B-52 pilot who had seen several of Hammond's performances attempted to copy the "pitch-up" maneuver at an air show in Kamloops, Canada—with near disastrous results. The navigator on this flight said, "We got down to *seventy* knots and . . . I felt buffeting" during the recovery from the pitch-up. At 70 knots, the B-52 is in an aerodynamically stalled condition and is no longer really flying at all in the aerodynamic sense of the word. Only good fortune or divine intervention prevented a catastrophic occurrence in front of the Canadian audience.

A second example occurred at a military exercise at Roswell, New Mexico, when another young pilot was administratively grounded for accomplishing a maneuver he had seen Hammond do. "It was a flaps down, turning maneuver in excess of 60 degrees of bank, close to the ground." His former instructor said of the event, "I was appalled to hear that somebody I otherwise respected would attempt that." The site commander was also appalled, and sat the man down and administered corrective training. The negative example set by Hammond had begun to be emulated by junior and impressionable officers and had resulted in one near disaster and an administrative action against another junior officer. This was precisely what many had feared and is a classic example of the subtle ripple effects of unchecked rogue behavior.

The response to this event from the senior commander on the base sheds some light on the nature of the rogue's ability to exert what some have called a "social anesthesia," or numbing effect, on superiors. In testimony after the crash in June 1994, this commander stated under oath that Hammond "never acted . . . anything other than totally professional . . . *nothing I saw or knew led me to any other belief* about Bob Hammond." This testimony was from a commander who personally witnessed Hammond's flagrant and willful tech order and regulatory violations at his own 1993 air show. Regarding the 1993 air show, the commander went on to state, "*I made it absolutely clear that everything that was going to be done in this demonstration was going to have to be on the up and up and in accordance with tech order and in accordance with the regulations . . . and I was sure that it was.*" This is denial of the highest order, as all of the violations of regulations were caught on videotape, and the commander knew it.

It is interesting to note that the site commander at Roswell, New Mexico, immediately recognized a high bank maneuver by a B-52 as a violation of tech order guidance and took administrative action against the offender—a Bob Hammond wannabe.

What was going on here? Did this commander not know or understand the flight manual limitations or the regulations? Was he misinformed? The truth is worse than any fiction. The wing commander stated that he looked to his director of operations for guidance, who in turn looked to his chief of standardization (Bob Hammond) to ensure that the regulations were followed—and so the demonstration proceeded under the guidance of an aviator who had a long track record of willful violations and poor airmanship. A B-52 pilot interviewed about this state of affairs said, "It was worse than the blind leading the blind. It was more like the spider and the fly," referring to the abilities of Hammond to bend the leadership to his will, another earmark of the rogue.

Situation Six: Yakima Bombing Range, March 10, 1994

Hammond was the pilot and aircraft commander on a single-ship training mission to the Yakima Bombing Range to drop practice munitions and provide an authorized photographer an opportunity to shoot pictures of the B-52 from the ground as it conducted its bomb runs. Hammond flew the aircraft *well below* the established 500-foot minimum altitude for the low-level training route. In fact, one crossover was photographed at less than 30 feet, and another crewmember estimated that the final ridge line crossover was "somewhere in the neighborhood of about *three* feet." One crewmember stated that he felt the aircraft would have impacted the ridge if he had not intervened and pulled back on the yoke to increase the aircraft's altitude. The photographers stopped filming because "they thought we were going to impact . . . and they were ducking out of the way." At the conclusion of this madness, Hammond also joined an unbriefed formation of A-10 fighter aircraft to accomplish a flyby over the photographer. This mission violated ACC Regulations regarding minimum altitudes, FAR Part 91, and Air Force Regulation (AFR) 60-16 regarding overflight of people on the ground. There were several occasions during the flight when other crewmembers verbally voiced their opposition to the actions being taken by Hammond. Following the flight, these same crewmembers went up the military chain of command with their story and stated that they would not fly with Hammond again under any circumstances.

During the flight, crewmembers strongly verbalized their concerns about the violations of air discipline and regulations. At one point, Hammond reportedly questioned the radar navigator's masculinity when he would not violate regulations and open the bomb doors for a photograph with weapons on board. On another occasion, following a low crossover, the navigator told Hammond that the altitudes at which he was flying were "senseless." But the real hero on this flight was Captain Eric Jones, a B-52 instructor pilot who found himself in the copilot seat with Hammond during the low-level portion of the flight. On this day, it would take all of his considerable skills, wits, and guile, to bring the aircraft safely back to the home base. After realizing that merely telling Hammond that he was violating regulations, and that he (Jones) was uncomfortable with that, was not going to work, Jones feigned illness to get a momentary climb to a higher altitude. Jones also said he needed some hands-on training and flew a few passes on the range himself at safe altitudes. But in the end it was once again Hammond at the controls. The following is Jones's recollection of the events that took place then:

We came around and [Lieutenant] Colonel Hammond took us down to 50 feet. I told him that this was well below the clearance

plane and that we needed to climb. He ignored me. I told him (again) as we approached the ridgeline. I told him in three quick bursts *"climb-climb-climb."* . . . I didn't see any clearance that we were going to clear the top of that mountain. . . . It appeared to me that he had target fixation. I said *"climb-climb-climb"* again, he did not do it. I grabbed ahold of the yoke and I pulled it back pretty abruptly. . . . I'd estimate we had a cross-over around 15 feet. . . . The radar navigator and the navigator were verbally yelling or screaming, reprimanding [Lieutenant] Colonel Hammond and saying that there was no need to fly that low . . . his reaction to that input was a laugh—I mean a good belly laugh.

Upon returning from the mission, the crewmembers discussed the events among themselves and came to the conclusion that they would not fly with Hammond again. Jones reports, "I vowed to them that never again would they or myself be subjected to fly with him. That if it required it, I would be willing to fall on my sword to ensure that didn't happen." The next day, Jones reported the events to Major Don Thomas, the squadron operations officer, stating, "I did not ever want to fly with Lieutenant Colonel Hammond again, even if it meant that I couldn't fly anymore as an Air Force pilot." Thomas told Jones that he didn't think it would come to that, because he "was joining a group of pilots in the squadron who had also made the same statement."

The staff at the squadron level began to take action when Jones reported the events to Thomas, who had also already seen a videotape taken from the ground during the photography session the previous day and was aware of the severity and degree of the infractions. Although he was admittedly a good friend of Hammond, Thomas had seen enough. He immediately went to the squadron commander, Lieutenant Colonel Mark McCloud. Thomas recalls, "I had an intense gut feeling that things were getting desperate. . . . I said, 'I feel like I'm stabbing a friend in the back. I like [Lt.] Col. Hammond but we need to remove him from flying. That Yakima flight needs to be his finis-flight.' I guess I was just trying to protect Bob Hammond from Bob Hammond." The squadron commander concurred, but it was agreed that in order to restrict the wing chief of stan-eval from flying, the order would have to come from a more senior commander. McCloud went to see Colonel Pollard, the deputy commander for operations. At the meeting, McCloud laid the facts on the table and made his recommendation to ground Hammond. The DO thanked him and said he would get back to him with a decision after he had heard the other side of the story. Pollard consulted with Hammond and was told that he (Hammond) was just trying to demonstrate aircraft capabilities to the more junior crewmembers. Hammond was verbally reprimanded by Pollard (undocumented) and promised not to break any more regulations in the future. The DO then called a meeting with Hammond and McCloud to announce his decision. He informed them both that he had reprimanded Hammond but that he had decided against any restriction on his flying. At that point, McCloud made a decision to restrict his crews from flying with Hammond unless he was personally in the aircraft. According to McCloud's wife, "Mark said afterwards that he knew that he was not going to let [Lieutenant] Colonel Hammond fly with anybody else unless he was in the airplane . . . that he was going to be flying whenever Bob flew." He was true to his word, all the way to his death.

By failing to take action against Hammond, the DO had set the stage for a bizarre and dangerous situation. Two men (McCloud and Hammond) who were professionally at odds, to say the least, were to be paired in the cockpit for the next several months. McCloud had confided in his wife that he did not trust Hammond to fly with his aircrews. Captain Eric Jones related the following encounter with Hammond (after the DO's decision)—it is classic rogue rhetoric.

> I was sitting there and he came over and said, "That little [expletive deleted]," referring to Lieutenant Colonel McCloud, "tried to get me grounded. But I solved that, the three of us." And Lieutenant Colonel Hammond told me, speaking directly at Lieutenant Colonel McCloud, that he didn't respect him as a man, as a commander, or as a pilot. Apparently Lieutenant Colonel McCloud had said something about him being dangerous and Lieutenant Colonel Hammond indicated that he told him that he was just a "weak dick."

The DO had not adequately considered the implications of his actions when he allowed Hammond to continue to fly. Within his operations group there was, in essence, a small mutiny going on. Many of the crewmembers were no longer willing to fly with his chief of standards and evaluation, even under orders. He had alienated his bomb squadron commander, who was now having to spend time tracking Hammond's flying schedule, to ensure that his crewmembers were not put in the unenviable position of choosing between risking their careers or risking their lives.

The Yakima mission brought to a head many emotions that had been lying beneath the surface at this base. In addition to the problems in the operations group, the officers' wives, civilians, and even the kids on the high school playground were discussing the antics of Bob Hammond.

The rift that existed between McCloud and Hammond extended beyond the men themselves. A B-52 aircraft commander stated, "Everybody was lining up on one side or the other, Bob had his groupies, and then there were the rest of us." McCloud's wife also felt the effects and strain. She related a conversation she had with Hammond's wife. "I was at Debbie Pollard's going away luncheon and I never really had a chance to meet [Hammond's wife] in the whole year. . . . Somebody mentioned something about one of the air shows, and she just turned to me and she said 'You know, there is not anybody that could do anything to stop my husband from flying the way he wants to fly.' "

The children were no more exempt from the controversy than were the wives. Patrick McCloud, Mark's oldest son, came home from school one day extremely angry at the daughter of the deputy operations group commander. When his mother asked him why he was so upset he replied, "Well, all year long she just kept telling me that the best pilot in the squadron was Bob Hammond. . . . It annoyed me. But the thing that really annoys me the most now is that she said that if anybody is going to roll the B-52, Bob Hammond is going to be the one to do it, and I can just see him doing it some day."

There is also some evidence to suggest that the local civilian community was aware of the controversy swirling around Hammond's flying practices. Many family members of aircrews would physically leave base housing any time they knew Hammond was on the flying schedule, to protect themselves and their children from his reckless acts. In addition, one civilian complained to the local TV news that a B-52 was in 60 to 70 degrees of bank over the local supermarket and that something needed to be done about it.

But it was the crew force morale that was most affected. Captain Shawn Fleming, a B-52 instructor pilot and a weapons school graduate, was an opinion leader within the squadron and summed up the feelings many 325th BMS aviators had about Hammond's airmanship and the wing leadership's actions related to it:

> **Everybody had a Hammond scare story. Hammond was kind of like a crazy aunt . . . the parents say "Ignore her" . . . and the hypocrisy was amazing. For him to be in the position of the Chief of Standardization . . . is unconscionable. When Hammond did something . . . he's patted on the back by the leadership, "Good Show." What's the crew force supposed to learn from that? You got the "He's about to retire" [and] "That's Bob Hammond, he has more hours in the B-52 than you do sleeping." Yeah, he might have that many hours, but he became complacent, reckless, and willfully violated regulations.**

By June 1994, the organizational climate at the base was one of distrust and hostility. "Everybody was just trying to get out of here," stated one B-52 crewmember. In spite of these facts, Hammond was selected by Colonel Pollard to perform in the 1994 air show. "It was a nonissue," Pollard said. "Bob was Mr. Air Show."

Situation Seven: Air Show Practice: June 17, 1994

Hammond and the accident crew flew the first of two scheduled practice missions for the 1994 air show. The profile was exactly the same as the accident mission except that two profiles were flown. Once again they included large bank angles and high pitch climbs in violation of ACC regulations and technical order guidance, even though the wing commander had directed that the bank angles be limited to 45 degrees and the pitch to 25 degrees. (These were still in excess of regulations and technical order guidance.) Both profiles flown during this practice exceeded the wing commander's stated guidance. However, at the end of the practice session, Colonel Pollard, who was on board at the direction of the wing commander to ensure the safety of the flight profile, told the wing commander that "the profile looks good [to him]; looks very safe, well within parameters."

Because the bomb squadron was scheduled to close, most of the B-52 crewmembers had already been transferred to new assignments. But those that remained were not comfortable with the situation. Major Thomas, the squadron operations officer, was also uneasy. "I had this fear that he was again going to get into the air show . . . that he was going to try something again, ridiculous maybe and kill thousands of people."

It wasn't just the flyers who were getting nervous. The flight surgeon testified that he was told by a crewmember during a routine appointment that he refused to fly with Hammond. This, coupled with a concern that Hammond was scheduled to fly in the 1994 air show, led the doctor to take his concerns to both the wing chief of safety, and the chief of aeromedical services at Fairchild. The chief of safety told the flight surgeon not to worry because "Lt. Col. Hammond was a good pilot and the maneuvers had been done before."

Major Terry Makon, the nurse manager in emergency services, attended an air show planning session in which Hammond briefed that he planned to fly 65-degree bank turns. The wing commander quickly told him that he would be limited to 45 degrees maximum. Makon recalls Hammond's response in a prophetic discussion between her and a coworker who was also in attendance at the planning session.

> **Hammond's initial reaction was to brag that he could crank it pretty tight. . . . He said he could crank it tight and pop up starting at 200 [knots]. Bob and I looked at each other, and Bob is going, "He's [expletive deleted]", and I said, "I just hope he crashes on Friday, not Sunday, so I will not have so many bodies to pick up." . . . Those words did return to haunt me.**

During the planning session briefing to the wing commander, Hammond briefed his aggressive profile. As the briefing progressed, the wing commander made it clear that (1) there would be no formation flight, (2) bank angles would be limited to 45 degrees, and (3) pitch angles would be limited to 25 degrees. During the first practice mission, the commander's guidance was repeatedly violated, but once again no action was taken against Hammond.

It appears that, at this point, the leadership had given up on enforcing standards with regard to Hammond. Further, they appeared to be unable to read an atmosphere of impending disaster that permeated nearly every aspect of the organization. On the afternoon of June 24, *Czar 52* taxied to runway 23 for departure. At 1416 PDT, the aircraft impacted the ground, killing all aboard.

Conclusions and Implications

Leadership is a social phenomenon, existing in direct proportion to the degree to which subordinates are willing to follow. When followers cease to follow, leaders cease to lead. This is true even if the "leaders" hold high military ranks and fill positions of great power and responsibility. Describing what occurred is interesting and insightful, but determining why it occurred is absolutely essential if we are to avoid similar rogue-induced catastrophes in the future.

Followers Stopped Following

Just as "up" has no meaning without the concept of "down," leadership must be defined in terms of followership. On an individual basis, Hammond refused to follow written regulations and B-52 tech orders, as well as ignoring the verbal orders and guidance given by the wing commanders and DOs. Even when verbal reprimands and counseling sessions focused on the specific problem of airmanship, he steadfastly refused to follow their guidance. At one point, only weeks prior to the accident, he clearly stated his feelings on the issue of guidance from senior officers.

> **I'm going to fly the air show and, yeah, I may have someone senior in rank flying with me. . . . He may be the boss on the ground, but I'm the boss in the air and I'll do what I want to do.**

The aircrews quickly perceived this as an integrity problem within the leadership. The flyers, and eventually other members in the wing, simply lost faith in the leadership's ability to deal with the rogue pilot. Captain Brett Dugue summed up the pilot's frustration this way, "You've got to be kidding me, if they allowed him to fly a 50-foot flyby at a change of command, do you think me telling anybody about him flying low on a bombing route is going to do any good?" As a result of this loss of faith, the aircrews began to employ other survival techniques, such as feigning illness and openly refusing to fly with Hammond.

The lesson learned and the implication for dealing with rogue pilots is that trust is built by congruence between word and deed at all levels. Subordinates are quick to pick up on any disconnect. They are closer to the action, have more time on their hands, and love to analyze their leaders. Retired Air Force General Perry Smith writes, "Without trust and mutual respect among leaders and subordinate leaders, a large organization will suffer from a combination of poor performance and low morale." He was right on target in this case.

Standards Were Not Enforced

A rogue aviator was allowed, for over three years, to operate with a completely different set of rules from those applied to the rest of the wing aviators. The institutional integrity of the bomb wing leadership was severely damaged by this unwillingness to act. The entire leadership structure appeared to be operating in a state of denial, hoping for the best until the base closed or Hammond retired. Why? Either the wing leadership did not understand or know that the rules were being violated, or they chose not to apply them uniformly. The first case illustrates possible negligence and incompetence; the second hints at a lack of integrity.

In the words of retired Army Lieutenant General Calvin Waller, "Bad news doesn't improve with age." Leaders dealing with a rogue must act upon information or evidence of noncompliance. If they elect not to act, they should communicate their reasons for not doing so. Failure to do either invites second-guessing and criticism, often eroding the critical element of trust between the leader and the led. Leaders must also learn to recognize the traits of the rogue aviator, for while Hammond stood out like a beacon, many other rogues still operate today to a lesser degree.

A Key Position Was Filled by the Wrong Person

Selecting an aviator who exercised poor airmanship as the chief of standardization and evaluation was a poor choice, but leaving him there after multiple flagrant and willful violations of regulations sent an extremely negative message to the rest of the wing flyers. Individuals who hold key positions are looked up to as role models by junior crewmembers. They must be removed if they cannot maintain an acceptable standard of professionalism. Even if Hammond had not crashed, the damage he had done through his bad example of airmanship is incalculable. Not only did many young officers see his lack of professionalism as a bad example, but they also observed several senior leaders witness his actions and fail to take any corrective action. What this said to them about Air Force leadership in general is uncertain, but in at least one case, it led an otherwise satisfied Air Force pilot to try civilian life.

> **I wanted no part of an organization that would allow that kind of thing to continue for years on end. We [the crewmembers] pointed it out to them [the leaders] over and over again. It was always the same response—nothing. I'd had enough.**

The implication for current and future leaders is simply to select key personnel carefully, with an understanding that they are role models and will help shape the personality of the entire organization. If a mistake is made by selecting the wrong person for a key position, remove that person if there is cause, so that you don't compound the original error. Rogues are dangerous enough without adding the credibility offered by a key organizational position to their power.

A Final Perspective

The crash of *Czar 52*, like most accidents, was part of a chain of events. These events were facilitated through the failed policies of several senior leaders at this bomb wing. These failures included an inability to recognize and correct the actions of a single rogue aviator, which eventually led to an unhealthy command climate and the disintegration of trust between leaders and subordinates. However, in most aircraft mishaps, the crash is the final domino to drop in the cause-and-effect chain of events. In this case, however, scores of young and impressionable aviators matured watching the quintessential rogue pilot as their role model for over three years. They remain on active flying status in various Air Force wings, passing along what they have learned. Because of this, the final domino in this chain of events may not yet have fallen.

Rogue behavior is certainly unnecessary in the modern world of aviation, but there was a time in America when rogues were necessary to move aviation forward. Chapter 3 looks at that unique period of American history.

Note: All quotations were taken from the USAF 110-14 Accident Investigation Board Report of the B-52 Mishap at Fairchild AFB, June 24, 1994, or from personal interviews conducted by the author.

CHAPTER THREE

When Rogues Were Required

T HROUGHOUT THE COURSE of this book, the term "rogue" has held a negative connotation. That is not always the case in society as a whole, where Hollywood versions of likable rogues, such as Maverick in the movie *Top Gun* and FBI agent Fox Mulder in the popular television series *The X-Files*, create the false impression that it takes a rogue to really get things done. Although this notion is seriously flawed when applied to modern aviation—even combat aviation—there were times when rogues truly were necessary to move aviation to the next level. This happened at least twice, and possibly three times, in the first three decades of this century. The first was during the initial decade of powered flight, known as the "exhibition era." The second occurred as aircraft became capable as instruments of war. The third was the period just following World War I, when barnstormers roamed the skies over America, a period that also included the institutionalization of commercial and peacetime government flying. Let's begin with the earliest of the necessary rogues, those that fanned the flames of aviation enthusiasm in the first decade following the Wright brothers' event in 1903.

Rogues Required: The Dawn of Aviation Enthusiasm

Following the Wright brothers' inaugural flight on December 17, 1903, technological advances in aviation came rapidly. By 1909, the world was ready for its first international air meet, a winner-take-all event in Rheims, France. The winner of the first Gordon Bennett Aviation Cup—and the $5000 prize that went with it—was an unlikely engine manufacturer from the United States named Glenn Curtiss. How this came to be is interesting especially in terms of how a rogue motorcycle racer became a disciplined airman, and what this meant for the future of aviation in a crucial decade of advancement.

Glenn Curtiss grew up racing bicycles as a young lad and eventually graduated to motorcycle racing all over the eastern United States. His love for racing, combined with his chosen vocation as an engine manufacturer, evolved into one of the most bizarre stories in the history of humanity's quest for speed. In the early 1900s, it was natural for a young man who loved to ride motorcycles to eventually become involved in the business of manufacturing them. As Curtiss developed his business, he found it highly profitable to manufacture engines for other purposes as well.

One example of such a venture was to provide power plants for the huge airships of the day. To ensure high quality and customer satisfaction, Curtiss made it a habit to manufacture *two* engines for every customer's order. In this way he was able to guarantee customer satisfaction, and if the first engine worked satisfactorily he had a small inventory in case another customer should call with a short-notice requirement for the same type of motor. One day an order came for a huge, eight-cylinder engine to power one of the largest airships in the world. Although Curtiss realized that it was highly unlikely that there would ever be a requirement for a second engine of this mammoth size, he followed his standard routine of manufacturing two engines. Upon delivery, the first engine was found to be in perfect working order, so Curtiss was left to ponder a use for the second engine.

Curtiss was one of the most successful motorcycle racers of his day. His success was based in large part on his total disdain for danger and unrelenting and aggressive riding style. These traits had earned him the nickname, "The Hellrider," and he was widely respected by other racers, many of whom kept a healthy distance from him in the turns on the racetrack. If there was such a thing as a rogue among motorcycle racers of the day, Glenn Curtiss typified the term in spades.

But as the legendary hellrider stared down at the huge engine, pondering its use, in the spring of 1907, he concocted an idea that would make all he had done before fade into insignificance. Curtiss ordered his metalworkers to build a motorcycle frame that would hold the huge engine, and he began looking around for a race event that would allow such a monstrosity to compete. He found one in Ormand Beach, Florida, where an upcoming event had an "open and unlimited" competition category. Curtiss knew this was going to open some eyes.

Glenn Curtiss understood speed. He had set two world records on motorcycles: the first in 1903 at 60.6 miles per hour, and the second at just over 89 miles per hour in January 1904. At the time, there was not a regulated system for determining exactly how you would validate such records, and others had unsubstantiated speed record claims. Regardless of the actual land speed record of the day, Curtiss was about to shatter it. Stories are told of women who fainted at the mere sight of the monstrous motorcycle as it was rolled out of the trailer at the raceway. The strip upon which Curtiss would race was constructed along the beach and would require him to drive beneath the pier at high speed. He analyzed the risk, shrugged his shoulders, and fired up the mechanical beast. Riding the huge motorcycle on a modified bicycle seat, with only a leather helmet for protection, Curtiss blazed down the track at over 136.29 miles per hour! It would be years before anyone approached this mark again. The hellrider had fulfilled his final need for speed by setting a new world record. He ceased building motorcycles a few years later and turned his interest to aviation. Strangely, he left his rogue tendencies on the ground, but he would need others to further the development of his new vocation, building aircraft.

Curtiss was initially not very interested in flying aircraft, but he was very interested in selling his engines to the Wright brothers. The Wright brothers, however, were exceedingly paranoid and highly suspicious of anyone who they thought might be trying to cash in on their success. Because of his inability to sell his engines to the Wright brothers, Curtiss joined the Aerial Experiment Association with Alexander Graham Bell to develop aircraft on their own. He would now need to learn how to fly.

As in his other endeavors, Curtiss became a perfectionist at flying aircraft. But contrary to his rogue approach to driving motorcycles, Curtiss was far more careful in the air. In winning the Rheims air meet in 1909, Curtiss was extremely disciplined. A heavy underdog to the Frenchman Louis Blériot, Curtiss crafted a plan that would protect his irreplaceable aircraft until the final winner-take-all race. He did this in the face of intense peer pressure from Americans at the site who wanted him to fly in the demonstration events preceding the final race. Curtiss explained his philosophy:

> It is hard enough for anyone to map out a course of action and stick to it, particularly in the face of the desires of one's own friends; but it is doubly hard for aviators to stay on the ground waiting for just the right moment to go into the air. It was particularly hard for me to stay out of many events in Rheims held from day-to-day, especially as there were many patriotic Americans there. These good friends did not realize the situation. America's chances could not be imperiled for the sake of gratifying one's curiosity.

These are hardly the words of a rogue, and those who knew Curtiss from his motorcycle racing days could not believe they were talking to the same person. Perhaps it was age or the wisdom of experience, but, for whatever reasons, Curtiss approached flying cautiously. So it was that Glenn Curtiss, the famed hellrider, was forced to hire a rogue to test and display his many new aircraft. This rogue's name was Lincoln Beachey.

History's Greatest Rogue

The following is a quotation from a book review by Kirk House:

> Carl Sandburg wrote a poem about him. Curtis LeMay, Jimmy Doolittle and Charles Lindbergh watched him fly as boys. Orville Wright and Glenn Curtiss said he was the best they had ever seen. Lincoln Beachey basked in the adulation but remained cynical about it, saying "they come to see me die."

Lincoln Beachey was born in 1887 in San Francisco (Figure 3-1). He flew his first flight only one year after the Wright brothers' first flight. According to a documentary entitled *Engines of Our Ingenuity*, Beachey was drawn to flight like a "moth toward flame." That analogy would prove all too true.

In 1910, the legendary Glenn Curtiss needed a pilot to test his new designs. At first, it seemed like Beachey was an unlikely candidate. His

Figure 3-1. Called by many "history's greatest rogue," Lincoln Beachey was fearless in the air at a time when rogues were required as a means of advancing the fledgling enterprise of flying. *(Chicago Historical Society photo)*

performance at the Curtiss flying school was abysmal. He was constantly crashing and destroying valuable equipment, but Curtiss recognized the fine madness of the rogue pilot and hired him to fly on his exhibition team to publicize his aircraft. In a very real sense, Lincoln Beachey was the first test pilot to put various aircraft through their paces.

John Lienhard, from the University of Houston, writes the following about the actions of—and the need for—a man like Lincoln Beachey:

> **Beachey performed and perfected every kind of stunt, flying into the mist of Niagara Falls, flying to an altitude record of over two miles, nose-diving from 3000 feet with his engine off, while on-**

lookers screamed, fainted, and vomited. He did one of the first loops in the air (and several thousand more afterwards). In an age of flying box-kites, nine out of ten exhibition fliers died. It was only a matter of time and Beachey flew constantly. In 1913, his notices said he'd entertained 17 million people in 126 cities. Each routine was closer to the edge than the last. He finally laid off for a year. Then he came back to San Francisco with a new plane. He did a series of loops for the crowd and climbed and dove far faster than he had ever done before. When he tried to pull out, the wings tore off with a sickening crunch.

Although Beachey survived even this horrific crash, he drowned before rescuers could arrive. Over 50,000 spectators on the shores of the San Francisco Bay had witnessed aviation's greatest showman fly his last stunt. Lienhard points out why this rogue pilot was so essential: "But he'd done the first thing that had to be done if we were to take to the air. He made such a theater of flight that we all had to join in."

It wasn't long before the specter of war gave a new group of young men the opportunity to invent new ways of dying and presented a new stage for the rogue.

The Birth of Combat Aviation

Prior to World War I, flying was reserved for those who had the technical skill and financial resources to develop their own aircraft. Men like Wilbur and Orville Wright, Glenn Curtiss, the French air racer and aircraft builder Blériot, the "Great Farman," and a handful of others were the select few who graced the skies prior to 1910. Early aircraft did not have enough horsepower to really do much more than hold a single person aloft for a short period of time. Flight controls and instrumentation were in their embryonic stages.

Even great minds like Igor Sikorsky and Blériot had difficulty in understanding the aerodynamic forces that were acting upon their aircraft, and this made mere flight exhilarating enough. Early daredevils who did not have employers like Curtiss had very little to work with—aircraft were expensive and training programs for the everyday chap were nearly nonexistent.

As aircraft engines became lighter and more powerful, and as flight controls and basic instrumentation became more developed, the aircraft became useful for a new purpose: as a weapon of war. The world in the early 1900s was careening toward war, and aviation manufacturers were getting ready. Unfettered by doctrine, laws of war, or regulations, the rogue aviator was bound to emerge in this new environment, and he was needed to some extent.

The First Combat Rogue[1]

Although lighter-than-air aircraft had been used in Europe and in the American Civil War, the first combat in powered, heavier-than-air aircraft took place in 1911. Italy and Turkey were at war in Libya, and both sides possessed military aircraft. In less than six months nearly every mode of employment now used in military aviation had surfaced, including reconnaissance, air defense, air superiority, transport, ground attack, and bombardment. Not surprisingly, the brave airmen who flew these first combat missions had no experience, doctrine, or regulations to guide them, and a few aspects of rogue behavior began to surface.

Far from being a rogue organization, however, this group shed a special light on the nature of good airmanship as well as identifying early tendencies of the rogue. Unspoiled by previous training or indoctrination on how tactical airpower should be employed, they merely responded to what worked and rooted out behaviors that were incompatible with military success.

The first air combat took place against a backdrop of desert ground warfare on Libyan soil, where the Italians and Turks were fighting over economic interests in an ebb-and-flow campaign in and around Tripoli. The Italians, under the command of Naval Captain Umberto Cagni, had occupied Tripoli on October 5, 1911, and were expecting an enemy counterattack of unknown size from an unknown location at any moment. Seventeen days later, the Turk counterattack came and, to a large degree, succeeded in pushing the Italians back from their defensive positions. The Italian high command was in desperate need of reliable intelligence as to the locations and strength of the enemy. Faced with uncertainty, the Italians turned to Captain Carlo Piazza, the commander of the newly formed air flotilla for assistance in obtaining aerial observation of enemy troop locations, strength, and movements. The air flotilla was composed of 5 fully qualified pilots, 6 reserve pilots with "lower qualifications," 9 aircraft, 1 sergeant, and 30 men. Within the confines of this small group of combatants, the roots of tactical combat airmanship and the first indications of rogue combat pilots would take shape.

Piazza flew the first operational military mission on October 23, 1911, lifting off at 6:19 A.M. in a French Blériot aircraft. Exactly one hour and one minute later he returned to the field and reported "several enemy encampments, each with 150 to 200 men." With this simple report, Piazza changed the nature of warfare forever, by eliminating the element of surprise obtained by hiding behind terrain. War had taken on an additional dimension. Even in the light of this successful first mission, the euphoria of flight that has been present since the days of the mythical Icarus was reported in the combat journal of the air flotilla.

Two days after Piazza's first flight, the Italian airmen discovered that the added dimension did not offer immunity from bullets, when Captain Ricardo Moizo decided to buzz enemy formations to demonstrate the superior capabilities of the airborne war machine. He quickly learned that such rogue behaviors had a price. He returned to the airstrip with three bullet holes in the wing of his Nieuport and received a stern warning about taking unnecessary risks with his valuable aircraft. The rogue combat pilot had surfaced.

With the role of the aircraft becoming increasingly important in the military plans of the Italians, it became apparent that tactics and regulations would need to be developed to protect the valuable resources from the enemy as well as from the shenanigans of the rogue pilot. The flotilla commander, Piazza "laid down the rules for his young pilots without experience in warfare." These rules established the first tactics, risk management procedures, and regulatory environment for combat aircraft. They were designed to guide the actions of the pilots by balancing the need to accomplish the military mission against the value of the aircraft and crew. From the earliest moments of combat aviation, it was understood that it made more sense to make "what if?" decisions on the ground, rather than in the complex and dynamic environment of flight, where emotions and euphoria can lead to rogue behavior. Unfortunately, this scenario would be revisited—writ large—in the Great War that followed less than three years later.

World War I in the Air

By 1914, aircraft had reached the stage of reliability where they could be used in combat with some regularity. Initially, these flights took the form of observation and artillery spotting, and the ground commanders were very skeptical about their effectiveness. It wasn't long before their skepticism disappeared, as artillery-induced casualties mounted to astronomical numbers, greatly aided by aerial spotting. Targeting spotter aircraft with both ground and airborne assets became a priority—a big one. The pilots themselves were beginning to realize their importance and feel the heat.

One of the first of the daring reconnaissance pilots, and an early rogue, was *Leutnant* Hermann Göring, later to command the entire *Luftwaffe* in World War II. Late in the summer of 1916, Göring sat in a briefing room where his squadron commander asked for volunteers to fly what amounted to a suicide mission deep into French territory. Great War historian Kelly Wills relates the following story in the World War I journal of aviation, *The Cross and Cockade*.

> Everyone groaned when the mission was announced—except Göring. He quickly got up, tapped his observer on the shoulder, and the two of them went to their aircraft and took off. When they returned several hours later their plane was riddled with bullet holes, but they had the photographs.

Göring was known to take incredible and often unnecessary risks, but this got him noticed by his superiors, resulted in promotion, and fanned the flames of other would-be rogues.

The Lone Wolf

The effectiveness and devastation caused by the spotter aircraft gave rise to the new breed of rogue—the first interceptor fighter pilots. The era of the lone wolf fighter pilot, going solo in one-on-one combat with his white scarf flying in the wind, was relatively short. Men like the legendary Manfred Richthofen, Max Immelmann, Rene Fonck, and George Guynemer racked up kill after kill, and the longer they stayed alive, the more unequal the combat between them and other "green" pilots became. Coldly efficient, these killers developed aerobatic maneuvers that at first appeared foolhardy, but eventually became standards that are still flown by fighter pilots today. Of all the early aces, one stands alone as an innovator in spite of his rogue tendencies: Oswald Boelcke.

Perhaps no combat pilot has done as much for the systematic education and training of other pilots as the great German ace Boelcke. Yet like many great pilots of this era, his recklessness and rogue tendencies would eventually result in his demise. Boelcke began his flying career in 1914 and flew with his brother Wilhelm in reconnaissance missions, mostly over the Argonne forest region. He was decorated for his daring and production, and moved up to more heavily armed aircraft. He recorded his first of 40 confirmed kills on July 4, 1915, and began an aggressive style of offensive attack that would at first characterize him as foolhardy among his peers. As his tally rose, however, others, including the great Max Immelmann, emulated his tactics. Boelcke was promoted to squadron commander and personally selected and trained Manfred Richthofen as his student and heir apparent.

In June 1916, Immelmann was killed and the German high command decided it was time to give Boelcke a much-needed rest before he too was lost. He was assigned to a public relations tour and during the next few months wrote a paper entitled "Air Fighting Tactics," more commonly referred to as the "Dicta Boelcke." It is still taught at military fighter weapons and tactics schools to this day. This type of scientific approach to combat certainly does not indicate rogue behavior. Yet rogue tendencies were there, and they eventually resulted in Boelcke's demise.

On October 28, 1916, Boelcke was on patrol with his protégés Richthofen and Lieutenant Bohme when they encountered seven enemy aircraft. Although outnumbered by more than two to one, they dove to attack. This was typical of the bold Germans. While engaged with a British fighter, Bohme collided with Boelcke, and the squadron commander's Fokker Eindecker spun toward the ground. The aircraft crashed near friendly German forces. Although the crash was severe, Boelcke's body was not badly broken up and he might well have survived had it not been for the fact that he refused to wear a helmet or a seat belt while flying, although regulations required it. In spite of all the discipline, knowledge, and skill, it was this one rogue tendency which likely killed the man who had won Germany's highest award for valor, the Blue Max, and set the standard for fighter tactics for generations to come.

While the combat pilots of World War I pushed the envelope of airmanship out of necessity from 1914 to 1918, another group was expanding the envelope in a different manner. The stuntmen and daredevils who stormed the skies of America in the second decade of the new century were a breed apart and would further American interest in aviation at a critical stage of its development. In addition, the military pilots who returned alive from the European combat theater would join in the parade upon their return.

The Barnstormers

Following the epic tragedy of the Great War, the War Department of the United States was forced to sell off thousands of obsolete war birds. In addition, the men who flew them were also cast off now that they were no longer needed for combat. The government was getting rid of these still-functional (albeit barely) aircraft at absurdly low prices— some as low as $300 for a Curtiss "Jenny" (JN-4D). C. R. Rosenberry, an aviation historian, states the obvious, "It was a fair bet that the unwanted pilots and machines would get together." The result was an era of aviation history that was uniquely American. There was a frontier to be conquered—the hearts and minds of the American public—and these intrepid souls were more than ready to be the "mountain men of the sky."

There were several reasons why these men were ideal for this task and why they were ready-made rogues. It is also important to point out that *these reasons no longer exist in today's flight environment.* Having just served in a war that took over nine million lives, these men likely saw themselves as living on borrowed time. In addition, stunt flying in the United States must have seemed like child's play after surviving combat with the likes of Boelcke, Richthofen, and a host of other German aces.

The American pilots who returned from World War I came home to a hero's welcome. They had seen the world and experienced the excitement and exhilaration of combat aviation. It was easy to understand why they wanted to continue to fly. While the Europeans of the same period moved directly from a combat aviation environment into passenger-carrying operations, the Americans were not yet ready to take this step. The infrastructure of runways and support systems did not yet exist. Europe had the aviation infrastructure from the multiple bases of operation in the war, so profit—not public support—was the motive for their flyers.

These American legends became known by many names, including "flying gypsies" and "lone eagles." The name that stuck, however, is indelibly etched in the psyches and secret ambitions of many modern aviators: the "barnstormer." They would put the roar in the Roaring '20s.

Touring Rogues: The Homeless Pilot

There were approximately 1200 privately owned aircraft in the United States in the early 1920s. Of these, roughly 600 were operated by what one historian calls "itinerant pilots," a breed of "nomadic, hand-to-mouth vagabonds." According to Rosenberry, these pilots would develop ingenious methods for determining the most profitable cornfields to land upon. Captain Basil L. Rowe, an ex-barnstormer, explained the theory:

> **Flying haphazardly around the country, I developed a system for picking the most profitable place to land. I would buzz the town a couple of times, if the people continued about their business, I did the same, but if the animals and fowl took off . . . and the kids tried to follow me—it indicated virgin territory.**

The barnstormers made money any way they could, including stunt flying, giving rides to awestruck civilians, and even running rum during Prohibition. As the novelty of flight began to wear off, the pilots were required to try more daring stunts at the same time that their aircraft were aging and breaking down. The results were predictable, but the feats that these men and women accomplished in the aging aircraft were almost unbelievable. In one rather incredible record, Chuck "Speed" Holman accomplished 1093 consecutive loops. Looping around bridges was another favorite stunt, and the press coverage of such flyers began to list the bridges at which they had accomplished this feat, as well as other bizarre claims to fame.

But the "good, clean fun" of barnstorming was soon overshadowed by the myriad of tragic endings. According to the 1923 version of the *Aircraft Year Book*, a first effort at tracking accident and incident statistics, there were 179 serious accidents reported, 85 deaths, and 162 injuries. These numbers may have reflected only a fraction of the total, as many of these accidents occurred in rural areas and were never reported. Rosenberry cites the causes:

- Wing collapses
- Stunting at low altitude
- Plane taken up with only one pint of gas
- Bad landing on a bad field
- Fabric on wings so rotten it broke at finger touch
- Plane plowing into crowd
- Control stick broke
- Stunt pilot fails to come out of barrel roll and tailspin

The question of the day was "What shall be done with the gypsy flier?" Eventually, regulations crept into the barnstormers' lives and the Air Commerce Act of 1926 started to bring the curtain down on rogue flyers.

As the barnstormers began to fade from the scene, rogue pilots had to find new ways to practice their trade. Some courted fame, others employment, but always the rogue tendencies found their way into the cockpit.

Amy Johnson

Amy Johnson was an unlikely rogue. As the Roaring '20s moved into full swing, the American public and the world were introduced to several women flyers, including the legendary Amelia Earhart. The British, not to be outdone, offered Amy Johnson. There was only one small problem: Amy couldn't fly very well. John Lienhard called her "a hopelessly unrealistic dreamer. She took up flying in 1928, after she'd been jilted. At the time, it seemed like a romantic way to die." It took Amy more than twice as long as normal to solo her first aircraft. Somehow after only two years of experience, she managed to get herself selected to fly a new experimental airplane to Australia. She made it, but the flight was extremely difficult and filled with crash landings and self-induced problems. Lienhard sums up her trip:

> **When her battered airplane limped into Darwin, Australia, she was given a hero's welcome. She was the first woman to make the trip. The *Daily Mail* gave her a £10,000 prize and scheduled her on a flying tour of Australia. The stress of the tour was worse than the stress of the flight. It left her close to a nervous breakdown.**

Johnson continued to set obscure records—and continued to crash often as the result of taking shortcuts, poor planning, and other rogue behaviors. Lienhard sums up her impact:

> **By then Amy Johnson had somehow—Heaven knows how—helped tell us what we needed to know: that aviation was both exciting and safe. In the end, Amy Johnson had become what she'd set out to be. She really was an authentic hero of aviation.**

It is indeed ironic that she taught us this lesson by being an average to below average flyer and by taking risks that many thought were outrageous, given her level of experience. As Johnson accumulated fame and glory, many began to understand that flying couldn't be that difficult.

The difficulty lay in developing a reliable system that could tap the potential of aviation for more than demonstration and entertainment. One of the first attempts was the use of aircraft to deliver the mail. History would reveal that it took a few rogue pilots to keep the system alive in the early days of airmail.

The Mailmen

In 1916, the U.S. Congress appropriated $100,000 to see if aircraft might have utility in speeding up the mail service. By May 1918, a route and delivery system had been designed between New York, Philadelphia, and Washington. The air express got off to an inauspicious beginning, attempting to take off from Washington without any fuel. This took place in front of President Woodrow Wilson, Mrs. Wilson, the head postmaster of Japan, and a host of photographers and congressmen. After draining gas from every vehicle in sight, the aircraft finally made it airborne, but the pilot got confused and headed *south* instead of north. He eventually figured out he was lost and landed in a cornfield, breaking his propeller. But things would get better.

After the initial few months, the system settled down, but the need to expand meant getting a few daredevil pilots who could carry the mail west over the mountains. Max Miller and Ed Gardner were the perfect pair. Both former stunt pilots, they welcomed the opportunity to approach danger with a purpose. Rosenberry states, "If an unknown route was to be charted, an untried plane put through its paces, Miller or Gardner drew the chore and relished it." One of these challenges was the first attempts to overfly the Alleghenies en route to Chicago. This route was to become the final resting place of many airmail pilots and was dubbed the "graveyard of the airmail." The experience would pale to insignificance later when pilots tried to cross the Rocky Mountains at night without aeronautical charts.

But the real challenge was the sheer volume of the mail, and it soon became obvious that night flying would be required if the airmail was to become a reliable part of the postal service.

The Night Flight of Jack Knight

By 1921 the routes had been established from New York to San Francisco, but flights were made only during the day. The new administration of Warren G. Harding (who would be inaugurated on March 5, 1921) was promising "to get government out of business," and the railroads were making a big lobbying effort to shut down the costly airmail operation. Rail was certainly cheaper, and at the time a good bit safer and more reliable. In less than three years of operation, the airmail service had lost 26 men in the line of duty, and much of the mail that went down with them had never gotten through. The post office needed a public relations coup, so it decided to attempt the foolhardy: a coast-to-coast night delivery. The event was publicized nationwide and set for February 22, Washington's birthday. This was certainly not the most ideal time of the year in which to attempt a night flight across two mountain ranges. But politics drove the perceived need, and rogue mentalities and actions were needed to save the postal service's aerial program. The mission would be flown.

A handful of volunteers consisted of both pilots and ground crews who would light bonfires in fields to help the pilots navigate. Two aircraft took off from each coast and headed for each other, planning to meet in Omaha. One eastbound plane went down on takeoff from Elko, Nevada, killing the pilot. The westbound effort got only as far as Chicago, where a blizzard grounded the effort. In the middle of the plan sat Jack Knight, who was supposed to fly the 276 miles from North Platte to Omaha (Figure 3-2). Rosenberry describes the young pilot: "He was a wiry, frail looking man, and his nose was wrapped grotesquely in adhesive tape, having broken it a week before in a forced landing on a mountainside."

Because the pilot who preceded him had broken the tailskid on the aircraft upon landing at North Platte, Knight wasn't able to take off until three hours late, at 10:45 P.M. He landed in Omaha at 1:10 A.M., "looking forward to coffee and a warm bed," but to his astonishment,

Figure 3-2. Jack Knight weighed the risks and made a dramatic night flight from Omaha to Chicago in the dead of winter. (*United Airlines photo*)

there was no aircraft there to meet him. The airport manager called the project off, but Knight wouldn't hear of it. "I'm going to take the mail to Chicago," he said.

Knight had never flown this route, and the "bonfire brigade" had long since gone home, assuming the mission had failed. Snow and cloud cover made stopping for fuel extremely difficult, and at one point Knight had to circle a dark field until an employee heard the plane and came out with a flare. The engine flamed out just as Knight touched down on the snow-covered runway. Knight's official report dismisses the close call, as well as the challenge for the rest of the flight. "Lost 10 minutes at Iowa City locating the town and field, and remained there until I got a weather report from Chicago, as weather was bad."

The early newspapers picked up the story on the telegraph and ran morning editions detailing the lone pilot's all-night flight against the elements. Rosenberry describes the Chicago arrival:

> In Chicago, many of the night-club patrons spontaneously decided to stay up the rest of the night and greet him. Thus it was that, when Knight rolled to a stop at Checkerboard Field at 8:40 A.M. he was uproariously greeted by men and women in evening dress, kissed by the ladies.

It had cost the life of one pilot and taken a rogue effort, but the next day, Congress approved $1,250,000 for continuation of the air-mail service.

It would be 10 more years before the need for bravado and high-risk night flights would begin to disappear, and it would take the efforts of a man whose name has become synonymous with aviation professionalism.

Rogues No Longer Required: Professionalism Creeps In[2]

In 1930, Elrey B. Jeppesen began his aviation career with a job flying mail between Salt Lake City, Utah, Cheyenne, Wyoming, and Oakland, California. This was not the most forgiving terrain to be flying over, especially at night, without the aid of reliable weather forecasts, accurate terrain maps, or radio aids to navigation. But the mail had to get through, and this was the highest-paying route—$50 per week and 7¢

per mile (14¢ at night)! "That winter began with 18 pilots flying between Oakland and Cheyenne. Before the season was out, Jepp attended the funerals of four of them." It wasn't that these pilots were foolish or undisciplined. They were not attempting to take navigational or procedural shortcuts. It was simply a matter of a lack of—as yet uninvented—instrumentation and no reliable or complete terrain maps for pilots to use when determining their next course of action. The costs were simply too high, and Jepp set out to remedy this situation.

"Captain Jepp started recording field lengths, slopes, drainages, lights and obstacles. He illustrated airport layouts and the terrain, and noted local farmers who had phones and would provide weather reports." He quite literally established the first METRO weather system and developed the first set of approach plates in an attempt to protect his friends and himself. He knew that to survive they must fly in a more disciplined and systematic manner. Jepp took no unnecessary risks; his disciplined approach is clearly evidenced by his description of how he mapped the elevation of Blythe Mountain, a particularly dangerous peak just outside of Salt Lake City:

> **I climbed it with three altimeters strapped to my back, and I took the temperature when I went up. I took the readings to the physics department at the University of Utah and had them figure the elevation. Then I added 500 feet to it to be safe. [Later developed technology showed that] I was off by 200 feet, so with the 500 added . . . I was 300 feet in the clear.**

There is much for us to learn from the methodical approach taken by this pioneer of disciplined flight operations. For Jepp, it wasn't enough to climb the peak with a single altimeter—he took three. Although he was quite good at mathematics and the equations for temperature conversion were available to him, Jepp took his readings to the experts at the physics department to provide a level of certainty beyond that which he himself felt adequate to provide. Finally, because he recognized the limits of the technology of the day, he added a 500-foot margin for error "just to be safe."

Of course, the rest of the story is the stuff of aviation legend. His mapping business—which he once offered to United Airlines for $5000—grew from selling his "little black book" to other pilots for $10 a pop, to a multimillion-dollar profit margin per year. Today, more than 2000 charts are updated every month at Jeppesen corporate headquarters in Englewood, Colorado.

The professional approach to safety demonstrated by Elrey Jeppesen was the first of many efforts to bring rational decision making back into aviation. Rogues were no longer required to advance public interest in aviation. In fact, it was just the opposite: the public was convinced that aviation was here to stay, and now they wanted professionalism and safety—not stuntmen and daredevils.

A Final Word on the Bygone Era

There are two special places for rogue aviators. The first is a place that Eddie Rickenbacker calls "the kind of show that requires the forfeit of aircraft and crew." These are situations such as we have seen in this chapter, when the need to promote aviation, win in combat, or establish the airmail delivery system outweighed the risk to pilot and craft. The second place for the rogue pilot is in our memories, because we should all be grateful for these brave men and women who paved the way for those of us who fly today. But the rogue does not belong in the cockpit with us today, except as a fond memory.

Returning to the modern era, Chapter 4 looks at how an accident investigator in Australia uncovered a rogue who had been operating with relative impunity right up until his final rogue act.

CHAPTER FOUR

Discovering a Rogue: An Accident Investigator's Sobering Journey*

Often rogues aren't recognized as such until a post mortem *analysis—a sort of psychological autopsy—is done. A mishap or accident investigation board most often accomplishes this. Doug Edwards was a senior military officer and seasoned fighter pilot in the Royal Australian Air Force (RAAF) when he was called to duty as a head of a Court of Inquiry (the equivalent of the USAF Mishap Board President) to investigate a mishap involving a gifted young fighter pilot. What he discovered—as well as how he discovered it—is sobering, but beneficial in understanding the many faces of the rogue pilot. This is his story. (Note: As Doug is Australian, his English is slightly different from the American style. His spelling and punctuation have been edited to conform to American usage.)*

Called to Duty

The basis of Australian law is our Constitution. Drafted in the 1880s, it closely follows the leading democratic model of the time, that of the United States of America—and why not? Why try to reinvent excellence? So, our Constitution is like yours, with Montesquieu's doctrine of the Separation of the Powers a powerful influence on its design. There are three discrete "Chapters," one each for the Executive, the Legislative, and the Judicial powers. So zealously are the internal roles and prerogatives of each of the arms of Government guarded that when one encounters an "outside" delegation it is with some wonderment.

* This chapter was written by Doug Edwards.

These thoughts pass through my mind as I fly to Williamtown, home of the Royal Australian Air Force (RAAF)'s Tactical Fighter Force. I am to head a Court of Inquiry into a fatal aircraft crash. The realization that it is a court, *a real court*, not some administrative tribunal, becomes clear from the terms of reference. I am to investigate everything the least bit relevant, with delegated powers as if I were a judge, to compel evidence if necessary, on oath or affirmation, to determine all issues pertaining to this particular accident, including questions such as manner of death and the responsibility of others in the cause(s) thereof. These are grave matters, indeed, normally determined in the Coroner's Court. The state does not lightly hand over its judicial authority. This signal of respect for a military proceeding has a sobering influence over my deliberations.

The Crash Scene

Pretty soon we are at the crash scene, standing around the "crash kit," getting to know each other. It's midafternoon. My investigating team comprises another pilot, a medical officer, an aeronautical engineer, and my ace up the sleeve, a psychologist. I'd heard just enough about the accident, before I left Canberra, to think "Human Factors," and to get on the phone to ask for some help. The bloke they've sent turns out to have a Ph.D. in psychology, but we don't know that right away and are thus neither skeptical nor intimidated, and by the time we do learn, he has established himself as a valued member of the investigation.

Nothing at the site can be moved until I say so. So we get on with it, walking around, talking observations into tape recorders, assigning jobs to the other folk who are there, like sending one pair off to drive around and see if they can round up any eyewitnesses. What's being recorded is basically a stream of raw data with the occasional "easy" conclusion thrown in. *Impact point thirty nautical miles from base, can't have been airborne for more than five minutes, little fuel used from the six thousand pounds he'd taken off with, therefore aircraft was still at heavy weight,* and so on.

That the final maneuver was a spin is quickly discovered. A delta-wing aircraft spins when you suck in a lot of backstick at low speed with just the slightest amount of roll command in. The nose pitches up to about 45 degrees, whereupon the adverse yaw swings it rapidly across, rotating around the axis of travel—in the direction opposite to that of the roll command. When a right-handed pilot under pressure pulls full backstick, it is common, in that right-handed action, for the hand to come not straight back, but toward the strong-hand side of the body, introducing a little right aileron. We determine from the crash pattern that the aircraft has yawed left into the spin. More food for thought.

We know it was a spin because the radar nose cone, and the pitot head that protrudes from it, are buried in the sand at the first point of ground contact. The aircraft has hit nose down, inverted, and nearly vertical, as it would be after one-half of a turn of the spin. The flight path heading is northeast. Upon impact, the nose section broke off and stayed there. Further down the wreckage trail, we find the cockpit section, badly damaged. It has nearly separated from the fuselage, the fracture line being along the rear cockpit wall, just ahead of the equipment bay. The main chunk of wings and fuselage has slumped to the ground last, having rotated through a complete 180 degrees. That is, the engine exhaust is now facing in the direction from which it came. That the main part of the wreckage is nearly intact indicates the impact occurred at relatively slow speed. *Yes, surely a spin. But how, and why?*

He has come down in a pine forest—Pinus radiata—Monterey pine. They are called 'radiata' because, when grown alone or well spaced, they radiate branches in all directions, each tree almost like a ball. If planted close together, as in plantations, they shoot up tall, on straight trunks, just the thing for housing planks and floor boards. This has proven to be poor growing territory for these pines, though. It's mostly sand with little nutrient. While the trees have grown all right, up to 60 feet, they are thin and scrawny, and they snap readily when struck by something hard, like a jet aircraft.

In the crash kit is a *theodolite*. We use it to measure the angle of the final flight path, the chute carved by the Mirage's plunge down through the trees. It's only seven degrees, a gentle enough dive. But it doesn't make any sense. This is a jet that cruises at 420 knots and lands at 180. The spin entry just described will only occur at 200 knots. *How could he have got to be at treetop level and that slow?* It's the nearest thing to hovering, and this Mach II jet is no helicopter. There is no known training or operational maneuver or procedure that will get him to that altitude and airspeed. It's baffling, a mystery.

One of the helpers checks back in, one of the pair who'd been sent to scout for witnesses. They have found two farmers, each of whom had been plowing, one on either side of the flight path, and at right angles to it, and about three to four miles distant. That's a long way away, seeing it's a small aircraft—35 feet long, 27-foot wingspan, 15 feet from ground to tip of the tail fin. However, they're all we have. I hand this bloke the theodolite, tell him to go back to the witnesses, and tell him what to do with the farmers when he gets there.

Which is to ask each farmer to stand where he had been when he saw the jet, first sighting, last sighting, anything interesting in between, and then to point along each line of sight. Get them to walk around a bit, then go back to the spot and point again, to get a range of sightings to average out. While doing this, both remarked how they had paid immediate attention, when they heard the Mirage coming. Since their farms were in the low-level flying area for Williamtown, they were experienced observers of military jet traffic, especially those flying near to the ground. But today was a surprise, they said, as the cloud bases were quite low. "The planes rarely came under such conditions." So they looked, all right, and watched. Both men keenly recalled and showed where and how they saw the flight path.

Getting each of two people to point to where they saw something, then recording the azimuth and elevation angle of each "point" in order to gauge the instantaneous three-dimensional location of a fast-moving object from their intersections, does not conform to the standards of scientific precision you would want of, say, the surgeon operating on your cerebral cortex. However, as relayed by my investigator, the pictures are the same from each witness. The Mirage had pitched up abruptly and entered a sharply banked turn. It then disappeared into the cloud. It reappeared out of the cloud soon after, still banked and diving steeply. They saw the wings roll level and dive recovery commence. The plane appeared to have nearly bottomed out of the dive when they lost sight of it among the pine trees. Before long, black smoke told them the rest of the story. Now I am armed with even more detail. As well as their accounts, the sleuth has a bunch of numbers from the theodolite shots in the forest.

I walk the mile or so to the southern boundary of the pine forest. It's dead flat between here and the base, so I can look back along the track he would have flown. The weather hasn't changed since this morning, basically a moist southeasterly, an onshore stream, giving low stratus cloud, 800-foot base, tops at 12,000, occasional showers. He would have taken off on runway 12, crossed the coast, turned left to parallel the beach, turned left again to fly inland towards the low flying area, and, entering it, turned right to head northeast, straightening at the first point he's seen by a witness. He would have leveled at 500 feet after takeoff, to stay under the cloud, and flown out to here at 420 to 450 knots. Nothing unusual in that, except it was hard to see what the purpose of the flight might have been, what training value it could impart. *What was he thinking?*

And why the gutbusting pitch-up and roll? Nobody pulls up into cloud while rolling hard. Yet, that's what a couple of very credible witnesses saw. *Unless . . . unless something's gone amiss with the flying controls. That must be it! Say, a control rod had become disconnected, allowing one elevon to go full up, that would account for the roll. The pull-up could be explained by the pilot's instinctive reaction to the roll, to get a bit of height under him while he sorted the problem out.*

The engineer had imagined this hypothesis before me. He joins me at the forest edge to explain how it's not the answer. He's located and followed all of the control rods, examined every connection, and found no failure, nor any damage not plainly attributable to the final impact. I had a feeling that would be the case, as the loss-of-control theory was hardly consistent with the observed leveling of the wings and dive recovery. They could only have been flown under total control. Back to square one.

As we walk back along the line of the flight path, we encounter pine fronds and branches lying on the ground, some hundreds of meters from the final impact point. Looking up, it is possible to make out a line of damage in the treetops. Like a stone skipped across the water, the aircraft had entered the treetops, then pulled clear, before finally settling back into the forest.

It's late in the day by now, getting dark. We've traveled from distant places and been exposed to tragic and dramatic circumstances. The officers' mess bar will be open—this is an Air Force with reverence for its drinking tradition—and there is a helicopter parked thoughtfully nearby at my disposal. Time to head back in for the night.

The Wake

After dinner, I note that *the wake* is grimly in full swing in the bar. I overhear one pilot telling some nonflying types that the crowd at the next air show will probably set a new record. You usually get 30 to 40,000 people to a base open day, he explains. But back a few years, one had pulled over 150,000. That was a football Grand Final crowd! Huge! The traffic around the base had been chaotic. Stuck in the traffic, many people just pulled their cars off the road to watch the flying displays from a distance. It was surmised that the heightened public interest in the base was related to the fatal crash a few days before, during practice, of the solo display pilot. If this theory is correct, the pilot is saying, then the forthcoming air show will attract another massive crowd. Because once again, the display pilot has crashed during practice.

Interesting. I hadn't realized the mishap pilot was to be the display pilot for the next air show. Indeed, it is odd, as he had only been back in the Mirage a month or so, hardly time to regain enough familiarity to be doing low-level aerobatic displays. However, I am preoccupied, and don't follow this line of thought any further. I seek out a table away from the noise to play with those theodolite readings on some graph paper.

What stars those farmers prove to be as eyewitnesses! There is remarkable consistency between the readings, I can locate where he was when they first—and last—saw him. At the point where he's lost to sight, their separate lines of sight intersect at 800 feet, the cloud base. That's confirmed by a further intersection, where they had seen him coming out of the cloud. If only some of this would explain what the pilot had been up to. Pilots do not pull up into cloud then dive out, especially not while rolling rapidly. *Or would he? If so, why? What sort of bloke was he?*

Getting to Know Tom

I had never met Tom, the dead pilot, though before long I will know him as well as I have ever known anyone. The learning process begins, as one at a time, pilots detach from the huddle near the bar and come over and sit beside me. A picture builds. Medium height, medium build, looked smart in uniform, very self-assured, inclined to strut. There were no grounds for this self-esteem, I am told. Sure, he had good hands, but he was surrounded by good pilots. By and large, no one was much better than anyone else. Among people not well known for reticence, Tom had projected the self-image of *the superior pilot*. It's no wonder no one seems to have liked him.

He hasn't been on the base for long, not this time, at least. In his last posting he was at East Sale, the training base, at the Central Flying School (CFS), teaching pilots how to be instructors. CFS is regarded as a prestige posting, as only the best instructors at the flying schools get to teach the trade to others. Fighter pilots don't see things that way, of course. They figure they're already at the top of the prestige ladder. Besides, fighter pilots are rarely assigned to CFS, there being so much demand for instructors at the conversion unit, and then to return to the squadrons, to be the seasoned hands. Nope, being at CFS was nothing special to the boys at Williamtown.

Tom had followed a well-trod path, graduating from the pilots' course high enough to get sent to fighters. He then moved to a conversion to the jet, to a tour in a squadron, and did well enough there to get selected to the instructor course. After two years at a school, he moved to CFS; two years there, then back to Williamtown to instruct at the conversion unit, teaching young pilots to fly the Mirage. At the flying school and at CFS he had flown the Macchi, a single-engine jet trainer, two seats in tandem. The Macchi had a straight wing and tip tanks, an aerodynamic combination that made it extremely agile. It'll get around a loop in 1500 to 2000 feet. A really tight loop in the much faster delta-wing Mirage uses up 5000 feet at the minimum.

One of these tipsy pilots is telling me how he had done his instructor course while Tom was at CFS. He said how arrogant he was. "Aren't all fighter pilots?" I ask him, "That is, at least, how other people always seem to see us. It's an occupational hazard. Get used to it." No, this was different, I am told. The arrogance was displayed in how he flew. An example was when he was leading this pilot, as wingman practicing close formation, through the low flying area. "Why the low flying area?" I ask, "That's not the usual place to practice formation." "He was obsessed with low flying," he tells me. "At one point we flew over a lake so low I could see him leaving a trail in the water like a speedboat. Even if we'd been authorized for low flying, which we weren't, there'd be a height limit of 150 feet. But we weren't authorized to low fly. Yet he did this all the time."

I find that bit about the "speedboat wake" hard to believe. I'd seen a bloke doing it years ago, in an F-86 Sabre. You had to get down to three feet or so for that stunt. Nobody did that sort of thing anymore. That had been back before the Air Force turned professional. No pilot would think of such crass behavior nowadays—would they?

"That's exactly the height he was flying at," I'm calmly assured, "I sat just a bit above him, and he was down at no more than three feet above the water. I took him to task about it after. He dismissed my complaint with scorn."

Pretty soon, this bloke leaves, to be replaced by another pilot. This one had seen a dozen or more of Tom's solo displays in the Macchi. The instructor school at CFS had the RAAF aerobatic team. It put on exhibitions nationwide. For most of the time he was at CFS, Tom was the solo display pilot, coordinating his stuff with the team performance, filling in the blank spots, so to speak. My informant tells of a couple of Tom's exploits, and I'm all ears from his first words.

"It was at another RAAF Base" he says, "and the cloud was so low—it looked about two thousand feet—we thought the show would be cancelled. But no, in sweep the six jets, pulling up into a loop as their first maneuver. For at least one third of it they're completely in the clouds. We can't believe it. The remainder of the display is restricted to the horizontal plane," he goes on, "but even so, there was really not enough space between cloud base and the deck, not for doing this sort of thing safely. We watched in real anxiety. Nobody wants to see a prang."

I can't believe this—at an Air Force Base?! The spectators must have included about a platoon of senior officers, including the base commander. Assuming he was the teeniest bit career-smart, not to have ordered immediate cancellation of the display was none too bright, but even so, surely someone said something later?

Well, yes, they had, but they were assured that where the team did the loop was clear; the leader claimed he never lost sight of the ground. Outside the fighter force, CFS had real standing, and CFS had spoken.

"That's one of the oldest fallacies in the book" I exclaim (or words to that effect). "Cloud can be thin enough that you can see through, looking vertically, several hundred feet of it. But your aerobatic reference is the *horizon*, miles in front of you. You might be able to see 'down' through some cloud, but you surely will not be able to see the distant primary maneuver reference, the horizon. But that aside, where was Tom on that day. Did he fly?"

He had, and he'd gone into the cloud base repeatedly. Twice he'd done it during stall turns. Not only that, neither stall turn attempt had been successful, he'd "fallen out" of them. This is mind-boggling. A stall turn is a maneuver where you pull to the vertical, and use rudder to bring the nose across, enough so that at the very top, with zero airspeed, the aircraft will gently continue the turn till it's in a vertical dive. In a Macchi, the stall turn has a probability of success of about 80 percent. There just isn't quite enough rudder authority to get it around with certainty, every time. In low-level displays, you only *ever* do maneuvers that have *100 percent* chance of success. There is simply no time to recover if you mess it up. To even contemplate permitting periods of loss of control in a low-level display sequence borders on insanity.

But it's worse than that. When you do manage to fly the stall turn properly, it is *efficient*, in aerodynamic terms. The flight path is smooth. When you fall out, the flight path is inefficient, not at all smooth, with all sorts of possibilities for extra drag. Energy thus being depleted, the height at which the pull-out from the ensuing dive can be begun is reduced. You can see the problem for displays close to the ground. And here had been this bloke falling out of stall turns in cloud! This pilot truly must have been a rogue!

I hear more of the same as the night goes on. Different observers, different places, but the same story, pressing on with displays when the cloud was too low, both the team and the solo pilot. In and out of cloud—not cancelling when they should. To my horror, a little personal stuff creeps in. One or two people—they've been drinking, remember—describe Tom's womanizing. Being the only fighter pilot on that base, and the display pilot, had collateral benefits. Some women found him attractive. He betrayed their husbands. I hear how this and other aspects of his lifestyle distressed his wife, how they fought incessantly. *I need to stop all this, so I head for my room.*

But I'm thinking, next morning, from early on, thinking, thinking. . . . Accident investigating can be a lot like operating a VCR—play, stop, rewind, play, fast forward, back up, play some more, wait a minute, rewind, and so on. The team and I go into replay mode the next day, following through everything Tom had done since arriving at work—just yesterday. The weather is much the same, we note, more stream weather, the southeasterly running in from out to sea, cool and moist, bringing stratiform cloud, low base—500 to 1000 feet. The tops, today, go all the way to 20,000. Some drizzly showers exist across the area. There is an occasional, isolated *Cu*, a cumulus cloud embedded in the grey overcast, the product of just enough warming to trigger and sustain a thermal updraft in that particular place in the otherwise uniform layer of damp cloud. Hidden within the drab stratus blanket, the typical fleecy, cauliflower-lumpy outlines of these cumulus build-ups cannot be seen. However, the updraft does have the effect of raising the cloud base directly underneath to about 4000 feet. These clear patches will pass overhead from time to time. We learn this at the morning briefing, at the Base Operations center. When I ask if those periods of higher cloud base would have been around yesterday, the meteorologist says, "Yes."

After the briefing, the crews drive to their various squadrons. As Tom would have done, we go down to the conversion unit. Being driven there, my thoughts follow some of what must have been going through his mind 24 hours before. Weather like this—and there's no mistaking the situation, it's clearly visible out the crew coach window—it's too poor for students at this stage of their training—will defeat the flying scheduler's best-laid plans. Tom would know that, and that the schedule would most likely be rearranged for this eventuality. "Weather days" are common, but there are still training events that can be accomplished. Among other things, ground school lectures would be put on. Tom would probably score one, and have to deliver a lecture. The weather's not too bad for the old hand pilots, though. Any instructor who needs some proficiency work would be able to go up. Tom was asked to present a lecture, and he did book a practice sortie for himself, for after that. Nothing abnormal in that. No smoking gun here.

The Proceedings

We are allocated a room. It's already been set up like a court, me at the top table, places for witnesses to sit, Bibles at hand, all the other reference books you could ask for, stenographers to take down every word. Before taking evidence, we have to agree on who to call. I tell the team what I'd heard last night, the bit about flying displays under low cloud. This is serious. If the case is established that he had learned some bad habits while at CFS, then his former supervisors—the ones who should have pulled him into line—have failed in an important command duty.

In legal terms, this means their reputations are at stake. They must have the allegations against them put to them, then be given the chance to refute. *I'd rather be out flying than dealing with this garbage.* We agree to summon two officers: Tom's immediate superior at CFS, who had also been the aerobatic team leader, and the Commanding Officer of the school itself. I phone them, and tell them why they are to be examined, and that they will be given the chance to defend themselves against any attack on their repute, and so on. They agree to fly in later in the day. I know both men well, and count them as friends. The distasteful job is done by 10:00. In a gloomy mood, I head for outside, for some fresh air.

Across the road the Mirages are lined up. It is a pretty plane. In the 1960s, when it was built, the threat that the strategists worried about was going to come in high and fast. It was to be countered by interceptor fighters with the ability to get rapidly to 35,000 feet or so. Once there, they were to accelerate to high supersonic speed, climb to 50,000 feet, then zoom to 60,000, and fire the killer missile from head-on. The delta wing was the popular aerofoil design for that. (The Mirage's U.S. counterparts were the larger but similarly shaped F-102 and F-106.) It was an aerodynamic compromise, well known to all concerned. Sure, it had low drag at high speed, but at low speed, the penalty was low lift— that is, it would not fly well at slow speeds. While economic in low-level cruise (for example, at anywhere between 350 and 550 knots), its handling characteristics below 300 knots were awful. In a circuit (traffic pattern), it flew downwind at 240 knots, flew the approach at 200, and landed at 185. The word "agile" would never cross your mind when thinking or talking about the Mirage (Figure 4-1). No, it would not be your first choice for a sparkling aerobatic display.

Just beyond the conversion unit's Mirage fleet is a line of Macchis. Before transitioning to the fast jet, would-be fighter pilots get checked out in the tactics and weapons work in the trainer, an aircraft they have flown at the pilot's course and are very familiar with. While reflecting on this—my gaze has just drifted from the Mirages to the Macchis—I note a sensation akin to pleasure. The feeling of gloom that I had carried out of the building has abruptly and perceptibly lifted.

It's the weather that's done it. The cloud mass is passing overhead at about 25 knots. It has been, for the most part, low cloud, 500 feet ceiling. Suddenly, one of those patches of higher base dominates the scene. There is much more ambient light about, under it, and you can see

Figure 4-1. Mirage. This high-performance aircraft requires considerable vertical space to perform aerobatics—a fact this rogue forgot to account for. *(U.S. Air Force photo)*

much further. This increase in visibility has manifested in me as an uplifting of the spirit, a corresponding "brightening." It's a powerful psychological influence, when you think about it, like a switch being thrown—click!—and warmth and confidence instantly displace melancholy. . . .

And it is an important clue. This is a time in history when "management by objectives" is just achieving eminent acceptance in Australia. It fits the military environment well—we take pleasure from *reaching* the objective—not in *failing to achieve it.* Here's this seriously committed pilot flying along under cloud, his aim being to practice some aerobatic maneuvers. He encounters one of those patches of higher cloud base. *Click!* Do it. He's done it plenty of times before, so he pulls up and rolls.

He must have had a barrel roll in mind, and he must have visualized that it would fit within the confines of the lighter area. The trouble is, his past experience in these circumstances has been in the Macchi. *He has imagined a Macchi-sized barrel roll.* That'd fit easily into the amount of clear airspace he has just found. A Mirage-sized barrel roll will be three times the size. And then there's the question of aligning the axis of the roll with the horizontal.

In the barrel roll, the horizontal reference is—yes—the horizon. But that's not in sight, owing to the surrounding cloud mass. Indeed, the point at which his glance will fixate will be the line of the cloud base, thus supplying a reference plane canted downward. The higher he goes the steeper will be the tilt. As he flies over the top of the roll, he can only see ground. It's not until he is well into the dive that he can see far enough ahead to realize how steep it is. He rolls wings level and pulls back hard for recovery.

It all fits. The pull-up and roll, as seen by the witnesses, were the entry to the barrel roll. He didn't actually fly up into cloud, he merely disappeared from view behind it, into the small clear area passing overhead. The axis of the roll being steeply depressed, when he emerges and is seen again he is in a steep dive, still rolling, still flying the maneuver, still intent on meeting the objective. Then he realizes his dangerous situation, levels the wings, and attempts to pull out of the dive.

And he nearly makes it, bottoming out of the dive at 40 feet above ground level. But he's in among the treetops. The branches up there are soft and light and do no damage to the plane and he flies clear, climbs out of the trees. But the intakes have filled with shrubbery and the engine flames out. He begins to lose speed. Grimly hauling back on the stick—an instinctive move, keep the jet flying by sheer willpower— there is a 10-second period during which he could have ejected, opted for survival. He would even have had time to visualize himself walking back into the crew room, arriving back among all those pilots he had let know that he thought were his inferiors—him now a proven failure, having lost a jet, through his own fault. *Click!*

Analyzing a Rogue

Professor James Reason postulates multiple "defenses" against human errors. In this case, the defenses included the military code of discipline. Unbelievably, this pilot had slipped through that net. Indeed, when I did interview his previous commanders, I found evidence of high regard for Tom as a pilot, the sense that he was capable enough to do things the "ordinary mortal" pilot could not. They were wrong—so much for human judgment. Yet these were people who would have had no trouble, because of their positions as senior commanders, in acquiring status as experts in such matters.

More important, in the leader-follower paradigm, Tom had no leader for all that time at the instructor school at CFS. *His pilot seniors had deferred to him.* He had projected the image of superior competence and they had bought it. This could only reinforce his own exaggerated regard for his flying skills. He thus became his own role model, leading himself, solo, along the route to hubris. Tom, and Tom alone, commanded Tom. No wonder a rogue emerged.

Military officers giving evidence under oath later denied all the stories about him that I had heard on the first night. In later years, in less formal circumstances, I learned that all of the tales were true. Indeed, much of this later evidence came from people I had interviewed at the time. This, of course, occurred years after, when they had forgotten that they had lied on oath, and spontaneously offered the truth. Reality is everyone's mental "default setting." The truth will come out. Sadly, after several more instances of the military "code of silence"—covering up wrongdoing in the causes of accidents—the civil authority withdrew the concept that had allowed the military to investigate fatal mishaps. Now, Coroner's Courts inquire into fatal military accidents in Australia.

The role of emotion in decision making is grossly underrated in the aviation community, no doubt as "real men" don't talk about such things. Yet there is an abundance of evidence that emotional decision making might be at work when we are listing our options in flight—as Tom would have done when he encountered the break in the weather. It is emotion—how we feel—that closes the deal, that makes the final choice. The emotional reward will be the approbation (he believes) his peers will send his way after he has hacked the mission though the going was tough.

Think for a moment about all of the "I learned about flying from that" stories in the books and magazines. Bad weather, ice, lost at night, low on fuel, in cloud but not instrument rated, pressing on under the overcast, just scraping in. They do make far better reading than "I could see the weather was too bad so I turned around, came home, and canceled the flight," don't they? But good stories are usually about bad decisions. Pilots should be open and ruthlessly honest about their thought processes. Moreover, they should train their decision routines in the presence of emotion so as to know how it affects their judgment. I wish this was the end of this story, but sadly it is not.

Another Domino Falls

Tom had a younger brother. He, too, entered the Air Force, only to be discharged from the pilot's course for illegal low flying. I wonder where he learned that. He later got a job with an airline. One day, he was asked to ferry a T-28 home after an air show, leaving before the show was over. After takeoff, he attempted a barrel roll in front of the crowd and crashed, killing himself and his passenger. The maneuver was not requested or authorized, nor was he endorsed to perform it.

Perhaps this is an argument for a genetic link to rogue behavior, but I think not. More likely, the younger brother saw the adulation and "fringe benefits" that came his brother's way as a result of his flying and lifestyle. He had picked an undisciplined role model—a fatal flaw made by many rogues.

My Own Master

Experiences such as this have led, over time and in different places, to the practice of personality testing. People who manifest certain personality characteristics are dissuaded from careers as pilots. This may or may not have merit. For example, if I get to be so angry—legitimately angry—because of another person's appalling behavior that I want to kill them, I am not given that right under law. The practice of self-restraint—of not simply indulging one's natural responses to stimuli—is unexceptional enough. So, too, should pilots establish and adhere to a proper code of conduct. If the tenets of a military code are insufficient restraint on overconfidence, what chance is there for a lesser set of externally imposed rules? The case for self-regulation rests.

In the end, there is but one defence against accidents caused by rogue behavior—the pilot's personal code. The opportunities for malpractice as a pilot are limitless, the wide-open spaces, nobody looking, no way to get caught. The sense of reward—the pleasure registered as a result of such things as illegal low flying—is no doubt heady. But you can surely get just as much pleasure from the pride that comes with dedication to sound judgment and common sense. As a pilot who follows a personal code of behavior, you are both the honorable follower and the respected leader. What better way to go? You only need to know yourself.

To drive home the point that rogues exist in all aviation cultures, we move next to a location several thousand miles to the northeast of Australia. We return to the early days of aviation in the Soviet Union, where we find one of the most celebrated and unique pilots in all of history.

CHAPTER FIVE

Valery Chkalov: Russian Rogue*

The Rogue's Paradox

Where is the line between safe but aggressive flying and rogue flying? Are rogue pilots always dangerous to fellow flyers or can their behaviors serve to improve the safety of flight for others? Are rogues always villains, or can they also be heroes? Are pilots—or the public at large—capable of making this critical distinction in behavior? History shows us that truly gifted rogues might live to fly another day, and their success may actually foster safe operations on occasion. They may even become heroes, as in the case that follows. But in the vast majority of cases, a rogue pilot's ability to cross the line of compliance will result in disaster or at the very least prompt other pilots to try their luck with potentially tragic consequences.

But extraordinary pilots—even rogues—deserve special attention. These special cases actually move the line of what is possible or, in flying lingo, expand the envelope. Although many of the early flyers are deserving of this description, none is shrouded in such extensive myth and hero worship as the famous Russian rogue, Valery Chkalov (Figure 5-1).

In fact, discovering the truth about Chkalov can be very difficult, even for practiced historians. To begin with, there isn't much written on Chkalov in the English language. One of the only detailed sources is *Russian Lindbergh: The Life of Valery Chkalov*, written by his close friend

---

* This chapter was written by Tony Kern and Noel Fulton.

Figure 5-1. Valery Chkalov, a hero of the former Soviet Union, represents the rogue's paradox—the tragic flaw of immense skill unbound by discipline—that often underlies rogue behavior. (*Transaero Airlines photo*)

and crewmate Georgiy Baidukov and translated to English by Peter Belov. The problem with *Russian Lindbergh* is that it was written in 1975, in the midst of the cold war. It is more a hero story than a biography. Chkalov, after all, was a national hero. The book hesitates to criticize Chkalov in the slightest way for any action. Everything is cast in the best possible light with a political spin. For example, Baidukov tells how Chkalov's father was involved in a dispute with a "sly" and "savage" local merchant who forged documents in order to cheat the hardworking father—classic communist prose. Through his extraordinary courage and physical abilities, Chkalov helped his father win a bet, humbling the merchant. This story may or may not be true but it immediately establishes Chkalov's courage and, perhaps more important, his ideological purity to a Soviet audience. But in the midst of this idolatry are bits of truth that are verifiable through other sources. The picture painted by the rest of this chapter represents the truth as best as we could determine it.

Chkalov straddled the line between hero and rogue for most of his aviation career. He was aggressive to a fault. Extremely undisciplined, he was respected by some, feared by others, and virtually everyone who knew him testified to his unparalleled knowledge and skill in the air. There can be no question of the fact that he willfully violated multiple regulations, aircraft limitations, and rules of engagement (ROE). By our earlier definition (a rogue is as a rogue does—Chapter 1), Chkalov was clearly a rogue pilot on many occasions. Although his heroism is well documented, the extent of his villainy may never be known for reasons already explained. Chkalov invented procedures that made flying safer for his fellow Soviet pilots, but his example may have led other less skilled flyers to disaster. Perhaps better than any other example in this book, Chkalov personifies the paradox that is the rogue pilot: immense skill and knowledge unbound by discipline, a tragic flaw in the Shakespearean sense of the word.

The Early Years

Valery Chkalov was born in the Volga River region of Russia in February 1904, the 10th child to working-class parents. His father, Pavel, operated a steamboat on the Volga River. Perhaps the aggressive nature of his adulthood could be traced to a quest for identity among nine siblings—a situation made much worse when his mother died in childbirth when he was six years old. He grew up swimming in the Volga and was, by local accounts, an extremely strong and well-liked lad. Life has always been a struggle in Russia. As the 10th child in a working-class family, Valery must have been strong merely to survive.

When he was 15, Chkalov went to work assembling airplanes at the Fourth Aviation Depot. He devoted himself to learning everything he could about how airplanes were put together and developed a keen interest in moving beyond mere mechanics into operating the aircraft. It is here that the young Chkalov established one of the main pillars of outstanding airmanship, a deep understanding of how and why an aircraft flies. His aggressiveness for the rest of his career would be partially justified by the depth of this knowledge—a knowledge that others who died trying to emulate him did not possess.

Building aircraft was not enough for the young Russian. In spite of his young age, Valery was constantly pestering the commander of the plant for a pilot nomination to the military flight school. After two years his persistence paid off, and Chkalov finally received his appointment to the Yegorevsk Military Theoretical Flight School, a sort of basic education and flying ground school. Upon his appointment, he became the youngest student at the school.

Is there any significance to this idea of being the youngest? One of the common traits of rogues from all professions is that they can lay claim to one or more adjectives from the following list: *youngest, first, highest, lowest, fastest, closest, only.* To rogues, these adjectives all equate to the same word: *best.* Once a superlative adjective is applied to a rogue, second place is simply not good enough.

At the Yegorevsk Academy, Valery worked hard learning physics, basic aerodynamics, math, and "political preparation." He fared well in all of these subject areas—well enough to graduate near the top of his class and earn a chance to move on to flying school. The next stop was the Borisoglebsk Flight School, where he learned basic flight maneuvers in an Avro trainer. Here the young Russian mastered the basics and pushed himself to become one of the elite students in his class. Chkalov again distinguished himself by becoming one of the top 10 graduates. From Borisoglebsk, a select few pilots—the cream of the crop—went to the Moscow Aerobatics school to learn aerobatics in World War I fighter aircraft such as German Fokkers and English Martinsides. Of course, Chkalov was among them.

It was in Moscow that Chkalov's more aggressive characteristics began to emerge, at least in terms of documented evidence. On multiple occasions, he was chastised for being cocky, flying excessively steep turns, and even intentionally spinning aircraft—a prohibited maneuver at that time. After barely recovering from an *inadvertent* spin, Chkalov *deliberately* spun the aircraft in the opposite direction, breaking a steel wing support in the process. He was extremely lucky to recover with this extensive damage to the primary wing structure. Lady Luck would continue to ride as Chkalov's copilot for most of his career, but we will speak more of that later. Despite—or perhaps because of—his daring and natural ability, Chkalov was beginning to earn a reputation as a gifted pilot in some circles of Russian military aviation.

Chkalov finished his formal training at the Advanced School of Gunnery, Bombing and Aerial Combat at Serpukhovsk, where there continued to be considerable evidence of aggressive noncompliance with existing directives. At the end of the day, however, Chkalov's raw talent once again overcame his commanders' concerns over his lack of discipline. In November 1924, Chkalov received the rank of fighter pilot and joined a line unit.

Fighter Pilot, Rogue Pilot

Upon graduation from Serpukhovsk, Chkalov was assigned to the First Red Banner Fighter Squadron and immediately began to exhibit rogue behavior. On one of his first flights in an aging Newport-24 his mechanic warned him, "Just take it around in circles. Don't try any derring-do; the Newport might disintegrate." Valery started off with a few basic traffic patterns, but the need to prove himself soon overcame the warning of the mechanic. It wasn't long before Chkalov flew the aircraft through various aerobatics in direct contradiction to the mechanic's warning and in defiance of existing operational limitations. When the squadron commander was made aware of Chkalov's actions, he attempted to make a lasting impression on the new recruit. He severely reprimanded him and put him in the guardhouse. It was the first of many visits for the young pilot.

It wasn't long before his commander realized that it would take more than the guardhouse to curb Chkalov's actions. Within a few months of his first stunt, while practicing aerial gunnery on target balloons, Chkalov became so frustrated at missing the target with his guns, he actually rammed a balloon with his aircraft! On another occasion Chkalov violated the rules of engagement for a mock dogfight with his commander and used this violation to defeat his boss in simulated combat. One report has it that the ensuing reprimand resulted in a heated confrontation and fistfight between the young rogue and his commander. Chkalov was placed back in the guardhouse, but he wouldn't stay there for long.

His continued aggressiveness in practice combat made it difficult for other more experienced pilots to practice and fly with him. Chkalov usually got the better of his peers and superiors because they were following the rules of engagement and limitations of the aircraft, and he was not. This is one of the primary mechanisms used by rogues to create an unsafe atmosphere in a competitive organizational environment. To compete with an unchecked rogue, others must follow his lead into the regime of poor discipline and noncompliance. The problem here is that, while someone like Chkalov may have the skill and knowledge to pull it off safely, his competitors may not.

Following yet another episode of the overaggressive young pilot endangering his colleagues, the experienced fighter pilot Pavlushov, Chkalov's direct superior, commented to the squadron commander, "Chkalov has no fear and if it were not for my own cautiousness, he would cut into my machine. . . . He has become unrecognizable . . . like an animal." Strong words indeed from an accomplished and highly experienced peer.

Here is yet another example of the dangers inherent in rogue behavior. The rogue is often unconcerned with the hazards they pose to others who share the same sky or who may be beneath them on the ground. The rogue wants to *win*—fly lower, fly faster, take a shortcut, show off, get home, and damn the rules. Chkalov stated several times that he felt "oppressed by these limitations," referring to the operational limits and rules of engagement for practice combat. He ignored them all without a second thought, endangering everyone in the vicinity whether they are standing on the ground or flying.

Chkalov's Contributions

It would be easy to dismiss Chkalov as just a dangerous rogue pilot. He obviously cared little for regulations that he felt were limiting. But it would be a mistake. Sometimes, the rogue can push the envelope outward. Like a mythic hero, the rogue can return from near death with a gift that improves safety for all. A Russian expert on Chkalov describes an occasion when Chkalov's daring actually improved flying safety, instead of diminishing it:

> **Autumn was approaching. They were shifted to their base field. There were fewer and fewer chances to fly. A limitation also had been set: while performing acrobatics in the [Fokker] D-7, it was forbidden to leave the field, because while performing maneuvers the engine sometimes would quit and it was impossible to start it up, even in a dive. Because of this problem several planes had already crashed on forced landings and the pilots received serious injuries.**
>
> **Chkalov once again walked around thoughtfully and would**

not go out for several evenings. This was a rare thing for him. . . . Obviously, there must have been serious reasons for the young man to have even stopped reading. The first fine day explained everything: Chkalov was doing seemingly inconsequential maneuvers before everyone at the field when he deliberately made his engine quit. Chkalov did not bring his plane in for landing at the field as ordered by the First Red Banner Squadron; he put the plane into a steep dive, and, close to the ground, pulled up with a sharp turn to the side opposite to the revolving engine shaft. As a result the blade started to rotate and, when the ignition was turned, the engine started and continued to function normally. Chkalov noticed from the air that his illegal demonstration was being observed and he repeated the maneuver several times.

When Chkalov taxied up to his stand . . . the other pilots were waiting. They did not let Chkalov jump out of the aircraft onto the ground; they grabbed him and began to toss him into the air. Finally the pilot stood on the ground and strode to the squadron commander to give his report. But Antoshin (the commander) embraced him and said: "Thank you very much! Now write the instructions. Then we'll oblige everyone by ordering them carried out without any changes."

Chkalov just gasped: "I . . . and instructions? That's a paradox!"

Sometimes, by accident or by design, rogues place themselves in such deadly situations that getting out alive requires new skills and procedures that then get passed on to other pilots. Sometimes rogues are heroes. Consider the difficulty in disciplining such flyers. True, their day-to-day actions endanger their lives and others. But occasionally rogue pilots improve safety for everyone or get a critical mission done when no one else can. Where does a commander or supervisor draw the line? Following this act of sheer brilliance, Chkalov's commanders had an increasingly difficult time with disciplining him, but they made the attempt nevertheless.

Back to His Old Tricks

Despite these heroics, Chkalov still spent considerable time in the guardhouse for his reckless behavior. He was sentenced to 10 days in the guardhouse for completing *over 200 consecutive loops* on a bet with a fellow pilot—a feat difficult to comprehend, let alone believe—yet it is reported as fact by Baidukov. Even for this outrageous maneuver, he did not serve the full 10 days. On another occasion, Chkalov spent time in the guardhouse for doing acrobatics at extremely low altitude in violation of existing regulations.

A Rogue's-Eye View of Regulations

Chkalov's thoughts on the matter illustrate the mentality of the rogue with regard to following flying regulations. "They say: 'not according to the directives.' *But what if the directives improperly set the norms for me?*" Let's analyze this statement, because on the surface it sounds like a fair and logical argument.

The rogue's argument for noncompliance goes something like this: "The rules were meant for less skilled pilots and I cannot possibly achieve my full potential within the overly restrictive confines of regulatory compliance." There are two primary problems with this argument. The first is that the rest of the aviators with whom a rogue shares the sky make decisions under conditions of "assumed compliance," meaning that they base their actions and decisions on the belief that others will be following the rules. When men like Chkalov routinely violate the rules and others know it, it breaks down the trust between flyers that is so critical to safe and orderly operations.

Trust is also essential in combat. The famous American ace Eddie Rickenbacker is quoted as saying, "Even in combat, a 50-50 chance is all a pilot should ever take—unless the show is one that demands the loss of pilot and aircraft." Chkalov would have had serious difficulties flying in Rickenbacker's famed Hat in the Ring squadron, one of the most successful and aggressive outfits ever to roam the skies.

The second problem with the argument against following directives is that it shows that rogues are more worried about themselves than about others—stressing individual improvement over team safety. Once again, this erodes teamwork and trust and paints the rogue pilot as one concerned more with personal fame and glory than with unit cohesion and team accomplishment.

So where should we set the regulatory boundaries? Should we write regulations to protect the least skillful pilot? What of pilots like

Chkalov with extraordinary skill? How can they be given enough leeway to realize their full potential without endangering everyone else? Whether or not a pilot feels "restricted by limitations" or "confined by regulations" is ultimately irrelevant. The conscientious flyer will pilot the aircraft in the expectation of *everyone* following the directives. When individual pilots decide that they are beyond such limitations, they endanger themselves and others. The only way a high-risk system like aviation can work is on the basis of assumed compliance and the trust that goes along with it. Consider a driver on a curving, two-lane road who considers the double yellow line a limitation on his or her superb driving abilities and an insult to the V-8 power under the hood. The aggressive driver crosses the yellow lines in a tight left turn, maximizing performance—trusting skill and luck to win the day—and runs head on into a driver following the rules. The safe driver drove the mountain road expecting any oncoming traffic to follow the rules and stay on their side of the road. The safe flyer follows the rules and hopes everyone else does the same. When pilots neglect rules or don't make use of all available information, disaster waits around some—if not every—corner. Stephen Coonts, the famous author of *Flight of the Intruder* and many other action novels, writes in the Navy's *Approach* magazine:

> **Even though the probability of a mishap is low, you'd think people would be reluctant to gamble with their lives. But people are addicted to it. They play the lottery, bet on sports. They go to extraordinary lengths to meet interesting specimens of the opposite sex because the hoped-for rewards justify the tremendous known risks. Success at a risk-free endeavor is impossible—everyone intuitively understands that. Risk makes life worth living, life itself is a gamble. Random chance rules our lives. What you are trying to say is this: Most people try to minimize the negative effect of random chance on them, or, said another way, they want to be the dealer. In aviation, we know how to do that: Know your [regulations], keep emergency procedures fresh and ready to use, stay situationally alert, be mentally and physically ready. If you are, you'll have the tools to make the best of whatever situation random chance throws at you. You'll be lucky.**
>
> **I've never thought much of the old saw, "I'd rather be lucky**

than good." I think the good are lucky. Not the morally good, but the professionally good. There is just no substitute for sound, thorough preparation to avoid or cope with foreseeable misfortune. People who drive straddling the centerline can get around a few curves, but sooner or later they're going to meet a Kenworth coming the other way. That's not just predictable, it's inevitable.

Apparently Chkalov never grasped the essence of calculated risk. Eventually he would meet his own Kenworth coming around the corner.

The Rogue Reprimanded (Again)

Even a great Russian hero like Chkalov can go too far, and a bizarre (for anyone but Chkalov) series of events actually led to his discharge or "demobilization" from the Soviet Air Force. This came after the same leadership awarded Chkalov a commendation for his aggressive and frequently reckless flying. This was certain to have sent mixed signals to all who knew of the situation, but it seemed that the Soviet Air Force leaders were unsure about just how to deal with this talented, but rogue, flyer. The challenges have changed very little for today's frontline commanders and supervisors.

The first in this series of events was one of the most foolhardy stunts imaginable. Chkalov flew his plane underneath the Trinity Bridge near Leningrad with less than three feet of wingtip clearance on either side! The story goes that Chkalov was riding to the field on one foggy morning when he suddenly jumped off the bus on impulse to study the architecture and height of the bridge. He carefully studied the forms, trying to memorize the height and width of the steel and granite span over the icy river below. At the first available opportunity, Chkalov flew his fighter over to the bridge to scope it out from the air. He flew several circles and passes at the bridge before his final run. His circles attracted pedestrians who came out onto the bridge to watch the curious aerial display. Finally Chkalov lined up with the river and threaded the needle to the horror of the crowd upon it. Word of such activities have a velocity all their own, and the rumors of the stunt reached the airport almost before Chkalov. The squadron commander was furious and asked Chkalov to "imagine that our pilots are going to try exactly the same thing tomorrow. What do you think will happen?"

Chkalov, apparently unconcerned with this possibility, answered know-ingly, "They'll crack up."

This complacent attitude about setting a bad example characterizes rogue pilots across the decades. In this case the military leadership understood that serious breaches in flight discipline that go unpunished will spread as other pilots attempt the same feats, yet instead of ground-ing Chkalov permanently to avoid this potential for disaster, Chkalov merely spent more time in the guardhouse. He didn't learn anything and, apparently, neither did the leadership, as he was shortly thereafter selected for a plum assignment.

The bridge stunt was just prior to the 10th anniversary of the Octo-ber Revolution. A huge parade was being planned in Red Square. Oddly—or perhaps not—the military leadership chose Chkalov to rep-resent the Leningraders at an air show during the festivities. Baidukov writes about the dilemma:

> **The position of the Air Force was a ticklish one. On the one hand, here was an almost unequaled master of aerobatics, the best ae-rial gunner and the foremost fighter pilot in aerial combat. Chkalov had saved the life of more than one pilot in the squadron by discovering a way to start the D-7 plane in the air when the motor had stopped while hovering in aerobatic maneuvers. . . . On the other hand, no other pilot had spent so much time in the guardhouse for breaking set procedures and flight regulations: for flying at extremely low altitudes, for flying under a bridge, for turning 250 loops in a row, and for many other things.**

Chkalov was given no restrictions in his demonstration and received a special commendation for an exciting performance. It seemed that the air force was reinforcing Chkalov's behavior instead of discouraging it. But as Coonts stated earlier, "if you straddle the centerline long enough . . ."

The Beginning of the End. Flying lead on a team of fighters on a cross-country mission, Chkalov attempted to fly underneath a tele-graph line (setting a great example for his wingmen). He judged the line height by the telegraph poles but forgot to account for the inevitable sag. All of the planes struck the wires and crashed. Amazingly, there were no casualties, but the command authorities had seen enough. They decided to put Chkalov on trial as an example to other reckless flyers. Why then, and not earlier? Baidukov explains:

> **At this time the situation regarding accidents in the Red Army Air Force was truly tragic: hundreds of people from the battle units perished from either inexperience, reliance on worn-out old techniques, or the low quality of the first Soviet aircraft.** *But the largest number of catastrophes and accidents could be explained by the lack of discipline of the flight personnel and the low level of leadership at the fields and in flight* **(emphasis added).**

This is as close as Baidukov ever comes to condemning the actions of Chkalov. Chkalov was obviously one of those field leaders who failed to provide a good example to fellow flyers. It was also exactly that "low level of leadership" that turned a blind eye to Chkalov's stunts instead of grounding him earlier. Although Baidukov would never mention it, you have to wonder how many of those accidents were the result of pilots trying to duplicate the actions of rogues such as Chkalov. On January 2, 1929, Chkalov was dismissed from the air force and sentenced to a year in prison for his willful disobedience of flying directives. It seemed that the air force had finally had enough of Chkalov's antics—or maybe not. He was released just 19 days later.

Rogue for a Reason: Chkalov's True Calling as a Test Pilot

Chkalov spent some time as a transport pilot and continued to petition the air force leadership to be returned to fighters. Many of his former comrades, commanders, and instructor pilots (IPs) also wrote letters in support of the brass flyer. They felt that Chkalov's talents were being wasted. Chkalov himself considered his life boring and hardly worth the effort. He spent almost two years flying transports and teaching others to fly, when he was reactivated and sent to the Test Pilot Institute of the Soviet Air Force on November 11, 1930.

Chkalov threw himself into his new life with passion. He was working with the top pilots and designers of the prewar Soviet Union. Now, his job description required pushing the limits of new aircraft to safely test them before sending them out to the rest of the air force. But even in this environment, Chkalov's aggressiveness could get him into trouble. On one occasion, Chkalov and another test pilot were completing separate tests in different types of aircraft and landing next to each other at the test institute's field. Suddenly Chkalov added power, climbed, and then dived toward the other aircraft in a mock attack. The other pilot evaded the attack and launched one of his own. An aerial 'battle' began at an altitude of 200 meters.[4] Observers on the ground thought for sure that the aircraft would collide. The commander of the institute gave both pilots "complete freedom" instead of punishing them. It seems that Chkalov's superiors decided that the only way to deal with him was to let Chkalov go and hope for the best, but this is not the line of the air force now—test pilots are given certain freedoms and rightfully so. The environment is contained, and their job is to push the envelope.

Chkalov continued testing new aircraft for the air force and, later, for Soviet manufacturers. He seemed to mature with age, but he never lost the daring that had made him (in?)famous. Chkalov's mastery of the air improved safety for many of the Soviet flyers. He worked closely with designers and engineers to fix the problems that can be uncovered only by a skilled pilot in flight testing. Many of these fighters, such as the IL-15 and IL-16, went on to see service in World War II. Chkalov contributed to fighter tactics and training. And it was his daring that led to his greatest accomplishment in aviation of that era, one that rivals the Atlantic crossing of Lindbergh.

Hero of the Soviet Union

Chkalov was picked by Georgiy Baidukov to command the first transpolar flight from the Soviet Union to the United States. Baidukov picked Chkalov to command despite Chkalov's inability to fly in instrument conditions (by the gauges) without visual contact with the ground because, "we need the most courageous, most authoritative flier in the country," and just taking off in the overloaded aircraft would be half the flight. Chkalov and his crew spent many months planning and preparing for the historic flight across the north pole. This was not the time for rogue behavior. Every detail was carefully thought out. They made use of the best in navigation and weather forecasting. The flight was a model of airmanship.

At 1620 GMT, June 20, 1937, after 63 hours and 16 minutes in the air, Chkalov and crew landed at Pearson Army Air Corps base in Vancouver, Washington. The flight stunned the aviation world and the crew was accorded a hero's welcome in the United States. The flight had faced many dangers of weather and fatigue. The AN-25 iced up dangerously on numerous occasions during the flight. The crew faced bitter cold, altitude-induced nosebleeds, and severe hypoxia. They had planned as best they could, although they could not forecast all the problems of the flight, and critical, time-sensitive decisions were made accurately throughout the flight. Later flights across the poles by Russian flyers were safer due to the trail Chkalov blazed. The crew was decorated and hailed as Heroes of the Soviet Union upon their return, the highest award possible in that country. The flight was loudly proclaimed as the inevitable result of socialist planning and technology. It was a propaganda gold mine.

Chkalov himself was eventually elected a deputy of the Supreme Soviet, but he continued to fly. He died testing an IL-180 on December 15, 1938. Joseph Stalin was a pallbearer at his funeral.

It's difficult to evaluate the contributions of a pilot like Valery Chkalov. He flew in a very different time and a very different place. He was obviously a virtuoso in the air. His peers sung his praises almost without exception. His superiors were constantly frustrated at Chkalov's willful disregard of flying directives but gave him tremendous leeway to probe his own limits. His contributions to flying safety are easy to see: safer aircraft, emergency procedures, his transpolar expedition. We may never know how many pilots he helped and how many he killed. Chkalov's exploits undoubtedly contributed to the accidents caused by the lack of discipline prevalent in the Soviet Air Force of the 1930s. How many pilots tried to emulate Valery Chkalov on their last flight?

It's hard to imagine a Chkalov in the air today. But the rogues are still there. Every group of pilots knows which one of their number pushes the occasional limit or ignores the occasional regulation. Most every honest pilot will admit to bending a rule from time to time. It may seem a good idea at the time. Unfortunately, with the dramatic increase in air traffic over recent decades, bent and broken rules more and more often lead to bent and broken aircraft, pilots, bystanders, and families. The "big sky theory" may have been true for Chkalov, but it's hardly true for the military, commercial, and general pilots of today. Every bent rule has dangerous consequences for the bender and the innocent bystander. Chkalov never killed anyone directly. He was lucky, for a time. Most rogue pilots end up in the same place for the same general reasons. If you'd like to visit, bring flowers.

While Valery Chkalov gravitated to different missions out of necessity, many rogue aviators self-select into certain niches in the aviation arena, where they can play out their undisciplined acts under less scrutiny. Our next chapter looks at these "special mission rogues" in action.

CHAPTER SIX

Special Mission Rogues

SPECIAL MISSIONS MAKE special demands upon the men and women who fly them. So far we have confined our discussion of rogue pilots to the mainstream—the military and commercial arenas of aviation. Let us now turn to some more specialized missions—agricultural flying and fire fighting, two of the most difficult and demanding jobs any pilot could ever ask for. The special missions are also fertile ground for the growth and feeding of rogue pilots.

Agricultural flying encompasses a variety of mission types, but perhaps none more demanding than that of the agricultural pilot, also known simply as "ag pilot" or "crop duster." The crop duster is required to take off at maximum gross weight (and often slightly above), navigate to a specific small patch of ground, and deliver a load of nutrients, insecticides, and the like, precisely and evenly along a specified track to coincide with the rows of crops, with very little overlap and no missed spots. Typically, at the end of each field will be either a row of tall trees, high-tension power lines, or both. To avoid dropping any of the precious cargo on an adjacent property—an act which could well result in a lawsuit or a shotgun blast from an angry farmer—the crop duster must time the delivery as expertly as any combat pilot with precision guided weapons. However, unlike the combat pilot who typically makes one pass across the target and escapes, the crop duster must pull up at the end of the field into a near hammerhead stall, execute a 180-degree turn, and repeat the process in the other direction. Add to this a list of hazards as long as an Iowa cornfield—blowing dust, glare, low-level wind shear, birds, fatigue, trees, and power lines—and you begin to see the difficult nature of the crop duster mission.

In spite of—or perhaps because of—the difficulty inherent in this mission, many pilots who are out to prove something to themselves and others are often attracted to this type of flying. Highly unregulated and nearly always unsupervised, the ag pilot's environment is an ideal place for those who desire to use the flying game to prove something about themselves. The following story is illustrative of one such rogue. A friend and colleague who flew with him to the end wrote it. All names are pseudonyms and the company is no longer in business.

Crop Duster

I should say right off that we lost the pilot involved. He was the son of the owner of the company for which I was flying, Wagner Air Ag. Jake Wagner was about thirty-five and had started flying as a teenager. His father had entered WWII under age and had ended the war as aircraft commander in a B-17 in the European theater. The 8th Air Force (in which the European B-17s flew) was a tough bunch. There was a period of time during the Combined Bomber Offensive of the early 1940s that an assignment to a B-17 unit was very near to a death sentence. Over 70,000 allied airmen from the British Bomber Command and the U.S. 8th Air Force were blasted from the skies over Germany and France between 1942 and 1945. Those that survived knew the lessons of risk management like few others who have ever taken to the skies. Charles Wagner brought that mentality with him when he formed his company.

Wagner Air Ag was well equipped. Charles bought and used 15 T-6s, between 8 and 15 Stearmans and N3Ns (depending on the season and recruits), a Catalina PB2Y, 3 P-51s, and 2 B-25s, all converted for spray work, with the possible exception of the P-51s. I think he got those for "sport" and to remind him of the good old days.

I began flying for Wagner's in the late 1980s. I was 18 and Charles was getting close to 70. I was brand new and had never seen an accident; Charles had seen a lifetime of flying and had never clipped a wire, wrecked an airplane, or been sick for a day from pesticide poisoning. In a word, he was *careful*. **Notice that I did not say** *timid*, **because the owner could still get the job done as often as and better than anyone in the company. He just didn't take any unnecessary chances. It is worth noting that only one pilot had ever died flying for Wagner's, a kid about my age, years and years ago, who tried to do a barrel roll around another airplane while ferrying to a field and nosed in on the recovery. Charles would never stand for this sort of thing, at least from any of us. He had a more difficult challenge with his son.**

Charles's son Jake had grown up in the shadow of his legendary father and must have just become rebellious against some of his ideas. Jake liked to take the airplane out when spraying rinsate (water used to flush the system) and do hammerhead turnarounds by the dozen. He would taunt me in a turn. . . . I would be rolled in real tight and beginning to feel a buffet in the turn—meaning I was as tight as I dared go—and would look up through the eyebrow panels to see him turning *inside of me* **. . . how, I will never know. Jake liked to push it—a lot.**

The day in question was part of a rush time; we were some 60,000 acres behind in requests, a heavy "greenbug" and Russian wheat aphid infestation was occurring, and we weren't getting the winds we needed to make headwind takeoffs or make the spraying effective. I know you may not understand this "ag jargon" but what it means is we were losing the battle against the bugs—and possibly our contract at the same time. It was a real crunch time for the company, and everyone knew it.

There was an enormous amount of pressure to fly, and we were averaging 18-hour days, arriving before sunrise to prepare the aircraft, flying all day, then staying at the field cleaning the hoppers until well after dark. Those of you in the military or commercial aviation may be shocked to hear that ag pilots operate for days—and sometimes weeks—on five to six hours' sleep per night, but it can be commonplace during a rush period. Refuels and reloads were often hot (refueled and loaded with the engine running), with pilots standing in the cockpit to relieve themselves as necessary. It was as close to hell as flying can get.

The business had become much smaller by the time I flew for the company, with three spray airplanes (and two personal air-

craft) and four pilots. We flew Cessna 188 AgTrucks. We operated from a tight airstrip, which required special procedures for take-off when hot and loaded. We would taxi to the end of the strip, run to full power, and swing the tail for a 180-degree turn to line up, using the speed from turnaround to give a little extra momentum. As the tail became light we would go full forward on the stick and pop full flaps (we used a Robertson STOL system to droop the ailerons); this would put the tail in the takeoff position. Immediately we would pull back and break ground, and the runway would be behind. It was a one-way strip, with tall high-tension lines on the other end. It was a tricky maneuver, to say the least, and the wind didn't always cooperate.

Our departure end was bounded by a railroad track on a six- or seven-foot berm, running perpendicular to the runway. It was fenced off by a standard barbwire fence. At times it looked as high to us as the Empire State Building. We would stay in the takeoff configuration for a mile sometimes before we were able to retract the flaps and climb over a parallel power line and go to the field. Everyone knew that the takeoff was the most difficult part of the flight, but we did it so often it became routine. I guess you may say we were set up for complacency, but most of us still treated the takeoff with a healthy respect. Except Jake.

During full up operations, three pilots would fly, and one would load and act as a safety observer for the launch and recovery in the event anything went wrong. I was loading on this day, being new and inexperienced. I was worried about what I had seen happening to Jake over the past few weeks. He was going through a divorce, and he had been through several others previously. He had a history of drug and alcohol problems, and was drinking at night. He did not drink on the job to the best of my knowledge, but you could tell that the stuff was taking its toll. Just the physical demands of the job were wearing me out. At the end of each day I felt like I had been run through a wringer. I don't know how Jake did it, but he kept going. He was exhausted and was leaving the airplane during the loadings for several minutes at a time to sleep in the hanger. He was a "whatever it takes" kind of guy, but I knew he was fast approaching some kind of personal limit, either physically or psychologically.

It was damn hot. The day before, with the mercury soaring over 100 degrees Fahrenheit, the heat had been blamed for inducing the cardiac death of a migrant harvester, just adjacent to the airport. Due to temperatures, we were flying reduced loads, down from around 165 gallons to about 125. One sixty-five was too much at the time, even with all the special procedures. I had been loading and sending out 130 gallons maximum and advised Jake to do the same. He told me he could carry more and demanded I load his plane up. I complied. I put it on his aircraft, fueled her up, and loaded his flags.

The three taxied out; I took my post to watch the takeoff roll. Charles took off first and circled back over to watch the other two, both his sons. Jake took the runway next. I noted a slight tail-wind register on the hangar wind sock and advised Jake about this over the radio. He advised me that I would do better to keep my mouth shut, and he pushed up the power. I was worried, but I had seen him do it so many times before that I was not overly concerned. Still, that tailwind combined with the over-gross takeoff weight made the hair on the back of my neck stand up, and shortly thereafter I knew why it was.

Jake was two-thirds of the way down the runway, and still his tail did not come up. I could see his acceleration was sluggish—well below normal. I observed him pop flaps and force the tail up, but almost at the end of the runway. He could have dumped his load, but for some reason chose not to. He literally forced the air-plane into the air, striking the fence. We later found both spray booms wrapped entirely around the fence posts, pulled from the airplane—the posts had to be cut off to remove them. He came down on the other side, in a very steep nose-down attitude, and disappeared from view. It was close to sunset, and there was a bright orange flash. I thought it was an explosion, but it was only the red dust thrown upward against the backdrop of the sun. He came upward nose-high and then disappeared from view again. I sat there horrified momentarily and then headed for what I was certain would be the site of the crash, and quite possibly Jake's demise. To my surprise, I found that he had not stopped at or near the end of the runway.

I later learned his rudder cables, which were coupled to the steerable tail wheel, had been severed. He was unable to retard the throttle that was stuck in a full-open position. In short, Jake was trapped in the world's most powerful tricycle with no way to steer. He finally dumped his load, but failed to shut down the engine. He proceeded through a quarter section of stubble milo and through another fence. He crossed a highway, penetrated another fence, and entered a shallow ravine. He came out of the ravine, through a billboard, back through the fence, and onto the highway. This continued until he struck a tree in the yard of the first house on the edge of town. The propeller was severed at the hub, and the right wing removed but for the attachment at the flap, by the trailing edge of the wing root. The fuel bladder was ruptured and sprayed the airplane. The engine was canted about 30 degrees, opening the cowling, and the fuel was ignited.

I arrived very shortly after Jake had ground to a halt, and the airplane had just begun to burn. I put out the fire. My coworker removed the canopy on the left side of the airplane, and helped pull Jake out. He was cut badly on the forehead where he had impacted the crash pad (a crushable part of the panel designed to collapse under impact), and his left knee was open to the bone. He staggered past me as I was extinguishing the fire and opening the battery compartment, I told him to lie down by a tree and I would see to him next. He was lucky to be alive. But the story was not over.

Epilogue

Put together and boiled down without all the background, you could see this one coming a mile away. It was a classic predictable accident. The catch to the whole affair comes when I can truthfully say he didn't die immediately from the impact, but rather from a far slower and far more painful demise. We did lose him, but only because he found his truck and, in his state of mind, left town and hid. He thought he was in a great deal of trouble, and he ran. I learned his version when he covertly entered the hangar, as I dismantled the airplane some months later, and asked me what had happened.

Jake died about six years later, by suicide—stabbed himself to death. His father, who had survived combat and over 40 years of active crop dusting, died a year later in his sleep . . . still no accidents and no sickness from the chemicals. His brother sold the business and moved away.

Analysis

Obviously, there were demons at work in this young man besides merely being a rogue pilot, but that is part of the point of this case study. Most pilots understand the term "compartmentalization," meaning the ability to leave your ground problems on the ground and concentrate on the problems at hand in flight. Occasionally the problems become so powerful or so numerous that it becomes impossible to lock them away during preflight. When you combine these stressors with the type of operational pressures that were present when this mishap occurred, you have a pressure cooker that will likely break the strongest personality. Everyone has a breaking point, and when it is reached, rogue behaviors are just one of a host of negatives that can occur.

Author's note: Until I began researching the historical essence of airmanship for my first book, I had no comprehension of the difficulty and sophistication of the ag pilot's mission. I now firmly believe that they, along with the group that is discussed in the following case study, are as skilled and professional as any military or commercial flying operation I have ever witnessed.

Fire-Fighting Rogue

If you start with all of the hazards faced by the agricultural pilots, add high-pressure altitudes, unknown terrain, box canyons, mountains, smoke, haze, multiple aircraft operations in a confined space, and—oh, yeah—searing flames licking at the bottom of your aircraft, you *begin* to see the challenges faced by the airborne firefighters (Figure 6-1). After reading this short list, you may ask yourself the same question I did when I first met these guys a few years ago: who in their right mind would ever want to do such a thing? Luckily for all of us, there is no shortage of pilots who are willing to accept these challenges to protect our precious natural resources. Once again, however, the environment is conducive to the adventure seeker and, as in every other field of aviation, rogues emerge.

Figure 6-1.   Air tanker. Fighting fires from the sky is as hazardous as most combat missions. The thrill and excitement it generates provide fertile ground for rogue pilots. (*U.S. Government photo*)

The following case was offered by an individual who has been flying both agricultural and fire-fighting missions for more than 20 years. He has flown in North and South America and fought over 200 fires from the air. The story begins over a fire many years ago in the southwestern United States.

Red-Hot Pilot

Blane always knew he was better than everybody else was—at least in his own mind. He had flown combat in Vietnam—fighters, naturally—and claimed he was never interested in flying for the major airlines. Of course, we all had heard that one before from many other pilots who didn't quite have what it takes to work for a major carrier, but for some reason when Blane said it, you really believed in it. Taken by itself, this condescension and the attitude of superiority was not really a problem. The problems arose when he took this attitude into the sky with him over a fire with 20 other pilots trying to build some sort of ad hoc team and come out of the situation alive.

I had only been flying ag and fires for about four years when I first ran into Blane—and I mean that literally. I was working for a small outfit out of Northern California; we were dropping fire retardant on a fire located about 50 miles from our home strip. The Santa Ana winds were kicking up, and the government decided it was time to bring in another contractor to help us out. Blane flew for them. He had been kicking around Ag, flying for five or six years, but he had just been hired on for his first stint at fighting fires in a multiengine.

Back in those days there weren't many regulations, but one of the cardinal rules of aerial fire fighting has always been not to reverse track after crossing the fire line until you are absolutely certain there are no aircraft following you down the chute. Blane undoubtedly knew the rules—he would not have been allowed to fly if he did not. For some reason, he chose to ignore them on this day and, as luck would have it, I was trailing him into the drop zone. Evidently he had experienced a malfunction in releasing his load and decided to pull up hard to the left after his run and take a 45-degree cut back across the fire to try again. As I mentioned before, this is a no-no of the highest order.

We were on our final heading into the fire drop zone and were 10 seconds out from the final drop point when I saw him coming at us from our 10 o'clock position. We couldn't have had more than 50 to 75 feet of altitude clearance, and he was on a definite collision course. To complicate the matter further, in the smoke and haze, I couldn't be certain of the position of other aircraft in the vicinity. But I knew they were out there. This was a fast-moving fire and there were helicopters and small single-engine air tankers (SEATs) all over the place. The only evasive action I could take was *down,* so I "bunted" the aircraft into the flames. We released our agent at the programmed drop point and executed a standard climb out. I was having difficulty seeing out through the scarred windscreen, but I assumed that the fire might have done the damage. After recovering our aircraft back to the home strip, we had to abort the remaining runs scheduled for the rest of the day due to aircraft damage we picked up during that evasive maneuver. Upon closer inspection, we found blistering under the aircraft caused by the intense heat and fire. More interestingly, we found the topside of the aircraft had been hit with a load of fire retardant.

It didn't take long to find out who the idiot was who had tried to kill us. Our boss called his boss and made the complaint. We were assured through the same channels that this would not happen again, so we decided to let bygones be bygones. I guess I chalked it up to inexperience on the part of some new guy. After all, I had made some pretty dumb mistakes in my first year flying against fire, too. He would learn like the rest of us—from experience. I was wrong. Experience only made Blane more unpredictable—and more dangerous.

A few weeks passed, and a rumor began to circulate about a multiengine air tanker pilot who had done an aileron roll over a nearby lake after dropping a load of fire retardant on a small fire in southwestern California. You must understand, most of the aircraft we were flying at this time (and still) were 1940s and '50s vintage, held together by chewing gum and baling wire. To even contemplate—let alone attempt—aerobatics was absurd. Further investigation revealed that it was not merely rumor, but fact, and apparently was routine behavior from a new guy with the company down south. You guessed it—Blane.

Why they continued to employ a pilot with such poor discipline I will never know, but I suspect it had something to do with him always pressing past the minimum to get the job done. Unfortunately in our business, there always seems to be room for those guys. Blane bounced around the industry for the next 10 years, leaving a trail of "I can't believe he did that!" everywhere he went. Blane was nothing if not a survivor. Unfortunately this was not the case for some other pilots who began to copy his rogue actions and stunts.

As word of his rogue behavior spread throughout the industry, Blane began to justify his actions by ridiculing the actions of others. For a time, he was surrounded by a group of young admirers who saw the Vietnam veteran as a role model. Finally, one of these young admirers killed himself ingloriously while attempting an Immelmann-type maneuver (half loop and half roll to reverse course) in a Cessna 152 after *deliberately flying into a box canyon*— a maneuver Blane had demonstrated to him and others. This had a sobering effect on everyone who saw Blane as the one who exemplified the *real* firefighter mentality.

Slowly professionalism crept back into our ranks. It's still creeping and we have a long way to go, but thankfully there aren't many Blanes left around. And if they show up, they don't stay around for long. I don't believe the culture would allow it anymore. I could be wrong, but I hope not. I don't know where Blane is today. He left the industry about a decade ago, complaining that we were getting soft.

Civil Air Patrol Rogue

The Civil Air Patrol (CAP) is an aviation-oriented, nonprofit, volunteer organization with three missions: Emergency Services in search and rescue and disaster relief, the Cadet Program (leadership development and aviation-related activities for youth, ages 12 to 21), and the Aerospace Education Program. The CAP was founded in 1941 to assist in the war effort. It later transformed its wartime mission of coastal anti-sub patrol to a peacetime focus on community service and leadership development. It is currently the official Auxiliary of the United States Air Force, and the Civil Air Patrol's programs are supported by the aviation experience and resources of its members and of the Civil Air Patrol corporation.

The following is a letter received by a Civil Air Patrol instructor who had seen all she wanted of undisciplined rogue behavior.

John and I flew a Cessna 172 to Mansfield so John could pick up another aircraft. As we got into the aircraft, I asked John if he'd like me to read off the checklist for a "challenge-response" team approach. He was flying that leg. His response was a less-than-enthusiastic, "Sure, whatever."

I began the checklist with the section on crew coordination and the safety briefing, but John was ignoring me and he was jumping ahead in the checklist. When I got to the step for circuit breakers, he said, "I already did that." It was clear to me that John did not know how to act in a multipilot cockpit, nor was he the least bit interested in learning from me.

Later, as we were taking off, John elected to do a short-field takeoff. I had no problem with John wanting to practice one for proficiency, but his execution of it led me to believe that he had attitude-based, as well as skill-based, problems. We rotated at 55 KIAS (normal), but then proceeded to climb out at that airspeed (it should be 65 KIAS). I called out, "John, airspeed." He *still* maintained 55 KIAS. I again called out, "John, airspeed should be 65." Again, he didn't do anything, and now we were down to 48 KIAS and the stall-warning horn was going off. I was just about to state, "My plane" and take control when John pulled up the flaps from 10 degrees to zero. As Cessnas like to do when reducing flaps, the nose came down and our speed increased. However, we were still climbing out at 65 KIAS, and the short-field technique says that after the flaps come up, you should transition to best-rate which is 76 KIAS. That whole experience really scared me—probably more than any student could have. I thought that we would have another Taunton—a fatal CAP crash in Massachu-setts—right there. It wasn't long before more indicators of John's rogue behavior surfaced.

It was a good day for training—clear skies with a slight cross-wind. John was instructing his student in touch-and-go's in the pattern at Otis, an Air National Guard base. Mike, another instructor, was also in the pattern at Otis, about to make a full-stop landing. As Mike and his student rolled out on the runway, John was instructed to go around because Mike and his student had not yet exited the runway. John had a better idea, and replied, "It's okay, I can S-turn and still land." Tower curtly said, "Negative, go around." John was not to be denied, however, and came back again with, "We can still make it." The tower con-troller, now clearly angry at the breach of discipline, replied very loudly and firmly, "CAPFlight 1925, GO AROUND!" Finally, John did. Wouldn't it have been better for John to teach his student to obey ATC instructions even if it is a bit inconvenient? The pattern was never all that busy while we were at Otis—a go-around would've cost them perhaps five minutes. But it appeared as if John saw this as an infringement on his judgment, and had to assert his ego against the controllers. That is the stuff landing dis-asters are made of.

Again while John was instructing his student the next day, he taxied for takeoff. A multiengine cargo aircraft, a military C-130, was in the pattern doing touch-and-go's. As the C-130 lifted off from the practice landing, John was instructed to "taxi into position and hold, expect a three-minute delay for wake turbulence." John replied, "Tower, we'll waive the delay." On many occasions, this might have been a legitimate decision based upon the liftoff point, crosswind component, etc. But on this day the conditions were ripe for wingtip vortices at the Cessna's rotation point, and John didn't give it a second thought. So now he's teaching his student that as long as your ego is at stake, you don't have to worry about wake turbulence. It is a matter of time until he kills someone. There is more.

John was teaching spins in the aircraft. While the teaching of spins is not prohibited for primary training, I have four problems with teaching it in CAP aircraft, but John didn't see any of these as restrictive.

- Spins are not allowed under CAP regulations.
- There were many loose items on board the plane which could have struck either of the pilots during the spin.
- They did not have any parachutes, as required by the FARs since spin training is not a requirement for primary flight instruction.
- The plane definitely was not in the utility category, as required by the Cessna POH to do spins.

John seems to be a frustrated pilot in the CAP, who feels the need to do something that will get people to recognize him as a "superior aviator." His next stunt was to brag about his aerobatic stall series.

John was bragging about teaching accelerated stalls with the wings "near vertical." When pressed about it, he admitted to "maybe 70 or 80 degrees." Besides the fact that this would be an aerobatic maneuver, it's totally unnecessary for primary training and could teach dangerous habits to a student. The purpose of the maneuver is to teach the student how the aircraft can stall at a higher speed during a high-wing-loading maneuver, not to teach poor discipline.

John is the proverbial "accident waiting to happen." He flies in an organization that preaches discipline and sound judgment, yet he routinely violates both. We have made his actions known to flight standards personnel, and hope to retrain or remove him, but until then, we will hold our breath. Even in the Civil Air Patrol, rogues exist and endanger us all.

A Final Thought on Special Mission Rogues

There are similar stories from other special mission categories such as search and rescue, aeromedical evacuation, and even from the missionary fields. The point is simply that niche flying is highly individualized with very little oversight, thus creating multiple opportunities for rogues to flourish. Therefore, these missions demand the highest degree of personal discipline, and peer pressure and an attitude of zero tolerance for deviations is likely the best method for dealing with the problem.

But even these tools are often ineffective if we cannot identify the aviator who is at risk of a rogue act. The next chapter looks at the phenomenon of "the failing aviator" to help us better identify those who can use our help.

CHAPTER SEVEN

The Failing Aviator

SOMETIMES EXPERTISE, charisma, and the "I'm better than you" attitude are not the only earmarks of a rogue pilot. An in-depth review of human factors and decision-making accidents reveals that a different kind of rogue is also present among our ranks. Such individuals use the aircraft and flight environment to compensate for inferiority in other areas of their lives. Occasionally it is not just inferiority but a combination of internal and external factors that results in accumulated stress. This stress will eventually manifest itself in undisciplined acts. These acts may result in one-time decision-making errors in the cockpit, or they may manifest themselves in more long-term failures of discipline such as excessive drinking, drug use, or abusive behavior at home or in the cockpit. When viewed together this has become known as the "failing aviator syndrome." It can occur to flyers who have been exceptional in the past, but who have been overcome by stress or change and can no longer cope with the dynamic environment of flight. At other times it occurs to flyers who never quite make the grade. In both cases, the failing aviator syndrome is usually accompanied by personality factors that do not handle failure well, and this leads to coping behaviors that can be—and often are—dangerous and destructive.

These failing aviators can be found in the cockpit of Piper Cubs, F-14 Tomcats, and major airline 747s. The results of their behavior vary from minor infractions with resultant disciplinary actions to much graver actions. For example, there is the strong possibility that a commercial airline pilot recently committed suicide with his airliner, taking nearly 100 passengers to the grave with him. The failing aviator could be any of us, now or in the future. Because of the gradual nature of the failing aviator syndrome, identifying and assisting a failing aviator can be difficult. They are not always easy to notice. They are usually people we are comfortable flying with, people whom we have trusted for some time, but for one reason or another they begin to experience difficulties. They might be hobbyists or combat pilots, or they might even work for the FAA, as in our first case study.

A Failing Fed

When I first read this mishap report it was a hard one to comprehend. A Federal Aviation Administration Beech Super King Air 300, operated by the Flight Inspection branch out of New Jersey, crashed into mountainous terrain in poor weather, because *the pilot elected to fly visual flight rules (VFR) into bad weather in mountainous terrain.* That bears repeating. The guys who inspect and certify our instrument approaches and landing systems, the guys who know the critical importance of reliable navigation systems to keep us safe near the ground, the guys who know more about terminal approach procedures and ground clearance than Elrey Jeppessen—these guys crashed because they were too stupid to get an instrument clearance! At first I had to check the date on the report to make sure it didn't say April 1. This had to be some kind of sick joke—but unfortunately it wasn't.

It began with the pilot in command (PIC) of a routine flight check mission, who became overly anxious to complete a job he hadn't been able to get done the day before on the Winchester Airport ILS. After completing the inspection, he took off VFR for Richmond, Virginia, even though the crew knew that the weather would likely require an instrument flight rules (IFR) clearance along the way. As the crew departed Winchester, they began to encounter low ceilings and requested an IFR clearance, but the air traffic controllers were extremely busy and were not able to immediately respond to the request. Instead of remaining clear of the clouds as the FARs require, the FAA inspection crew continued along their route of flight into instrument conditions, trying to hack the mission. Becoming increasingly uncomfortable with their deteriorating situation, they contacted ATC. "We're over the Linden VOR at 2000, can you get us a little higher?"

The Linden VOR sits on top of a mountain labeled clearly on the chart as 2472 mean sea level (MSL) and within an area labeled as "designated mountainous area." This crew was reporting level at *2000 feet in the same area!* It is obvious that they were already in way over their head, literally and figuratively. Ground witnesses in the area described a twin-engine aircraft orbiting in and out of the clouds. The hilltops were "shrouded in fog," reported another witness. The aircraft impacted a ridgeline at 1770 MSL, killing all on board.

Surely this must have been an inexperienced pilot, trying to prove something to his boss and organization. Unfortunately it was not. The pilot in command was a 55-year-old Airline Transport Pilot (ATP)-rated, single and twin certified pilot, with more than 6700 hours of experience—more than 2000 in the BE-300. His second-in-command was even more experienced, with more than 13,000 hours of flight time and more than 1000 in the Beech 300. How could this level of experience make such an elementary mistake? Could there be more at work here than a single lapse of judgment?

As the accident investigation unfolded, it revealed a failing aviator who had been sending off clear signals that something was wrong for over two years. The National Transportation Safety Board (NTSB) reporter listed several indicators, which are classic earmarks of the failing aviator.

- For the past two years, several coworkers had formally objected to the pilot in command's actions in flight.
- Eight of eleven second pilots requested scheduling preference to avoid flying with this pilot.
- The pilot had required three attempts to successfully complete type rating check in the BE-300F.
- He often omitted the briefing of flight crews on essential parts of the day's plan.
- He refused to accept responsibility that his failure to adhere to a checklist may have resulted in engine damage.

In addition to these indicators, there had been a recent upturn in the undisciplined actions of the PIC, including the following:

- He continued a VFR flight into IMC conditions.
- He failed to keep VFR cloud clearances and conducted flight below 1000 feet above the ground in marginal weather conditions.

- He lied to air traffic control when queried about weather conditions—he said he was in visual conditions when they were actually IMC.
- He performed a "below the glidepath check" in IMC conditions when the regulations require VMC.
- He disregarded checklist discipline on numerous occasions.

A further look into the life of the pilot in command revealed two DUIs in the past five years and a suspended driver's license for nonpayment of the state's auto insurance surcharge. His license was suspended a second time for failure to attend a mandatory drug and alcohol program. He was still driving with a suspended license at the time of the mishap.

Viewed as a whole, it seems impossible that this pilot could have gone unnoticed as a serious risk to safety. But over time, the gradual buildup of evidence did not seem so overpowering. Clearly this man had personal stress beyond the norm. He reacted to this by bearing down harder at work, which made him exceedingly difficult to work with. Without the social support from his colleagues, he began to measure his worth by how often he could get the job done, and he became obsessed with mission accomplishment. This in turn led to a pattern of failing judgment and greater risk taking. All of these are classic behavioral patterns of the failing aviator. Most of them were visible to his peers and supervisors. Why then, was action not taken to help? Perhaps all involved wanted to give this man the space he needed to solve his own problems, but when the behavior began to spill over into the cockpit, it was clearly time for formal action of some sort.

Once again, the significance of the failing aviator syndrome is that it can happen to any of us, given the right set of circumstances—just as it did to this FAA inspector, and to a senior captain with a major U.S. commercial carrier, in a fascinating story of a failing pilot, which hit the national news in 1996.

Captain WOW

According to an article published in the *Wall Street Journal*, a senior airline captain, who demanded to be called "Captain WOW" (for his initials) in the cockpit, was a rigid and domineering personality, who became prone to fits of rage at home as well as in the cockpit. The 58-

year-old, 265-pound former Marine had a history of violent outbursts. He once bashed a car with a nightstick. On another occasion he allegedly stabbed his second wife in the face with a fork during a fight (accidentally, he maintained). He pulled his third wife off of the toilet by her hair, while holding a cocked and loaded gun to his head and threatening to kill himself. "Stressed out" would be a gross understatement for these fits of rage.

In the cockpit, he was once reprimanded and grounded for six weeks for blurting out over the aircraft intercom, "I've already got your money, so shut the f– up!" in response to a first officer who was trying to return a $40 dinner tab. But Captain W hadn't always been like this.

An experienced pilot with combat time in Vietnam, he had won 2 distinguished flying crosses and 10 air medals. After leaving the military, he had a nearly spotless flying record for over two decades. Over the course of the last few years of a sound flying career, he had gradually become more and more hostile toward his coworkers. Had this not manifested itself at critical moments in the cockpit, it would likely have been seen as an aging captain who was coming up on mandatory retirement. Twenty years ago, before the advent of crew resource management (CRM) training, this type of behavior in the cockpit may have been acceptable. But not now, when new hires—even those from the military—have been brought up according to the gospel of teamwork and conflict resolution. On one European trip, it all came to a head. Martha Brannigan writes in the *Wall Street Journal*:

> **The mood was set from the first flight. The engineer refused to address Mr. W as "Captain WOW" saying in a later report to superiors that he didn't want to feed an "over-inflated ego." More importantly, the engineer charged that Capt. W had reacted hostilely when his crew tried to point out errors. . . . The conflict culminated at the gate in Frankfurt, Germany. 10 days into their assignment, Second Officer Sweeny's report to superiors said that Capt. W had "a screaming fit in the cockpit."**

In further testimony, it was revealed that this behavior occasionally went beyond mere differences of opinion. The first officer reported that the captain had broken altitude restrictions three separate times, to which the captain replied, "The altitude variations were minor and not a safety violation."

The flight engineer summed up the difficulties involved with working in an environment dominated by an aviator who demonstrated a combination of an aggressive personality, a failure to accept the team concept in the cockpit, and accumulated stress: "Capt. W's terribly bitter attitude, along with his violent, aggressive personality, make it extremely difficult for other crew members to perform their duties."

The airline had a number of complaints regarding Captain WOW, but deciding what to do about it was a much more difficult task. As they searched for the source of this behavior, they found an accumulation of debt and at least the appearance of a violent personality getting more and more out of control. The airline went as far as grounding him, but the process was extremely difficult and was administratively reversed on several occasions.

The stress of the entire episode was clearly apparent to one industry medical doctor, who reported that the captain exhibited "a narcissistic personality disorder"—a grandiose sense of self-importance that often leads to conflict with others. The Vietnam vet hadn't always been this way. He had once been a war hero and a model airline pilot, but somewhere along the way the stress had built up to the point where he became a failing aviator and a rogue pilot. These changes were obvious across his life's activities. His wife said he had become a "rage-a-holic." There are cues here that were present far earlier than they were addressed. Let's take a closer look at the role of stress in the pilot's psychological equation.

Personality Factors, Stress, and the Failing Aviator

Different personality types handle stress in different ways—some better than others. The CRM program of Transport Canada provides us with a simple but useful way in which to view these differences at a macro level. They suggest that people are either "hot reactors," who are almost immediately susceptible to stress in most situations, or "cool reactors" who are less likely to respond immediately to stress inputs, but who, nonetheless, are not immune to its effects over time.

Hot reactors are often very achievement oriented and see stressors as having an immediate impact on their ability to accomplish the mission. If you are in this category (as I am), you should realize your potential for worsening a problem through self-induced stress. This can often come about as a direct result of worrying inordinately about mission accomplishment. Additionally, hot reactors can become more easily distracted and run an increased risk of losing situational awareness. Finally, reacting too strongly to outside stressors can impair normal decision making and, hence, have a negative impact on flight discipline.

A closer look into the case of Captain WOW clearly reveals the hazards associated with being a hot reactor. On the European trip, the flight engineer reported that the captain busted several altitude restrictions as a result of his conflict with the crew. "Calling the crew insubordinate, he [Captain W] said, 'I felt like I was flying solo.' " Perhaps due to his hot reaction to the stress of the moment, as well as the accumulation of non-flight-related stress, he was indeed flying solo, at least in his own mind. Hot reactors don't gather much team support.

Cool reactors deal more effectively with mounting stress, but this is not necessarily a good thing either. Cool reactors can create a situation that can often mask the buildup of stress. Seen as unflappable, they can create a hazard both to themselves and to others on the cockpit team. When the cool reactor finally exhibits outward signs of stress, it is often seen as unusual and sometimes frightening to the rest of the crew. It may also indicate that they are getting close to their breaking point. Make no mistake about it, stress impacts us all and, regardless of personality type, we can be overwhelmed.

Before we move on, let's make sure that we don't leave you with the impression that all rogues in the air are overbearing control freaks. The following example demonstrates the other end of the spectrum and tells the story of a pilot who violated good judgment and cockpit discipline just to help the flight attendant get a head start on the beverage service. He certainly does not fit the typical pattern of the failing aviator. He was a happy and well-adjusted family man. But in this case, his "failures" occurred through a lack of discipline and attention to detail that sprang from his outgoing and friendly personality, which made them more difficult to see or address. While the captain in this mishap was certainly not failing at life in the same ways that others in this chapter were, complacency born of familiarity had clearly replaced solid cockpit discipline. It is important to understand that extremes at either end of the spectrum can result in rogue acts.

Just Trying to Help:
The Well-Intentioned Lapse of Judgment

It was just another milk run for the two pilots and one flight attendant on Jetlink Flight 2733. The Continental Express commuter lifted off from Runway 22R at Little Rock on time at 3:16 P.M. Twenty-seven passengers were on their way to Houston. The weather was fine, but most of the flight would be flown in high-level clouds. Some trace icing had been in the forecast. The crew checked in with Little Rock departure control and was cleared to join jet route J-180 to the west and to climb and maintain 10,000 feet.

The climbout progressed slowly. The aircraft—an Embraer 120 RT Brasilia—was relatively heavy with nearly a full load of passengers and considerable baggage on board. Six minutes after takeoff, Flight 2733 was climbing through 7500 feet and was cleared to continue its climb to an intermediate cruising altitude of flight level 220. After checking in with Memphis Center, the first officer asked the captain what altitude he wanted for a final cruise into Houston. He also discussed the performance data for a cruise to FL 260, and the captain responded, "I don't care."

As the aircraft passed through 8000 feet, the flight attendant came forward into the cockpit. This captain liked to keep the door open. "Hi!" the flight attendant said, and non-flight-related conversation followed for about one minute. Memphis Center called and offered FL 230 for a final cruising altitude and the first officer requested and was given FL 220. A passenger, seated in seat 1B, looked forward at about this time and saw the pilot "put his seat back, unbuckle his seat belt, and put his foot up on the aircraft console." A few moments later, the flight attendant returned to the cockpit and asked the pilot if he could climb any faster, because she didn't want to drag the beverage cart "uphill" during the climb. The pilot responded, "Okay."

The flight data recorder indicates that at this time the pilot more than doubled his pitch angle (from 3.2 degrees to 6.5 degrees) without increasing power. The captain and flight attendant continued their non-flight-related conversation, during which the first officer interrupted them to point out that they were "not climbing very fast." The captain replied that they were "heavy, really heavy" and continued his conversation with the flight attendant.

Less than a minute later, the captain noticed something was wrong and got back to the business of flying the aircraft. He called out to the first officer, "Frank, hang on, something ain't right." Within two seconds after his observation and call out, the autopilot disconnected itself, the stick shaker activated, and the stall warning horn sounded. Things had gone bad, and in a big hurry. The aircraft departed controlled flight and entered into what the accident reported as a "post-stall gyration." Not good.

As if the crew needed more to complicate the situation, the entire recovery process would have to be conducted on instruments, because IMC conditions prevailed from the point of departure to approximately 2000 feet above the ground. As the two crewmembers attempted to save the stalled and gyrating aircraft, severe oscillations were taking place. The flight data recorder showed bank angles of 111 degrees and pitch attitudes of greater than 67 degrees nose down. It is likely that the captain was also experiencing spatial disorientation, because during the majority of the recovery process, he never pushed the yoke forward. The aircraft spiraled through 15,000, then 10,000 feet, as the crew tried desperately to right the aircraft in IMC conditions. Finally, the first officer lowered the landing gear, and that somehow provided enough stability for the aircraft to be partially recovered at 6700 MSL.

But the excitement was not yet over. Unknown to the crew, the violent oscillations had done serious damage to the left engine. The aircraft had lost three of the four propeller blades and all of the upper cowlings, and had been bent on the engine mounts. With only single-engine power available and asymmetric thrust, the aircraft entered a secondary stall and began to depart again. Luckily, the crew was now proficient in recovery techniques and managed to get control this time in less than 1500 feet.

The aircraft was finally leveled off at 5500 feet, an emergency was declared, and the crew received vectors to the nearest airfield in Pine Bluff, Arkansas. The crew broke out of the weather in close to the airport, and the captain overshot the turn to final because of controllability problems. Being in no mood to attempt a single-engine missed approach back into IMC conditions, the captain elected to crash-land the aircraft with less than 2000 feet of wet runway in front of him. The aircraft hydroplaned off the end of Runway 17, slid through rough sod, past a vehicle and construction crew, between the ILS antenna and the

ILS equipment building, and came to rest in a rice field. Neither the crew nor rescue personnel were able to shut down the right engine and it continued to run for the next 15 minutes, but all passengers and crew were evacuated safely. Quite a bit to suffer through to make sure that the flight attendant didn't have to drag the beverage cart uphill.

A Different Type of Failing Aviator

The captain on this flight was anything but a problem for his company or anyone who flew with him. According to his chief pilot, he was a standout aviator, who could really apply the principles of CRM in the cockpit. He didn't drink excessively, had no former disciplinary problems, and was well liked and respected by the first officers who flew with him. He was living a normal, well-adjusted life. But what appears to have happened here was a creeping complacency. The crew had flown this route many times. They could do it in their sleep. Yet one small deviation—the decision to double the rate of climb to help out the flight attendant—coupled with some icing in the clouds, nearly killed them and their 27 passengers.

Pilots who fly a lot—especially those who fly the same type of missions over and over again—must realize that familiarity breeds contempt, and this mindset can lead to well-intentioned rogue behavior. This episode tests the limits of our definition of the rogue. The pilot was polite, practiced open communication, and shared responsibility in the cockpit. He had no history of problems with discipline. Everyone liked and respected him. Yet he was willing to take a step that violated good judgment and standard operating procedures. He knowingly and willfully put the aircraft in a region of increased risk, and he demonstrated apathy and complacency during this phase of flight. As the aircraft climbed out in IMC conditions, he consciously made a decision to double the climb angle without increasing power, and then unbuckled, pushed his seat back, put his feet up on the console, and chatted with the flight attendant. These actions are all well within our original definition of a rogue behavior. Remember, "stupid is as stupid does."

Our next look inside the failing aviator analyzes the other end of the experience curve, where inexperience and a new situation create too much excitement for a young man to handle. It will also help us distinguish between accumulated stress and the kind that leaps on a pilot in bunches with little prior notice.

The Stress of a Single Moment

Sometimes the stress of a single moment can overcome aviators, especially those who have other psychological baggage that might cause them to want to prove their mettle by demonstrating their prowess in an aircraft. One of the primary temptations has—and likely always will be—the air show. We are not just talking about the formal air show at your local military base, but also the impromptu air shows that are done for the benefit of a few friends or family.

It seems like everyone wants to be a demonstration pilot. We all love watching the Blue Angels and the Thunderbirds, and often wish we could perform like they do in front of an adoring crowd. But I am realistic enough to know that I cannot and, furthermore, that every year pilots lose their lives, and take the lives of others, by trying to perform maneuvers they are not qualified to attempt.

The air show temptation occurs when a pilot decides that "it's time to make a name for myself and impress somebody." Tragically, aviators often succumb to the temptation to "show their stuff" to friends and families. Far too often, the show the family and friends see is not the one intended and ends in the death of the pilot, often witnessed by the same friends and family he or she set out to impress. Following is an example of a young man who lets the thrill of the moment get the best of his judgment, and a rogue act is his last act.

Too Good an Offer to Resist

Several years ago, a military fighter pilot stationed in Europe was on a simple cross-country ferry flight. Approaching midway to his destination, he asked air traffic control for clearance off of their frequency for a moment to update the weather at his destination with a local American base "metro" (weather) shop. The news wasn't good. There were observed thunderstorms en route and forecast for his arrival. Using sound judgment, the young captain decided to divert to an intermediate base for some routine maintenance and to wait out the weather. While the aircraft was being repaired, the pilot talked with several other pilots and ground crewmen there and planned and filed the last leg of his flight at the local base operations.

Prior to starting his engines, he spoke with the local supervisor of flying (SOF) and asked him if it would be all right if he accomplished a "high-speed pass" on departure, prior to heading to his final destination base. The SOF approved the request. After cranking the engines, the pilot received permission from the tower for an opposite-direction, low-altitude, high-speed pass prior to departure from the airfield. After takeoff, the pilot performed a series of low-altitude turns to align himself with the runway. He made the pass over the runway at an altitude of 100 to 200 feet and at an extremely high speed. At approximately 1000 feet from the departure end, he lit the afterburner and aggressively pulled toward the vertical. Approximately 60 degrees nose high, the wings came off the aircraft and it burst into flames. There was no attempt at ejection.

A Youthful Rogue

The F-15 Eagle pilot was 24 years old and was on his first operational tour in the F-15. He had only 315 hours in type and 513 hours total flying time. The investigation revealed no physical or psychological problems. He was flying regularly and was qualified for the mission. He was considered to be among the better of the new guys, and he flew the jet well. Crew rest and duty day were not factors. The weather was clear. The pilot had planned and precoordinated a flyby with the local on-scene supervisor (SOF). This was a fairly routine occurrence and was condoned as being a morale booster for the local maintenance personnel, who seldom got to see the aircraft they worked on flying other than in the local traffic pattern at slow speeds.

But if this were such a routine event, why would the pilot feel the need to max-perform the aircraft to the point of destruction? The answer might well involve the need for a young and aggressive aviator to prove his mettle in front of a crowd. Unlike his home base, where he was considered a rookie, at this base, he wasn't the youngest, most junior member of the squadron. At this base—on this day—he would be *somebody*.

To speculate that this pilot was overcome by the excitement of the moment and that this excitement led to a rogue act might be considered a stretch of logic, but other circumstantial evidence suggests that it is exactly what occurred. Consider a few other facts discovered by the accident investigation board.

On the day of the mishap, the pilot failed to arm his ejection seat. He also forgot to fasten his parachute chest strap or to insert the presence or weight of external fuel tanks into the armament control panel. Without the proper configuration into the aircraft's computer system, the automatic over-g warning system would not be operational. As the mishap pilot made his flyby at an estimated 550 to 605 knots, he probably pulled back on the stick, listening for the warning tone of an approaching over-g. Pilots of high-performance combat aircraft are trained to take advantage of this aural signal as a means to keep their heads out of the cockpit. But as the Computer 101 instructor points out, "Garbage in, garbage out." Since he had forgotten to load the weight and fuel data, the tone never came, and the wings ripped off the *Eagle* at approximately 8.5gs due to the high speed and heavy gross weight. The thrill of the moment had made a kid into a rogue.

The Two Most Dangerous Words in Aviation

It has been said that the two most dangerous words in aviation are "Watch this!" But we have already seen that these words can have different meanings, depending on what it is that a pilot wants to prove. In the situation of the youthful rogue in the preceding case study, it was that he was the master of a very high-performance air superiority fighter. For Captain WOW, it was simply that he was in charge. For our next victim, it was to prove that he had what it took to be a naval aviator—an F-14 Tomcat pilot.

Trying to Prove His Worth—the Wrong Way

One of the last things Navy Lieutenant Commander Stan Gates (pseudonym) told his parents was to take the south route home so that they could get a good view of his takeoff. In January 1996, Gates had stopped off in Nashville on his way back to VF 213 squadron at Miramar Naval Air Station—"Fightertown, USA" of *Top Gun* fame. After visiting with friends and family, he fired up the Tomcat and requested a "high-speed vertical takeoff." Roaring down the runway at Nashville's international airport, Gates pulled the aircraft up into a near vertical climb, well in excess of the 65 degrees of pitch allowed by regulation. Very shortly after takeoff, the F-14 disappeared into a solid cloud deck. Moments later, the aircraft reappeared, diving out of the cloud deck, out of control.

Elmer Newsome, a 66-year-old native of Tennessee, and his wife Ada, three years his junior, were in the process of entertaining a favorite visitor in a residential subdivision a few miles from the international airport. Ewing Wair, 53, had stopped by to chat with Elmer and Ada on this cloudy January day. Perhaps the topic of the day was the weather or what they planned to do together when spring came. It didn't really matter what the conversation was about, as these were old friends who simply enjoyed each other's company. As they sat in the Newsome's brick home that Monday, they never could have suspected that this would be their last opportunity to share a story. They had the misfortune to be in the wrong place at the wrong time. A rogue pilot was about to take all of their tomorrows away. The three of them never knew what hit them. Also killed in the tragedy were the 33-year-old pilot, Gates, and his radar intercept officer (RIO), 28-year-old Lieutenant Graham Higgins. Five deaths resulted from an individual's desire to prove to those he loved that he had made it to the big time—Stan Gates was a Navy fighter pilot and he somehow interpreted that to mean the need to be reckless.

It could have been worse. Nearby, teachers and 540 students at the Paragon Mills Elementary School ducked when Gates's jet rattled the windows and doors at the school as it passed over. Students and teachers who rushed outside at the sound of the crash could clearly see the fireball from the school building. Terry Sensing, a physical education teacher, told reporters, "It scared me half to death; everybody in here started crying." The children and staff at Paragon now practice plane crash drills along with fire and tornado drills.

Why would a professional aviator feel the need to accomplish a stunt like this into a solid cloud deck? Perhaps part of the reason was Gates's need to be seen as a real Navy fighter pilot. He hadn't always been one.

Gates's first assignment had been as a naval flight officer (NFO), not a pilot. Based on his good performance, he had been selected to cross-train to the pilot position and had done just well enough to get into fighters. He was certainly not seen as the best of the best. In fact, Stan Gates was probably below average in terms of skill in the jet.

In most military circles, there is a stigma associated with those who come to pilot training after another tour of duty. This "crossflow" pilot is usually older than those he comes into the weapon system with. Typically, they have a higher rank than those they trained with, but a lower level of experience than those of equal rank. As such, they don't fit well into the formal or informal hierarchy. They often perceive a real need to prove themselves the equal of those who are their rank. The problem is that they are *not* equal; they are considerably less experienced. So they try to prove themselves in often inappropriate ways—such as performing vertical takeoffs into solid cloud decks.

Gates had lost another F-14 less than a year before this accident, and he had been found at fault. Flying off the deck of the *U.S.S. Abraham Lincoln* in April 1995, he had been a flight lead in an mock combat exercise west of Hawaii designed to teach fighter pilots evasive maneuvers. Sometime during the training mission, Gates had stalled the aircraft and went into a flat spin. Both he and his radar intercept officer (RIO) ejected safely. Following the inquiry into the mishap, Gates had been reinstated to the F-14 and came back up to mission-ready status. There were rumors of other instances of lack of discipline, but Gates continued to fly. Gates's squadron had now lost a total of four aircraft in 18 months. The Navy had lost 30 Tomcats in three and a half years. The movie *Top Gun* may have helped recruiting, but it sure didn't do much for the mishap rate in the F-14 fleet. In fact, the Hollywood version of airmanship may well have been an underlying contributing factor in many of the mishaps.

In retrospect, Stan Gates had shown several telltale signs of the failing aviator. He felt the need to prove himself, he had a history of discipline issues, and he had already lost an aircraft. What could have been done? Perhaps if he had understood what the professional culture of the naval aviator was, he would not have felt the urge toward exhibitionism.

The Real *Top Gun* Mentality

Shortly after the crash of Gates's F-14, there came a chorus of criticism. A human factors debate was played out in the public eye, with many people asking difficult questions about the personalities who fly in defense of our nation. The discussion that followed this incident centered on the term "*Top Gun* mentality." The secretary of defense used the term negatively. He cited the need to bring the *Top Gun* mentality under control.

Certainly, combat aircraft are not toys for exhibitionism. However, the layperson's understanding of the term "*Top Gun*" is based on fiction—the movie—which is loosely based on fact—the military's fighter weapons schools. Let's cut through these confusing layers and get back to the original concept of the term, the one based on fact. If these standards are clearly communicated, identifying the failing aviator becomes a much easier task.

Military operations in combat are truly the crucible of expertise. Donald Bringle, a career naval aviator and former Navy Fighter Weapons School instructor, comments on his view of the *real Top Gun* mentality in excerpts from a Naval Proceedings commentary in April 1996:

> **The real Top gun mentality is a positive force. . . . Never have I been associated with a more professional, highly talented, intensely dedicated group of aviators. The standards expected of every Top gun instructor, and consequently of every student, remain higher than those of any other organization in aviation.**

The standards that Commander Bringle speaks of are a necessary prerequisite to carrier aviation, due in large part to the demanding nature of the mission. Few of us will ever approach the airmanship and discipline demanded of carrier-based aviators, which is a tough admission for me to make as an Air Force pilot, but true nonetheless. The commander explains:

> **Every day of the year, on every carrier deployed overseas, there are nearly 300 young aviators on six-month deployments, braving extreme conditions, night arrested landings with no divert field in the middle of the Indian Ocean or North Atlantic, where the deck can pitch 30–40 feet in a cycle. Yet the leadership still launches the aircraft, and the young men and women launch without question, because that is what they are expected to do. In fact, they revel in the challenge of it all.**

The external demands placed upon carrier aviators have molded the vast majority of these aviators into a disciplined lot—at least at sea—in spite of Hollywood characterizations to the contrary. There is much to learn from the positive personality characteristics displayed by these professional aviators, and Commander Bringle leaves us with a few valuable insights into their internal makeup:

> **This lifestyle demands an individual who must have supreme confidence in his own abilities, yet maintain a high respect for the aircraft which he flies, and the conditions through which he has to operate the aircraft. . . . There has to be a sense of purpose for an individual to want to make a career of this. He does it for the love of flying, the camaraderie of his associates, and for the love of his country. This is the true Top gun mentality.**

Managing the Failing Aviator[1]

Appropriate management of the failing aviator is one critical key to mishap prevention. The goal is to reduce tensions in the individual to allow for adequate time and room to cope. Recognition of a problem in an individual is the first step. This can often be very difficult because the cues exhibited can often be subtle. Not every pilot responds to stress like Captain WOW did.

Another problem is a lack of opportunity for many to observe a pilot in action. Aviation, by its very nature, allows for little supervision or oversight, especially for senior captains or instructors. Those who do get a chance to observe are often the closest friends or teammates—like Gates and his RIO. These relationships do not foster the idea of bringing in outside interventions or reporting small infractions or violations. Usually, close friends or colleagues will try to help out on their own. But managing a true failing aviator is not a job for amateurs.

Yet another roadblock along the rehabilitation highway for failing aviators is their ability to mask, deny, or disguise the accumulating stress. Pilots are notoriously good at understanding the bounds of acceptable behavior, and if they step outside of these boundaries, they are usually quite capable of making up an appropriate excuse or rationalization. Other pilots are usually more than willing to accept these excuses from one of their own.

Enabling the Rogue

This tendency of other pilots, friends, and family members to protect a failing aviator may be the biggest challenge to overcome in rehabilitating such a flyer. Suppression of stress by an individual is to be expected, but enabling actions by others is shortsighted folly. Looking back at the case of Bob Hammond, the quintessential rogue from Chapter 2, it is easy to see that his rogue actions were facilitated not only by his family and friends, but by fellow aviators and, most absurdly, by his commanders. Following each of his now well-documented rogue events, there were those who not only condoned his actions, but congratulated him for it. This goes well beyond enabling and into active encouragement. To effectively manage a failing aviator, one must first educate the enablers, beginning with the sources of stress that wear down the failing aviator.

Environmental Stressors

There are many environmental stressors, but, to simplify, let's divide them into four categories: personal, family, social, and work-related. Personal stresses include those that are part of a pilot's basic personality type, such as obsessive behaviors, the need to be in control, or perfectionism. Family pressures may range from the illness of a spouse or child to interpersonal conflicts with the spouse—this is often a primary stressor for professional pilots who spend a lot of time away from home. Social stressors include such factors as financial and moral pressures, or a hectic, fast-paced lifestyle that starts to get behind schedule. Work-related concerns might include competition, job performance difficulty, trouble with the boss, or simple overwork. Helping pilots and the enablers to become more aware of these factors is a first major step toward stopping their rogue behavior.

Recognizing the First Signs

The most effective time to stop aviators from failing is before the bad habits or poor performance become ingrained into their patterns of behavior. Learning to recognize the early signs of debilitating stress is key in this process. Stress-induced changes include excesses in routine habits such as eating and drinking. Other common clues are increased agitation, aggression and irritability, fatigue, or a retreat from social activities. Fellow pilots should look for deteriorating flying performance—and increased risk taking, as well as the errors of judgment that appear most often of the omission type, such as the failure to use or complete checklists. If it appears that a normally conscientious flyer seems to care less and less about his or her performance, it's time to act. If these indicators are noticed, bring them to the attention of the individual in question, who is best equipped to handle it once the person gets past the denial.

Stress is very real—it is essential to life—but, equally, it can destroy life. An increased awareness by all concerned of the effects of abnormal stress, or of stress that a pilot is not coping with, is key to preventing rogue behaviors in failing aviators. Ignoring a failing aviator is fair to no one.

The failing aviator syndrome illustrates that not all rogues are undisciplined manipulators. Chapter 8 examines an even more difficult group to identify, the "one-act rogue," who shows few—if any—tendencies toward rogue behavior, right up to the moment of failed judgment and disaster.

CHAPTER EIGHT

One-Act Rogues

OF ALL THE CHAPTERS in this book, the one that you are about to read will generate the most controversy. Most pilots will disagree with its primary thesis. It will likely cause me considerable grief in the academic and operational circles in which I run. The main point of my argument here is simply this—even the finest, most disciplined pilots in the world are only one decision away from being rogue pilots—and a single act defines a rogue. Remember our definition in the Introduction—*you are what you do*—or, in Gumpese, "Stupid is as stupid does." If normally disciplined pilots survive a first rogue act, it is far more likely that they will attempt another at some point in the future. This phenomenon has come to be called "the slippery slope of compromised discipline." For this reason, it is critical that we all understand that there is no threshold of tolerance for rogue behavior. It bears repeating—a *single act* defines a rogue—and "one-act rogues" are just as dangerous at that moment in time as the most undisciplined pilot in the sky.

Many examples bear this out. For my first case study I have selected an inglorious moment from the history of the U.S. Air Force. It takes place in the aftermath of the Persian Gulf War in northern Iraq. The protagonists were—and most likely still are—solid aviators. But for a single moment in time, their flying records were spotless. At the moment of truth their discipline failed, and the results were horrific and far-reaching.

Friendly Fire: The Black Hawk Shootdown

On April 14, 1994, two American F-15 fighter jets misidentified, fired upon, and destroyed two U.S. Army Black Hawk helicopters with 26 individuals on board. Killed in the tragedy were Turkish, British, French, Kurdish, and American citizens. The investigation board found multiple factors contributing to the disaster, including misunderstood and miscommunicated procedures and rules of engagement and an AWACS crew that wasn't on top of its game.

But in the end, it was a breakdown of discipline by two fighter pilots—the last line of defense against systemic failures—who pulled the triggers after failing to adequately identify what they perceived to be Iraqi Hind helicopters. In a single act, the lives of 26 soldiers and diplomats were snuffed out and the lives of scores of family members were changed forever. Certainly, the lives of the pilots themselves will never be the same as a result of this one rogue act. Let's set the stage for the disaster.

Operation Provide Comfort: Background to a Tragedy[1]

At the end of Persian Gulf War, the United States was faced with the dilemma of how best to protect the enemies of Saddam Hussein who remained inside Iraq. The largest group that would require protection from the remaining Iraqi forces was the more than 500,000 Kurdish refugees who lived in the northern region of Iraq. To protect the Kurds, the United Nations designated a security zone, commonly called a "no-fly zone."

Iraqi forces continually tested the coalition's resolve by probing the no-fly zone with Iraqi aircraft, "illuminating" coalition aircraft with "fire control" radars (considered an act of war in any hostile region of the world), and even firing on friendly coalition forces. Coalition forces responded by shooting down an Iraqi MiG-23 and, bombing Iraqi anti-aircraft artillery and surface-to-air missile sites both inside and outside of the security zone. The war was over, but not the fighting.

Tensions continued to run high throughout the latter part of 1993. Kurdish refugees within the security zone were harassed by Iraqi forces, and United Nations relief trucks were sabotaged by Iraqis. On December 21, 1993, a small contingent of coalition personnel were attacked within the security zone. A coalition liaison employee was attacked one morning while leaving a support base in northern Iraq. In March 1994, Saddam Hussein publicly stated that he would be "forced to take other means" in response to the United Nations sanctions. Several non-government organization personnel had bounties placed upon their heads by the Iraqi government. On April 3, 1994, unknown assailants murdered a female civilian journalist employed by a French news agency, and the Iraqis were suspected. Tensions were running very strong in the area, and coalition aircrews and ground personnel remained in the highest states of readiness.

Peacekeeping

A military Air Force is trained to kill people and break things. It is not politically correct to say it, but it is the truth. To pull back from that combat mentality is extremely difficult, especially in an area that is still relatively "hot." The makeup of the American aircrews patrolling the northern no-fly zone closely mirrored that of those that had fought in combat there during the Gulf War. There were fighter aircraft and air-superiority fighters; for air refueling support, there were KC-135 and KC-10 tankers; and there were the ever-present E-3 Airborne Warning and Control System aircraft, commonly referred to as AWACS. There were certainly electronic surveillance aircraft patrolling the skies, vacuuming up electrons from communication systems, and, of course, there was the ever-present U.S. Navy aircraft carrier somewhere in the region.

Many of these same crewmembers had seen combat in Desert Storm, but this was a different kind of mission from the kick-butt-and-take-names approach of 1991. This was *peacekeeping*—a halfway measure between diplomacy and combat that no one is comfortable with, especially those with their fingers on the triggers.

For the tanker toads, the mission is basically the same, war or no war. It's an important mission, and the crew members are often seen wearing T-shirts that say "No One Kicks Ass Without Our Gas"—and it's true. The few differences that do exist for them are related to crew rest and safety. Other than the drag of being away from home, the peacekeeping mission is little different from training in the states on an air refueling track over Omaha. The tanker crews have it relatively easy.

For the AWACS crews, however, peacekeeping is an endless grind. Decimated by low morale due to excessive temporary duty commitments away from home and family, most crewmembers opt for civilian life at the first opportunity. In addition, the huge military drawdown after Desert Storm further cut the numbers of crewmembers available to share the load, making it even more difficult to keep even the most dedicated officers and enlisted men and women on the job—or on their toes.

The long hours and frequent tours of duty in garden spots like Saudi Arabia bred low morale and complacency. This was an important piece of the puzzle in this case study, because the U.S. Air Force has become increasingly reliant on AWACS, not only to locate the enemy and vector the fighters onto it, but also as an integral piece of the rules of engagement puzzle.

The Complex Role of the AWACS in Peacekeeping

AWACS operates as a form of gatekeeper to get into and out of a no-fly zone, as well as assisting in friend-or-foe identification for the fighters who are the real enforcers. The USAF 110-14 accident investigation of this event lists the common parts of a sophisticated mission package that the AWACS is responsible for controlling:

> **. . . daily flight operations are scheduled as mission packages. A typical package consists of a wide variety of aircraft with specific mission capabilities. When combined, these aircraft form a complex package capable of meeting tactical objectives. [It includes] a mission AWACS aircraft, six to seven air refueling aircraft (KC-136, F-135, VC-10), as many as 30 to 40 fighter aircraft (F-15, F-16, F-4G, F-15E, EF-111, Jaguar, Harrier) flying two and four-ship formations. In addition, Black Hawk helicopters maintain a visible presence in the security zone through air patrols and visits to Kurdish villages.[2]**

It becomes apparent from this list that one AWACS crew has a great deal of responsibility to safely conduct an operation of this magnitude, but it does closely reflect its wartime mission, so valuable training is obtained. The fighter crews faced a far more difficult and different sort of challenge.

The Fighter Pilots' Dilemma

Perhaps no one had it worse than the fighter pilots, who suffered in three ways from the new peacekeeping role. The first problem was a lack of realistic combat training. Unlike the tanker, reconnaissance, or AWACS crews, whose missions changed very little from combat to peacekeeping, the fighter jocks had to do a complete 180-degree shift in training philosophy. When preparing for combat, pilots will maximize training in offensive and defensive counter-air missions, dissimilar air-to-air combat, and weapons training. Budgetary and scheduling concerns preclude any of that in a peacekeeping role, where countless hours are spent "boring holes in the sky." To make matters worse, no-fly patrols are typically long missions, with little chance of seeing any action. Saddam learned his lesson well in 1991, and he is unlikely to challenge an American fighter pilot in the air with the few remaining aircraft he has left.[3]

Perhaps the most difficult part of patrolling the no-fly zone for many fighter pilots was flipping the mental switch from being an aggressive, offensive-minded combat pilot to flying a border-patrol mission that requires restraint. This is a problem that they share with Army and Marine foot soldiers in peacekeeping operations. After an entire career of training to kill, you are suddenly asked to lock your aggressive nature away and conform perfectly to a complicated set of rules of engagement that was written by international lawyers, not pilots or soldiers. And if you make a mistake, your picture is on the five o'clock news while some "talking head" public affairs officer from the Pentagon explains why you were so stupid.

This dilemma had even given rise to a bit of humor. Pilots said that the new fighter coming on line for the peacekeeping mission would be a two-seat F-15 "J" model—the "J" standing for the JAG (a military lawyer, known as the Judge Advocate General), who would tell the pilot when he or she is allowed to shoot. As we will see in a moment, it might not be a bad idea. In addition, the pilots referred to the never-changing mission as "Groundhog Day" after the movie in which Bill Murray relives the same day over and over again (Figure 8-1).

Figure 8-1. Peacekeeping in a warbird. It is difficult for fighter pilots to keep their edge after hundreds of hours of routine patrols. This may have been a factor in the friendly fire incident in April 1994. (*U.S. Air Force photo*)

Just Another Day for Three Aircrews in the Gulf

The day began early for all three flight crews. In Incirlik, Turkey, the AWACS crew woke up, had breakfast, and began their normal preflight routine of operational, intelligence, and weather briefings. They took off at 4:36Z ("Zulu" or International Coordinated Time) and powered up their systems. They declared themselves "on station" and ready to conduct business at 5:45Z. They immediately began tracking aircraft in southern Turkey and northern Iraq.

By this time, the Army helicopter crews, call sign "Eagle 1," were already several hours into their day. The Army likes to get up early. They were en route from Diyarbakir, Turkey, to Zakhu, Iraq, with a contingent of Kurdish, French, British, and American citizens to visit and inspect a Kurdish village. As the crew approached the entry point of the security zone, commonly referred to as "Gate 1," they made a radio call to the AWACS at 6:21Z to let them know who they were and what they were doing. Onboard the AWACS, a "friendly" tag of EE01 (Eagle 01 call sign) was attached to their radar signature.

Four minutes after the Black Hawks checked in with the AWACS (6:35Z), two F-15s, call signs "Tiger 1" and "Tiger 2," roared down the runway at Incirlik and headed toward their patrol area. As they leveled off at 27,000 feet, Tiger flight checked in with the AWACS and reported "ops normal." They began their airborne systems and weapons checks.

As the three mission elements proceeded with what had become increasingly routine, no one knew that in less than one hour, their fates would merge in two balls of flame on the desert floor.

Confusion and Breakdown

Back on board the AWACS, two separate controllers were responsible for handling the traffic in and out of the operational area. The first, the en route controller, handled traffic outside of the area, and the second, the operational controller, handled everything inside the area. A "senior director" oversaw the operation. Unknown to any of the crews, the Black Hawks were "squawking" the wrong Identification Friend or Foe (IFF) codes[4] as they flew toward Zakhu. As the helicopters entered a mountainous region near their destination, their primary radar return dropped off the AWACS radarscope at around 7:11Z (although a computer-generated track based on their last known heading and speed continued to be displayed). The F-15s were now 100 nautical miles distant and closing rapidly.

As the fighters entered the operational area, they checked in with the AWACS and received "negative words," meaning that nothing new had happened since the briefing they had received from intelligence that morning. This, of course, was not true—the Black Hawks were indeed "new," as they had not appeared on the morning air activity briefing. This would be the first of several critical breakdowns in flight tracking and communication.

First Contact

At 7:22Z something happened that got the fighter pilots' attention: their radar picked up a contact approximately 40 miles to the southeast.

They immediately reported it to the AWACS for confirmation. The AWACS area controller reported "clean there," meaning they had no radar contacts on the AWACS scope. Less than one minute later, intermittent signals were received onboard the AWACS from the Black Hawks, along with the character that identified them as friendly. For reasons unknown, this information either was not noticed or was not transmitted to the fighters.

As Tiger flight began to move closer to the contact, they tried repeatedly to verify the identity of the contact by electronic means, using the IFF. At one point, the flight leader *did* receive a positive Mode 4 response, but *after it would not come back, he determined it to be an anomaly in his system.* As the fighters closed to within 20 miles of the Black Hawks, they began their descent to conduct a visual identification pass.

Last Chance: Final Approach

The weather was clear and the unknown helicopters were traveling at approximately 130 knots down a valley floor, following a small road, as the Tiger flight closed in behind them. At approximately 7:28Z, Tiger 1 positioned himself about 1000 feet to the left of and 500 feet above the helicopter's flight path and observed "what he thought was a helicopter with a sloped vertical tail, sponsons (wings) on the fuselage, ordnance, and a dark green camouflage paint scheme." What he was actually looking at was a U.S. Army Black Hawk with external fuel tanks. What he "saw" was a Russian-built fully loaded Iraqi *Hind.* Tiger 1 transmitted that he had sighted a Hind and then quickly changed his mind—"No, Hip" (a different kind of Russian-built helicopter). It was difficult to see clearly with such a speed differential, and things were happening very quickly now.

As Tiger 1 passed overhead of the supposedly hostile helicopter, he began an orbit to the right to keep it in sight for further action, and saw a second helicopter. He quickly made a radio call to his wingman, "VID Hind, Tally Two, lead-trail," immediately followed by "Tiger 2, confirm Hinds?"—asking for verification from his wingman, who had more experience. The wingman replied "Stand by," and made his own visual identification pass. Following the pass, Tiger 2 called "Tally Two." The wingman testified later that he had intended his call to indicate that he had seen two helicopters, not necessarily to confirm their identity.[5]

The flight leader understood his wingman's transmission to mean that he had confirmed that they were Hinds. At about the same time, the AWACS operational area controller, who had been monitoring the entire intercept, stated "Copy Hinds." Now everyone was seeing an enemy.

Following the "confirmation" of enemy aircraft, Tiger 1 positioned himself 5 to 10 miles behind the lead helicopter, called "Engaged" to the AWACS (meaning he intended to attack), and ordered his wingman to "Arm hot" (prepare missiles for launch). He informed Tiger 2 that the leader would shoot the trailing helicopter and the wingman should destroy the lead helicopter—standard attack procedure so as not to warn the number-two "hostile" of the impending attack. At 7:30Z, Tiger 1 fired an AIM-120 radar-guided missile, destroying the trailing Black Hawk. Seconds later, Tiger 2 closed to approximately 9000 feet behind the remaining helicopter and fired an AIM-9 heat-seeker up its tailpipe.

The attack was efficient. There were no survivors. Approximately one hour later, mission controllers alerted the AWACS that two Black Hawk helicopters were unaccounted for, and asked them to begin search and rescue operations. Although no one would admit it in post-accident investigation testimony, they probably knew right where to look.

Error Chain or Rogue Behavior?

Like all mishaps, this tragedy had multiple inputs, any one of which could have prevented the disaster if it had been caught in time. Is it really fair to label this as a rogue act? Certainly many share in the responsibility, but only two people "visually identified" the helicopters and fired the missiles. Furthermore, Tiger 1 had received—albeit momentarily—a positive response at one point from the IFF system on board the Black Hawks. Could the monotony of the peacekeeping mission have set the stage for a couple of aggressive fighter pilots wanting some action? Although we may never know the answer to these questions, we do know how one of the shooters felt about his actions.

Human error did occur . . . it was a tragic and fatal mistake which will never leave my thoughts, which will rob me of peace for time

eternal. I can only pray the dead and the living find it in their hearts and their souls to forgive me.

Mistakes happen, but there was no rush to shoot these helicopters. The F-15s could have done multiple passes, or even followed the helicopters to their destination to determine their intentions. Hindsight is always 20-20, but to say that a mindset for action was not a part of this equation is to deny the obvious. A chain of errors does not excuse a highly trained pair of professional combat pilots for a gross miscalculation and failure of judgment. This was a rogue act.

In the next story, a normally solid instructor pilot is thrown off balance and makes a decision that hits every headline in the country.

Jessica's Last Flight

It seems that for every pilot, there is a given set of circumstances that will unravel his or her judgment. For some it is competition, for others it is the need to show off for friends and family. But for instructor pilot John Rexall (a pseudonym), it was a media frenzy centered around a little girl's brave and bold attempt at a new world record. According to the safety report, Rexall did not believe that there would be much media attention about this flight. When the trip was proposed, the pilot told his wife that the flight would be a "nonevent for aviation," and it was simply a matter of "flying cross-country with a seven-year-old next to you and the parents paying for it." The flurry of attention threw him off balance, and perhaps set the stage for a terrible decision.

The initial NTSB report was simply cataloged as follows:

Accident occurred APR-11-96 at CHEYENNE, WY
Aircraft: Cessna 177B, registration: N35207
Injuries: 3 Fatal.

To many Americans, however, the story of seven-year-old Jessica Dubroff's untimely death stirred deep emotions. The courage, initiative, and daring of the four-foot two-inch student pilot had been the center of attention in an otherwise slow news week. Jessica was trying to become the youngest person ever to fly coast to coast, and her radiant smile peeking out from under the bill of her baseball cap had captured the hearts of America during the first day of the trip. The Dubroff crew was engaged in a transcontinental record attempt involving 6660 miles of flying over 8 consecutive days. But when Jessica, her father Lloyd, and flight instructor John Rexall showed up at the Cheyenne, Wyoming, airport on the morning of April 11, 1996, they felt the sting of cold rain as thunderstorms approached the field and the wind gusted to nearly 30 knots. But the media was still there, so Jessica and crew delayed their departure, participated in media interviews, did their preflight procedures, and then loaded the airplane. After all, the world was watching. It would later be determined that the aircraft was 96 pounds over the certified maximum gross weight at the time of departure, but there was so little time to check on those items with all of the media questions to answer.

As the bad weather rolled into Cheyenne, the Dubroff crew was undoubtedly in a hurry to depart. Cheyenne is like many high-altitude towns in the Rocky Mountains. The weather rolls in fast, and can often be violent. But it usually passes just as quickly as it comes. Most pilots with mountain flying experience know this and are more than willing to give Mother Nature a chance to wear a kinder face. Rexall and his two fellow pilots were not experienced in flying in the Wyoming Rockies, and most likely were unaware of this phenomenon. They had a schedule to keep, more reporters were waiting at the other end of the flight. They had waited too long already, and were in a hurry.

This was clearly evident when they tried to taxi to the runway without removing the wheel chocks. Ironically, this cost them even more time, as they had to shut down the engine and have the chocks removed. As they approached the runway, they received a litany of weather warnings, and were advised of moderate icing conditions, turbulence, IFR flight precautions, and a cold front in the area of the departure airport. The airplane taxied in the rain to take off on runway 30. While taxiing, Rexall—the pilot in command (PIC)—acknowledged receiving information that the wind was from 280 degrees at 20 knots, gusting to 30 knots. At the same time, a United Express pilot facing similar conditions made a different choice. His commercial flight—with 19 passengers on board—decided to delay takeoff until more favorable weather conditions appeared on the horizon.

Dubroff's aircraft departed on runway 30, heading directly toward a nearby thunderstorm, and began a gradual turn to an easterly heading.

Witnesses described the airplane's climb rate and speed as slow, and they observed as the airplane entered a roll and descent that airport manager Jerry Olson called "a classic stall." The plane crashed in a residential neighborhood.

The formal accident report hints at peer pressure from the media as a possible cause for the failed flight discipline.

> **Probable Cause**
>
> **The pilot-in-command's improper decision to take off into deteriorating weather conditions (including turbulence, gusty winds, and an advancing thunderstorm and associated precipitation) when the airplane was overweight and when the density altitude was higher than he was accustomed to, resulting in a stall caused by failure to maintain airspeed. Contributing to the pilot-in-command's decision to take off was a desire to adhere to an overly ambitious itinerary, in part, because of media commitments.[6]**

The investigation that followed this tragic accident focused on the nature of the record attempt itself, pointing out that children should not be attempting world records in dangerous activities like flying. But they certainly missed the real point here. It wasn't the fact that a seven-year-old was attempting to set a new record that killed these people. It was a poor decision by the pilot in command, who apparently felt that this flight was important enough to warrant an overweight takeoff at extremely high pressure altitudes (which he had little experience with), into weather so severe that a commercial pilot had delayed takeoff. The peer pressure created by the media frenzy had overwhelmed a good pilot's normally sound judgment, causing an erroneous and fatal belief that it was vitally important that they launch from Cheyenne that morning. The circumstances had created a rogue.

Although a search of the FAA records found "no record of violations or enforcement procedures," there were indications of a lack of respect for weather phenomena. An instructor pilot from Rexall's home airport reported that he had witnessed Rexall attempt to land "several times when the weather was below minimums." He also stated that Rexall had designed his own personal instrument approach that went down to 500 feet. Perhaps getting away with violating the rules on these occasions led him to believe he could get away with challenging Mother Nature. He may well have set himself up for the big fall through several small compromises of discipline.

Our next case study looks at the sin of pride of performance that, once again, turns a good aviator bad with predictable results.

Too Much Pride

In the mid-1990s, a military B-1B bomber crashed short of the runway at Ellsworth AFB, South Dakota, after descending through the minimum descent altitude (MDA) on a TACAN approach. It clipped a telephone pole and crashed into a rising slope just short of the runway threshold. Fortunately, all four crewmembers survived the accident due to the quick reflexes and decision skills of the copilot, who activated the automatic ejection sequence for all four *after* the impact with the pole. The aircraft was completely destroyed.

It would be simple to chalk this mishap up to poor instrument proficiency or lack of flying skills on the part of the pilot, John Stahlman. Undoubtedly, the accident report stated that one of the causes was the pilot's failure to stop the aircraft's descent at the MDA, and this was true. This finding was accurate, but it did not get at the real cause of this accident. The aircraft commander on this flight was one of the most skilled at the base. Stahlman was an instructor pilot and flight examiner, thought of highly by almost all of the wing's aviators. He was also known to be extremely authoritarian, a take-charge guy. This made it difficult for other crewmembers to question his decisions in flight and to be assertive when they saw something that was not quite right—like a descent through the MDA without having the field in sight.

On this particular day, the crew was scheduled for a routine training flight that would consist of an air refueling, low-level bombing practice, and then a return to the traffic pattern for some instrument approach and visual landing pattern practice. The weather was forecast to be marginal, but above minimums for the return. This was not unusual in the Rapid City area, where the weather patterns are typical for the north central plains, low scud decks, blowing clouds and cold precipitation. Luckily, there were no real icing problems expected, as the B-1 engines have rather restrictive limits for operating in known or suspected icing conditions.

Upon completion of the low-level training, the aircraft began its descent into the Rapid City area. The forecasters were on the mark. The weather was marginal. It certainly didn't help that there were no precision approaches available for the B-1 to fly, but the localizer and TACAN approaches were pretty effective at getting in. Besides, the crew had the senior wing evaluator pilot on board, and if John Stahlman couldn't get in, nobody could.

The air traffic controller from Rapid City Approach vectored the B-1 to the final approach course for the localizer to the north runway. The crew ran the descent and traffic pattern checklists and received clearance for the approach. This was a single-frequency approach, so there was no need to contact the tower. At the final approach fix, Stahlman reduced power slightly and established a 1000- to 1200-feet-per-minute rate of descent en route to the MDA. The last ceiling and visibility report that had copied put the weather right at the MDA, so John was being as precise as possible. When they broke out of the weather, there wouldn't be a lot of time available to fix any problems he might create if he were a couple of degrees off the final approach course. No sloppiness allowed today.

As the aircraft approached the MDA, Stahlman eased the power back in and brought the nose up slowly. The B-1 cockpit is prone to spatial disorientation because of the long pointed nose of the aircraft and the pendulum effect of the underslung engines. It wouldn't do to get "the leans" in this kind of weather, so John was gentle with the controls and smoothly leveled off at the MDA. Now it was time to search for the runway prior to the visual descent point (VDP), from which they could execute a normal three-degree glide path down to the runway.

As the copilot searched outside for any sign of the runway, the pilot glanced up from the instruments to see the inside of a cotton ball. The crew continued inbound searching for some sign of the runway environment that would allow them to descend a little bit more. Regulations define the "runway environment" as airfield lighting, the runway, or buildings on the airfield itself. None of these were in view, so the crew continued to the missed approach point, executed the published missed approach, informed the controller that they had missed approach, and requested vectors for another try—this time they would try to get in using the TACAN approach. But Stahlman was beginning to have his doubts about getting in. He had flown an excellent approach to minimums and hadn't seen a thing. The weather must have deteriorated below minimums. But the crew checked with the base weather station and was advised that the local observation was still right at airfield minimums. This meant they were legal to try another approach. They still had enough fuel to hang around for a few more tries before they would have to divert to their preplanned alternate.

About this time, the crew heard another aircraft check in with approach control, requesting vectors to final approach at Ellsworth. They would be vectored inside of Stahlman's aircraft, and have the first shot at the runway. "Good luck!" John thought, as he recognized the call sign of the preceding aircraft—"Bone 23"—to be that of a less experienced pilot who wasn't even yet an instructor. As Stahlman's aircraft flew along radar downwind, the crew briefed the approach and listened as the radar controller cleared Bone 23 for the final approach.

"Bone 23, turn right heading 300, cleared for the TACAN approach. Contact tower upon landing on me on this frequency upon missed approach." Less than five minutes later, the offensive system officer (OSO), who was monitoring the command post frequency (the pilots did not monitor this frequency on approach because of the potential for distraction), told the pilots, "23 got in." Stahlman quickly asked the OSO to ask the crew where they had broken out on the approach. Thirty seconds later the OSO told Stahlman and the copilot, "Right at minimums."

The next approach was a mirror image of the first one, except that as they approached the MDA, Stahlman's level-off technique was even less aggressive. In fact, he brought the nose up for only a brief moment and then proceeded to descend through the MDA without the runway environment in sight. It is likely that he felt strongly that the ceiling might have changed a little in the three or four minutes since Bone 23 had made a successful approach, but if he pressed the approach just a little, he would certainly break out of the weather. Besides, if a less experienced pilot could get in, how would it look if John Stahlman couldn't?

The copilot called out that they were going below minimums, but then one or both members of the cockpit crew began to catch glimpses of the ground (*not* the runway environment). In fact, just off the left side of the aircraft the familiar yellow "M" of the McDonald's sign that was just south of the runway became visible on the upsloping terrain. The descent continued and suddenly the aircraft was out of the weather, but dangerously low and descending quickly well short of the runway.

Stahlman went to full power, hit the afterburners, and tried to pull the nose of the bomber up to get a rate of climb, but his actions were too late. The sink rate worsened as he attempted to max-perform the aircraft out of danger. The right wing clipped a telephone pole, cutting it off like a weed stem. The aircraft actually hit the ground on the crest of a small ridgeline and became airborne again momentarily. The co-pilot activated the automatic ejection system, and all four crewmembers were blasted clear of the aircraft a split second before it became a fire-ball in front of them. There were some ejection-related injuries, but all four survived, and three of the four are flying again today. The defensive systems officer suffered serious back injuries and did not return to flying.

Summary: Pride and Performance

John Stahlman made a seriously flawed decision to push the minimums on an approach. After hearing that another B-1 had successfully landed out of the TACAN approach, the senior instructor pilot (IP) pressed his approach below minimums and ended up in the dirt. One of the contributing factors in this mishap was the fact that the aircraft commander was a senior IP and flight examiner who had just heard a younger air-craft commander successfully land out of the TACAN approach. Although this was a routine training mission, and the crew had more than enough fuel to divert to a base with more favorable weather conditions, the senior officer was determined to take another shot at the TACAN approach. The fallacy in this decision is that weather, especially bad weather, changes rapidly. The fact that a younger, less skilled pilot was able to land out of the approach probably had more to due with a changing overcast cloud deck than his ability to fly the approach.

Epilogue: Gallows Humor and the McVASIs

Aircrew members are notorious for handling bad news poorly. We often deal with tragedy with inappropriate humor like *What was the last thing that went through ol' so and so's mind before he hit the mountain?* Answer: *The windshield.* Sick stuff, but it helps us get through it. Pilots are sort of like the TV show, *Men Behaving Badly*, except the jokes are worse. For example, within a week following the *Challenger* disaster, I must have heard 20 jokes. ValueJet has been another big victim of the aviation amateur comedians: *Think of us as AMTRAK with wings*, or *Even terrorists are afraid to fly with us*. Well, this B-1 crash gave a bit of fodder to our immature group.

It wasn't long before some words about the accident investigation leaked out of Ellsworth. It was rumored that the pilot had based his decision to continue the approach, at least in part, on seeing the McDonald's sign "at the usual position in the side window." Upon hearing this down south at another B-1 wing, we immediately sprang into action.

Most pilots know that vertical altitude slope indicator (VAS) lights are a system of red and white lights that assist the pilot in determining glide slope angle. Well, after hearing the story out of Ellsworth, we drew up a nice version of what we called the "McVASIs," based on what we thought this crew might have been thinking. If the "Drive Through" sign was positioned above the big yellow "M," you were low on the glide path. If it was below the "M" you were above the glide path, but if the "Drive Through" sign split the big yellow "M" precisely in half, you were safe to continue the approach. We drew this up with the recommended implementation language and as we howled at our own wits, someone mentioned the new piece of equipment that had just been installed in the orderly room. He called it a "fax" machine. We were told that it could actually transmit pictures over the phone lines. Pilots love new toys.

"Cool," we thought, and we agreed that this vital bit of safety information should be faxed to every bomb wing in America, along with our explanation on its development and guidelines for its use. We also decided that it wouldn't be right not to send one to the general at the Chief of Air Force Safety office at the Pentagon. Adhering to the Air Force value of "Service before Self," we decided that it would best be sent anonymously. So we proceeded to do so—not realizing that the return phone number was automatically printed at the top of each and every page we sent out. Within 20 minutes the squadron commander, who did not look amused, interrupted us in our gaiety. We left the squadron with precious little of our backsides still intact, but decided later at the officer's club that the joke had been well worth the cost.

Our last case study looks at the most tragic of one-act rogues, those who choose their last flight as the one to be undisciplined.

Finis-Flight

A few years ago, a large multiengine military jet aircraft (KC-135) disappeared from radar during a practice approach in instrument meteorological conditions (IMC). The investigation was relatively simple. The radar tapes revealed that the aircraft had left protected airspace and flown into terrain during bad weather. But a closer look at what prompted this action reveals a one-act rogue who pushed the limits on the last flight of his career. The pilot, who was also the squadron operations officer, failed to adequately plan the mission and follow prescribed instrument procedures. The mission consisted, in part, of a series of practice instrument approaches at a field that was below published minimums. Following the second missed approach and while proceeding inbound for a third practice approach, the aircraft descended below radar coverage. The aircraft subsequently crashed in a remote area 3½ miles north of the final approach course and 8¾ miles northwest of the field. All occupants of the aircraft were killed. Let's back up a bit and see how this highly experienced crew could have made such a basic instrument error as descending without course guidance.

The crew departed at 9:00 A.M. and flew at 13,000 feet to an airport for practice instrument approaches. Upon arrival at the VORTAC, the crew did not request ceiling and visibility information prior to the approach, as required by Air Force regulations—the first signal of procedural complacency, or perhaps an intentional act by a pilot who knew not to ask a question if he didn't want to hear the answer. After holding at the VORTAC, the crew was cleared for an approach. They were instructed to maintain 9000 feet until reaching a published segment of the approach and were given the local altimeter setting. The crew departed the initial approach fix (IAF) and flew without specific clearance to another instrument approach fix (IAF). They flew a distance measuring equipment (DME) arc until intercepting the final approach course and advised air traffic control that they planned to fly a total of four approaches.

The equipment at the airport was not cooperating; the TACAN portion of the VORTAC was off the air while the crew was flying the approach. The 9:55 weather observation, taken shortly after the initial approach clearance, was a 1500-foot ceiling and one mile visibility. This placed the field below approach minimums. The field remained below minimums for the duration of the flight, yet the crew continued to fly in violation of the regulations.

At 10:10 the crew was given missed approach instructions for their first low approach. They were told to execute the published missed approach procedure, climb to and maintain 9000 feet, and contact air traffic control. The crew then tracked inbound on the 054-degree course on the approach centerline but did not call when departing 9000 feet—another procedural error. They descended below radar coverage, passing 7000 feet. The aircraft passed over the airport without obtaining a visual on the runway (no surprise) and made a right climbing turn. The crew contacted the controller and requested a second approach. Radar plots indicate that the crew flew an improper missed approach, yet another indicator of procedural problems. The crew was then cleared to 9000 feet for the second approach. Once again they failed to update the weather observation.

The crew called inbound for the approach, and the air traffic controller replied: "Radar services terminated, and you can contact [Flight Service] radio [FSS] now, and again on your missed approach, climb out to niner thousand, and vacating five, give me a call on one three three six." The crew contacted FSS, calling inbound for the approach. They were given and repeated back the altimeter setting. At 10:29 the aircraft was tracking inbound on the centerline at 14 DME. The aircraft remained on centerline and descended below 7000 feet and out of radar coverage. The crew asked FSS to turn on the high-intensity runway lights and VASIs. The reply was, "Negative, I have no control on it. You have to do it with your own radio there"—another indicator of inadequate understanding of the procedures for this field. Witnesses at the airport confirm that the runway lights were not on and that the aircraft passed directly over the runway at 500 to 1000 feet. Once past the departure end of the runway, the aircraft made another right climbing turn into the weather. At 10:37, the crew contacted the controller, passing 7000 for 9000 feet on the second missed approach. The crew was given clearance for a third approach and instructed to maintain 9000 feet until established on a segment of the final approach course.

At this point the aircraft was at 10½ DME on the localizer course tracking 254 degrees and climbing through 7000 feet. One minute later, the aircraft had crossed the course, and was approximately a half-mile north of the course at 14 DME and at 9100 feet. The aircraft made a right turn and rolled out at 9000 feet tracking 052 degrees, a heading that paralleled the final approach course. At this point they were out of the radar coverage fan for the approach and had no DME information, a fact verified by subsequent FAA flight checks. Furthermore, the glide slope, navigation runway, and DME flags would have been in view on the pilot's instruments, yet the crew continued inbound. They were begging for trouble, and it was on its way.

At 10:40 the crew was given missed approach instructions. Radar contact was terminated, and they were told again to contact Flight Service. One minute later the crew contacted FSS, "With you, we, ah, descending seven thousand for approach." At 10:41:41 the aircraft descended below radar coverage. The last known position of the aircraft was at 7100 feet tracking 053 degrees, approximately 3½ miles north of the course and about 8¾ miles northwest of the field. Without adequate information to determine position, the aircraft impacted the rugged terrain.

The pilot was nearing the end of his tour of duty. This mission presented him with the opportunity to fly a memorable end-of-tour flight. The single significant medical finding relates to this end-of-tour or finis-flight attitude. His mission planning completely ignored weather factors, and he consistently exercised poor judgment during mission planning and throughout the flight. As the operations officer, most senior individual, and aircraft commander, he was the prime mover in this flight. He was responsible for maintaining crew discipline and ensuring that established procedures were followed. This disregard for discipline and procedures is typical of one who decides to fly a finis-flight in a grand or daring manner. In the military, finis-flights are common, and subsequent mishaps are not at all rare.

All crew members were current and qualified at the time of the mishap; however, the pilot had flown only once in the 30-day period prior to the mishap flight, completing one approach and landing. The copilot had not flown at all in the same period. The navigator had flown only one sortie in 60 days. The lack of recent flying impaired crew proficiency and may have been one reason why the remainder of the crew members did not catch or point out the multiple procedural errors.

The stated cause of this accident was that the crew positioned the aircraft outside the reception envelope of the approach navigational aids and descended without course guidance in IMC conditions. Yet the clear underlying cause was the desire of the instructor pilot/operations officer to go out in style. In attempting to do so, he pushed the crew into violating basic instrument procedures and paid the ultimate price. If his goal was to go out in style, he certainly failed. Controlled flight into terrain is an ugly legacy.

A Final Look at One-Act Rogues

In all three of our examples in this chapter, we see normally good pilots going bad for some reason or another. With the F-15 pilots in Iraq, it may have been that they were straining at the leash in an uncomfortable peacekeeping mission, and the thrill of the chase, once joined, was just too much for them to handle. With Jessica Dubroff's instructor pilot, the combination of fatigue, unfamiliar terrain, media pressure, and a history of getting away with challenging Mother Nature may have given him the idea that he could do it once again. John Stahlman was just overcome by pride of performance, usually an ally to good airmanship. In this case, however, his competitive mindset got the best of him, and he pushed his jet and his crew into a box that nearly proved fatal.

So what are we to learn from this chapter? Simply that rogue acts are often closer to the surface than we realize, and that each of us can succumb given the appropriate stimulus. It is up to each of us to take a look inside and guess at what it might take to push us into that region of the rogue.

The question remains as to the underlying forces at work when normally good pilots go bad. Our next chapter probes the inner mind to identify certain attitudes that might lead to rogue acts in the sky.

CHAPTER NINE

Bad Attitudes

MIKE TURNER, my college basketball coach, used to tell me that "mental toughness" and "extra effort" were far more important to winning than having a seven-foot-tall center. At the time he said it, I really doubted him. But part of my job as captain of the team was to keep the coach legitimate in the eyes of the younger players, so I played along, started diving for loose balls and playing hard every second as if it were the last ten seconds of the NBA finals. Before long everyone on the team was doing it. We finished the season with a league championship and ranked third in the nation, even without a seven-foot center. We had a motto that said "Attitude Is Everything." Although this might have been a bit of an overstatement, it worked for us, and it emphasizes the point we need to make for pilots. Good attitudes are critical to success in all of life's endeavors, but in aviation *bad attitudes can kill you.*

Psychologists tell us that there are two primary inputs to pilot behavior. The first is personality, a fixed and permanent part of your psychological makeup. The second set of inputs to the behavioral equation are more modifiable. They are the attitudes that come into the cockpit with you. There are good attitudes, such as assertiveness, respect, and a healthy approach toward the capabilities of your teammates. Then there are the other kinds, the hazardous attitudes that lead to rogue behavior.

Good news and bad news, the good first: psychologists and operators have been able to categorize certain hazardous attitudes into nicely defined packages, along with "antidotes" for pilots to use to prevent them. And the bad news? The word is not getting out, as evidenced by the dozens—if not hundreds—of accidents and incidents caused by pilots who fall victim to classic hazardous attitudes each year. Often these attitudes result in rogue acts.

Hazardous Attitudes and the Rogue Pilot

Aviators understand the need for control, but we typically think of it in terms of airspeed, altitude, and heading. Conversely, when we think of being *out of control*, we typically mean the aerodynamic stability of the aircraft. That is not the purpose of this chapter. Equally important from a flight discipline perspective is an inner control—*self-control*. We know that pilots fly for a wide variety of reasons. Some motivations lend themselves to a solid base of professionalism, and others lead to a predisposition for hazardous attitudes and dangerous acts.

It is critically important to identify hazardous attitudes, and equally important that we develop tools to counteract them. If we do not, situational factors can lead us over the edge into rogue behavior. The hazardous attitudes that are described here comprise an incomplete list, but they are the ones most likely to result in rogue acts. The important point is to recognize *any* attitude that may impact upon sound judgment and have a plan to counteract it. The following are of some of the more common hazardous attitudes that can lead to rogue behavior and get a pilot in deep trouble quickly. The first one is often disguised as a positive character trait—the "can-do" attitude. Left unchecked, it can cause the hard-charging, mission-driven pilot to become his or her own worst enemy.

Pressing

Pilots are typically achievement oriented. Often, they have come to flying as a means to conquer another personal frontier. Most are successful in other areas of their lives, and this didn't just happen by accident. These men and women take the same attitude toward mission accomplishment into the air with them that they have in the rest of their lives, and the result is often an inappropriate overemphasis on getting the mission done. "Pressing"—also known as "get-home-itis" or "Get-there-itis"—is one of the most dangerous of the hazardous attitudes. It likely leads to more rogue acts on the part of normally good aviators than all of the other hazardous attitudes combined. And as we mentioned earlier, it often comes described as a positive outlook on the job.

We have all seen—and many of us are guilty of—incidents where pressing too far led to poor judgment or unwise decisions. If you have committed one of these, and are reading this, then you are lucky to have survived the event. The mishap reports—and cemeteries—are filled with men and women who pushed one step too far in the name of getting the job done, or "hacking the mission."

Military pilots are notorious for putting the mission ahead of common sense. Ironically, more damage is often done by rogue acts in the name of the mission than would have been gained in benefits had the mission been accomplished. During Desert Storm, several aircraft were either lost or damaged when overaggressive pilots descended below a standard operating procedure (SOP) altitude to attack relatively low priority targets. Several were hit by antiaircraft artillery or surface-to-air missiles (SAMs) that could not have reached higher altitudes. In one case, a rescue attempt to get a pilot out of enemy territory after he had violated an SOP resulted in more casualties on the last day of the war.

Commercial pilots often press too far for different reasons, usually profit. Many airline pilots press lateral distance limits from thunderstorms, to get through to their destinations. In general aviation, "scud-running," the VFR pilot's attempt to stay out of the weather by hanging just under the ragged edge of a bad weather system, is seen by many as a badge of honor. In one incident, taken from the anonymous safety reporting system (ASRS) database, a helicopter pilot with only a VFR rating was lucky to survive to share his lesson.

The Customer Must Get Through

The weather in the Los Angeles basin was marginal visual flight rules (VFR), though acceptable for helicopters. The mission was to pick up the owner of a race track at the track, fly direct (VFR) to a country club near Palm Springs, and return approximately 1½ to 2 hours later. The weather east of Los Angeles was extremely marginal VFR; Riverside had measured 700-foot overcast, visibility 1½ miles, and fog. March Air Force Base was about the same. Beaumont was carrying an indefinite ceiling, visibility ⅛ mile. Obviously, the bad part was from March to Beaumont. I got

two separate weather forecast briefings, both of which were poor to say the least.

The flight was relatively routine (special VFR at Riverside and March) until just past March, when the ground began to rise into low jagged hills. I began flying toward the hills, still following the freeway. The ceiling got lower as the terrain rose and soon I was not only avoiding hills but dodging clouds as well. Events happened rapidly after that as I was still stupidly flying at about 100 knots. *Poof!*—into the clouds—ground contact lost! I knew "down" meant death, so I, a lowly VFR-only pilot, pulled aft cyclic and climbed into the clouds. Thank God I had an awesome 12 hours of instrument training and knew enough to go to the attitude indicator immediately. I stayed on it until breaking out in what seemed an eternity later, though probably less than a minute in reality. I had flown the same route a number of times before, so I knew that the *really* tall mountains were still many miles away. My immediate concern, upon entering the clouds, was power lines hidden somewhere ahead.

I managed to keep everything on an even keel all the way, but I've read the article stating that my life span as a VFR pilot upon entering the clouds was about 178 seconds. So, I suppose that if I'm ever stupid enough to do this again, I now have only about 108 seconds left. Figuring up all the possible FAR violations I made, I came up with a total of a whopping 62!

What caused me to do such a stupid, deadly thing? Hazardous attitudes, lots of them! The "let's take a look" syndrome; the "accomplish the mission, get-there-itis, pressing thing"; the macho, it can't happen to me attitude; and probably just poor pilot judgment. After all, as a helicopter pilot, the world is my airport. I can land virtually anywhere if I need to—as long as I can see the ground!

If this flight had resulted in a crash and the death of my passenger and myself, I think a case could be made for suicide and first-degree murder. I sincerely thank God and my instrument instructor for the ability to pull this one out of the hat.

What will I do when (not if) this situation comes again? I will be more assertive about the realities of flying in poor weather and tell my customer that the weather is bad and the flight will be delayed or canceled.

Overcoming the Urge to Press

Be honest with yourself. Just how bad do you want or need to get to the given destination, or accomplish the mission objectives? Sometimes you can see this hazardous attitude coming a mile away. Such was the case with this aviator, but she couldn't immunize herself from near disaster.

A Long Walk, a Late Dinner, and a Pilot Lucky to Be Alive

I had only been a flight instructor for about three months, and the guys (other instructors) with the company were always giving me a ribbing about "being weak" whenever I would bring the student back early for excessive crosswinds, approaching weather, or whatever. I was only 27 and I wanted badly to build some hours for an airline application, but I had also been trained by a conservative (by others' standards) instructor who had ingrained in my head the old saying, "There are old pilots and bold pilots, but no old bold pilots." I wanted to live to be an old pilot—but I nearly didn't make it.

I was flying with Alex, an eager 32-year-old who was picking up flying as a hobby to relieve stress from his stockbroker job. He was a great student, a quick learner who always did his homework and came prepared to fly. He aced all the procedural evaluations, and I guess you could say his flying skills were way above average for a new student. All of this might have led me into a complacent attitude, which set me up for the "pressing too far" trap.

We were scheduled for a cross-country out and back, which would complete Alex's training for his private pilot requirements, other than a few solo hours that he could complete on his own. Takeoff was scheduled for 9:45 A.M. We would be in to the satellite field by 11:30, grab some gas and lunch, and be back to the home strip no later than 3:00 P.M. Alex had to travel to the East

Coast for business the following week, so we were trying to get him completed before then. We needed the weather to cooperate, but it looked like we would get him done in time. But we really needed the out and back cross-country that day.

I was also in a bit of a rush. My fiancée Dave was coming into town at 5:30 that afternoon and I needed to be there to pick him up at the metropolitan airport, about 45 minutes from the strip we were flying out of. Of course, rush-hour traffic might be a problem, so I really needed to be on the road by 4:00 if at all possible. Dave and I hadn't seen each other in over a month, so I was really looking forward to picking him up. We planned to see the 7:00 movie and then go out to dinner. We had reservations at 9:30. I think you can already see that a lot hinged on getting back home in time. In retrospect, I should have seen the potential impact on my judgment, but the skies were fair and the winds were calm, so I wasn't overly concerned.

For the first time since we had started flying together, Alex showed up late. He apologized and we pushed the prebrief a little so that we could make it to the aircraft and hit the skyways. We caught an abbreviated weather brief—something about a 20 percent chance of thundershowers and the typical low-level wind shear associated with it—and launched. We were approaching the halfway point to our planned intermediate destination, when we started to get a few electrical gremlins in our Cessna. Nothing serious, but it looked like we might have a loose wire or something. We decided to press on. Alex needed the cross-country and the weather was good. We cut one pattern off the planned profile after we arrived, so we thought we were back on schedule.

After landing I sent Alex into the diner to order us lunch, and I took a look under the cowling to see if there was anything obvious with the wire harnesses. I saw what looked like a cracked insulation and possibly a partially broken wire, but I really couldn't be sure. I decided to call back to the shop and talk to my boss.

Bob, the flying school owner, answered the phone and told me that the aircraft hadn't had any problems before with the electrical system. He told me to use my own judgment but that the weather was beginning to "look a bit unstable" and to either get the plane fixed or to hurry back.

I inhaled a chili dog with Alex and decided to see if we could find the local aircraft electrician to have him take a peek at our generator. As I suspected, at 12:30 P.M. "Sparky" was at lunch, but was expected back "any minute." We decided to wait. At 1:20 he still hadn't arrived. (I found out later that he had been sitting next to us in the restaurant playing Pac-Man on the sit-down video game.) By this time I could see the cumulus clouds starting to build to the north, so I told Alex to start the walk-around, we were going to head back home before the weather got any worse. In retrospect, this was the worst decision I had ever made in my short aviation career.

We broke ground at 1:55, still plenty of time to get back home and get cleaned up to pick up Dave. But no sooner did we level off than our electrical system started acting up again, followed closely by an encounter with an angling cloud deck that was sloping down as we headed further north. This was not looking good. Although I am instrument rated, I didn't have more than 15 hours of actual instrument time under my belt, and the intermittent electrical system did little to inspire confidence. I thought, "maybe we should turn back and see if that electrician ever came back from lunch." But no, Alex needed this cross-country today, and Dave was already somewhere over the western United States on his way to Indianapolis—and the weather had to get better as we got closer to the field. Besides, the artificial horizon was holding pretty steady.

I decided to request an IFR clearance. I received my clearance and was told to climb to 5000 feet, which would put me in the clouds, where I didn't want to be with a possible short in the electrical system. "How do I explain this one?" I thought. I wanted an IFR clearance in case I needed it, but was more than a bit nervous about taking an aircraft with a known malfunction into IFR conditions. "Disregard the request, we'll maintain VFR," I reported back to the controller. I'm sure he thought he was dealing with an idiot. He was.

Conditions went from bad to worse. Rain started to splatter against the windscreen and there was considerable virga coming out of the clouds at our 12 o'clock position. I took the airplane from Alex and told him we were going back to the field we had just left. I started a slow 180-degree turn to the left, and halfway around I saw something that gave me a sickening feeling in my stomach. A big thunderstorm had popped up behind us and cut us off from any attempt at going back. I cursed my stupidity and started to sweat for real.

Turning back toward the home field, I decided that I had precious few options. I could get another IFR clearance and climb into the clouds with a bad electrical system and little instrument proficiency, or I could attempt to scud-run back home, skimming under the ragged edge of the cloud deck. I chose the latter. I told Alex to get out the VFR charts and scour them for towers and other obstructions along our new route. I was forced to gradually descend lower and lower until I was less than 1000 feet above ground level. With the forecast wind shear and related downdrafts—also known as "microbursts"—in the area, I was thinking that this could be a very bad trip indeed. The only blessing was that we were over flat farmland.

No sooner did I think about the wind shear and microburst than I felt the aircraft being pushed down. I advanced the throttle to full power and began to pull the nose up, but the airspeed began falling off too fast. I would either have to fly though this downdraft, or . . .

It was the hardest decision I ever made in my young—and rapidly fading—aviation career. I swallowed my pride and told Alex to begin the landing checklist.

"But we're still 45 miles from landing," he protested.

"No we're not," I replied.

We put the aircraft down in a driving rainstorm on a field parallel to a county road. The terrain was a flat but waterlogged field of corn stubble. The ground was initially firm, but the gear eventually sunk into the muck and we ended up tipping forward on the prop. We suffered minor damage, no injuries, and, luckily, no fire (I guess the rain did serve some purpose.) We ended up walking nearly three miles before we could find someone at home with a telephone.

I missed Dave at the airport, and we subsequently missed both the movie and dinner. Alex didn't get his required training and headed back east without his license. Both Dave and Alex got to help load a damaged aircraft onto a flatbed truck in the middle of the night. Bob let me keep my job. The jokes are worse now than ever before, but I am an older and wiser pilot.

The point is that I had no business taking a broken airplane into potentially bad weather with marginal instrument proficiency. When I told the story to my instructor, he just nodded his head as though he had heard similar stories a hundred times before. "I'm just glad you made it back," he said. "Many who make the same mistake don't." He finished the telephone debriefing with what has become the final question I now ask at every debriefing: "What did you learn?"

Overcoming Mission Hacking

If you find yourself taking risks that you normally would never consider, ask yourself why. When you find yourself saying that you *must* get somewhere, ask yourself what price you would be willing to pay for your arrival. Don't let your desires write checks that your aircraft and skills can't cash. Remember that this is the number-one hazardous attitude. Fine-tune your flight discipline antenna to recognize it, and then react with common sense. Stay inside your limits, and always leave yourself an out.

These last two case study scenarios were also partly associated with what is often referred to as the "Let's take a look" syndrome. It occurs when you think you might make a better decision after you encounter a particular phenomenon and see how bad it really is. The pilot in the second preceding case study got herself in trouble by thinking that she could alter her plan if the weather was really as bad as was forecast. She decided that there was no harm in taking off and taking a look. The reality of the sudden IFR encounter left her with only one option, and it was a bad one she was lucky to survive. Once into a situation, you have narrowed your options considerably.

Resisting the "Take a Look" Syndrome

Before you stick the nose of your aircraft into something you might regret, visualize the worst possible conditions you might encounter, and then analyze your options from that point. If they are options you are comfortable handling, press on. If not, sit this one out until conditions improve.

Antiauthority

Some aviators see the relatively unsupervised environment of flight as their chance to finally be their own boss. Although a pilot in command always has final authority over the conduct of his or her flight, as aviators we are required to abide by the rules and regulations. The authorities or air traffic controllers are not trying to fly your aircraft for you, but are merely ensuring that the airspace you are transiting remains accessible and safe for everyone who shares the skies. Noncompliance in aviation is not the act of a rebel, but rather that of a child—someone who is probably too immature to be in command of an aircraft. But rogues will never admit to this point.

Avoiding the Antiauthority Impulse

The capability to know and follow authoritative guidance is the mark of a professional pilot. The regulations are written for all of us. If you decide not to follow the rules, you are endangering the lives of others and casting disciplined pilots in a bad light. Avoid this behavior by recognizing hostility toward authority both on the ground and in flight. Realize that it can seriously impair your judgment. Great leaders must be great followers first. Closely related to the antiauthority hazardous attitude is simply the desire to prove oneself, referred to by the Spanish word *machismo*.

Machismo

Everybody wants respect, but when the desire for respect drives a pilot to rogue acts in an attempt to prove him- or herself to others, it is an attitude that is intolerable. This attitude is typically seen among men, but occasionally women may see the need to prove their mettle by foolish acts as well.

Ironically, dual-instructor crews are often most vulnerable to this hazardous attitude. Even with all of their accumulated experience, two instructors are often tempted to engage in a battle of egos in the cockpit, often resulting in unhealthy competition where flight discipline is the first casualty. Although the macho hazardous attitude permeates all sectors of aviation, it is conspicuous in the military and competition environments, where hot aircraft and supercharged egos often combine like a gallon of jet fuel and a match. Pilots who fly to prove something to themselves should be very wary of the tendency to let this turn into a hazardous attitude of trying to prove something to others. Prove yourself with disciplined professionalism. The pilot in the next story took himself over the edge and became a rogue.

Watch This!

Mike had just gotten his pilot license in January. He was flying out of a small strip in Texas that used to be an auxiliary field for the Air Force back in the 1960s. The field had been bought by a family that had turned it into a fly-in residential neighborhood with many homes and trailers located along the old taxiways, complete with hangar-garages to house both aircraft and the family car.

Mike's idol was a retired Navy fighter pilot who owned a Stearman and who practiced competition aerobatics directly over the field two or three times a week. Everyone knew that Mike wanted more than anything to be like "Dragon" (his Navy call sign). Mike was checked out in both the Piper Cub and the Cessna 172, but had flown a friend's Long-EZ and a few other experimentals on several occasions. He lived the life of an aspiring pilot and was surrounded by role models, both good and bad. Dragon had taken Mike under his wing and said he would instruct him in aerobatics, but first he wanted him to do two things. The first was to get 500 hours of pilot in command time, and the second was to read the book *Aerobatics* by Neil Williams.

Of course, Mike had read the book in the first week (likely without stopping to sleep), but building those hours was taking forever. Mike was young and in a hurry. Against the wishes and desires of his senior mentor, Mike began to hang out with a group of novice but affluent flyers who came down to the field often. This group had a reputation for being an undisciplined lot, and they fed off each other's acts—and each other's exaggerated claims. Mike had stumbled into a den of rogues, and he was not about to be outdone at his home field—especially not with Dragon watching. It was a lethal setup.

Mike took off in the borrowed ZLIN 526—the same type of aircraft that had recently won the European aerobatics championship—and immediately pulled up for a low-altitude Cuban-8. The first half of the maneuver was fine, but somewhere on the back side of the second loop, Mike lost too much energy and got himself in trouble. The "ground observer," a sort of half-coach, half-safety-observer who was talking to Mike on the radio, recognized the danger immediately and told Mike to "Knock it off." Mike answered the call "Roger" and rolled wings level inverted, still pointing 15 to 20 degrees nose low at around 500 feet AGL. There was still time to recover, but it looked as if Mike had frightened himself. He rapidly rolled toward wings level upright, but the rapid roll rate of the 526 (with which he was unfamiliar) caused him to overshoot the rollout, and he impacted the ground in 70 degrees of left bank.

Mike had no business attempting low-altitude aerobatics in a high-performance aircraft. His fate was sealed the minute he bought into the competitive attitude of an undisciplined group of pilots. His ego got the best of his judgment, and he killed himself in front of old and new friends alike.

Ironically, if Mike had gotten the message Dragon wanted him to get from the book, this tragedy might not have happened. Neil Williams speaks directly to this issue of experience in the Introduction of *Aerobatics*.

> **The aim of this book is to answer all the questions I wanted to ask when I started to learn aerobatics. . . . It is no substitute for good airborne instruction or even solo practice at a safe altitude. It all takes time, as does anything that is worth doing well. The tutor of Alexander the Great once remarked to his complaining pupil "There is no royal road to geometry." Neither is there a short cut to aerobatic flying.[1]**

Avoiding the Machismo Trap

Real machismo is characterized by humble confidence, not arrogance. Let your actions in flight be indicative of a confident and conservative approach to normal and emergency situations. Impress friends and aviation colleagues by your conscientious approach to planning and flying, and never attempt a maneuver to prove something to yourself or someone else, unless you are legitimately trying to improve yourself in a training environment.

Be particularly vigilant when you are flying as part of a two-instructor team. Regardless of the environments in which you fly, always remember the two most dangerous words in aviation—*"Watch this!"*

Invulnerability

Some aviators—usually pilots—feel bulletproof. They think disaster or bad luck will happen to the other person. These wishful thinkers are prime candidates to become rogues by running out of fuel or flying into thunderstorms or ice. This attitude often develops over time, perhaps after one has had several close encounters with bad weather, mechanical problems, and so on and survived. The more experience you have in the air, the more susceptible you are likely to be to this hazardous attitude. The law of averages are catching up with you. A wind shear doesn't care if you are a rookie general aviation pilot or if you have 30 years experience flying the line for a major carrier. It can and will kill you if you let it.

Fighting the Invulnerability Syndrome

Of course, we all know we can get hurt, and none of us actually believe that we can't be injured or killed. Yet often we find ourselves discounting danger in flight. It's just a matter of not realizing danger at the right moment. Delayed decision making is one serious manifestation of the invulnerability syndrome, and it can mask the seriousness of a situation, not out of a macho attitude, but from a more subtle belief that you will eventually come out of every situation in one piece. This does not argue for impulsiveness. You shouldn't reach for the ejection handles (literally or figuratively) every time that the master caution light comes on, but you must realize the danger residing in each situation, and react with appropriate promptness and respect.

The key to combating feelings of invulnerability is to realize that every year, literally hundreds of outstanding pilots—many that are more skilled and proficient than you are—get to meet Elvis, because they did not believe it could happen to them.

Impulsiveness

The opposite of the invulnerability syndrome is impulsiveness. Pilots can be a hasty bunch. As controllers, they want to take charge, and this often leads to situations where they act impetuously. This is especially true when they are confronted with situations that have no clear-cut answer. They want to make a decision and they want to make it *now*, and yet they may not have all of the required information to make the call.

There are many examples of situations where pilots acted in haste, later to regret their impulsiveness. An Airbus departing from London had engine problems, and the crew took prompt action to shut down the engine—the *wrong* engine, which is a critical mistake on a two-engine aircraft with one engine already gone. This critical mistake was repeated on an Army Blackhawk helicopter less than two years later, once again driving home the point that high-stress situations can overcome professional aviators if they are not aware of the hazards of impulsive actions.

Overcoming Impulsiveness

Airborne decisions seldom require immediate decisions or action. Analyze the situation, think before you act, and give your mind a chance to overcome the excitement and adrenaline of the moment. Many instructors give students a "wind the clock" step for reacting to an emergency situation, just to provide those valuable few moments to settle down and react rationally to a situation. In the front of several flight instructional manual's sections on emergency procedures are five words to repeat at the onset of any emergency: Stop—Think—*Collect your wits.* This is sound advice. Whatever technique you use, whether it's winding the clock or repeating a mantra designed to slow you down in a crisis situation, be aware of the pilot's tendency toward immediate action and prepare to counter it.

Complacency

Chuck Yeager, quite a rogue in his own right at many times during his 50-year aviation career, says that complacency is the single largest factor involved with experienced pilots who buy the farm. "When you let your guard down, when you think you know it all and start to get real comfortable—that's when an airplane bites *hard*." I have seen this occur more than once. In November 1994, a B-1B bomber crew flying a night training mission crashed into a ridgeline at nearly 600 miles per hour along a low-level training route they had flown dozens of times (Figure 9-1). Perhaps familiarity led them to ease up on their map reading, because the crew was in the most rugged portion of the route when they crashed, but their actions indicated that they might not have realized it.

Many rogue pilots are complacent because they have not bothered to learn enough to know what they are lacking as pilots. Airmanship is a complex phenomenon (see Chapter 11), and aviators who neglect certain aspects of it often sit comfortably while the situation deteriorates around them. When the situation is realized, rogue behaviors often result.

Complacency can set the stage for other hazardous attitudes. A few years ago a pilot of a Cessna 310 discovered two-thirds of the way to his destination that he had miscalculated the winds and the fuel requirements for his trip due to an abbreviated planning session. He had flown this route many times before. Weather deviations and a low-altitude jet

Figure 9-1.   Complacency may be a pilot's most deadly enemy. A U.S. Air Force B-1B bomber crew had flown this low-level route dozens of times, yet still lost situational awareness on a moonless night and slammed into this cliff at nearly 600 miles per hour. (*U.S. Air Force photo*)

stream resulted in his low fuel state, but rather than stop at an intermediate airport to refuel (which might embarrass him in front of his passengers), he elected to take an aircraft with a known pressurization leak to high altitude. He became hypoxic and disoriented, and eventually ran out of fuel and crashed, killing everyone on board the aircraft. The pilot was highly experienced and was known for his normally cautious approach to planning, but he had taken a shortcut on this flight due to overfamiliarity. When he realized his mistake, his pride got the better of him and drove him into a rogue act. The results were predictable.

Combating Complacency

John Olcott, the President of the National Business Aircraft Association, says that "maintaining vigilance in an atmosphere that nurtures complacency is an awesome challenge." The key to accomplishing this challenge is to keep your mind busy with flight-related activities, even during the most boring portions of a flight profile. Sharpen your estimation skills by trying to guess what the exact time or your fuel state will be when you hit the next waypoint. Play "what-if" emergency procedure games. *What if my engine quit right here? Where would I go? What checklists would I run? Who would I call on the radio? What resources do I have on board to assist me with a survival situation?* All of these questions are better asked *before* an emergency happens—and along the way they can help you overcome complacency.

A Final Perspective on Bad Attitudes

Hazardous attitudes can only hurt us if we allow them to manifest themselves in our behavior. By taking time to understand hazardous attitudes, and by looking for any hint of them in our flying activities, we can abolish them and avoid rogue behavior. But guarding against your own rogue acts is only part of the answer.

We must also look for hazardous attitudes in those we fly with. At a minimum, it will increase our vigilance. At the other end of the spectrum, it may save a friend's life and preempt an act that could kill others in the future.

Finally, watch for conditions that can set you up for a hazardous attitude—the need to get somewhere quickly, the unexpected request for a flyby, the flight with a senior or more experienced pilot who you feel can do no wrong. Simple awareness can be the most effective broad-spectrum antibiotic to cure the whole family of hazardous attitudes. Keep your eyes and ears open for cues, but most important, listen to your conscience.

There are times, however, when *external organizational pressures* are the forces that drive a pilot to rogue behavior. Our next chapter looks at rogues writ large, in the form of the "rogue organization."

CHAPTER TEN

The Rogue Organization

NAPOLEAN BONAPRTE once said, "There are no bad regiments, only bad colonels," implying that leadership is ultimately responsible for the actions of subordinates. In the case of Bob Hammond, our quintessential rogue of Chapter 2, this is at least partially true. In other cases, rogues seem to operate in spite of the best acts and intentions of their leaders, as in the case of the crop duster Blane. We began our discussion of rogues by agreeing with Forrest Gump that "Stupid is as stupid does," or that a rogue's *behavior*—even if it occurs only once—identifies him or her as a rogue at that moment in time. But what lies behind a rogue's intent? So far we have seen ego, competitiveness, and a bit of pathological social behavior at work. Now it is time to look at the flying organization itself as the driver behind rogue behaviors.

Three case studies illustrate three different aspects of the rogue organization. The first is a look at a driven corporate executive who creates an atmosphere that demands noncompliance. The second case study looks at a military organization that breeds a culture of noncompliance through complacency at multiple levels, leading to rogue behavior in otherwise professional aviators. Finally, we will look at the organization that cuts corners at every possible opportunity, coupled with a lax system of governmental oversight, leading not to rogue behavior by individual pilots, but to a rogue environment ripe for disaster due to systemic design.

A Company Out of Control

About 8:55 P.M., on May 30, 1979, Downeast Airlines Flight 46 crashed into a heavily wooded area about 1.2 miles southwest of the Knox County Regional Airport, Rockland, Maine. The crash occurred during a nonprecision instrument approach to runway 3 in instrument meteorological conditions (IMC). Of the 16 passengers and 2 crewmembers aboard, only 1 passenger survived the accident. The aircraft was destroyed.

The National Transportation Safety Board determined that the probable cause of the accident was the failure of the flight crew to arrest the aircraft's descent at the minimum descent altitude for the nonprecision approach, without the runway environment in sight, *for unknown reasons*. Although the NTSB was unable to conclusively determine the reasons for the flight crew's deviation from standard instrument approach procedures, it is believed that inordinate management pressures, the first officer's marginal instrument proficiency, the captain's inadequate supervision of the flight, inadequate crew training and procedures, and the captain's chronic fatigue were all factors in the accident. How could all of these factors be allowed to accumulate in one cockpit?

According to John Nance, the author of *Blind Trust* and an ABC News aviation correspondent, there was a whole lot more to the story. Downeast Airlines was a small commuter air carrier operating out of Rockland, Maine, a location notorious for its bad weather and sea fog. At first glance, it seemed as if it would be extremely difficult for a small company to make a go of it at this location, flying in an area where the weather was very often below takeoff and landing minimums for an FAR Part 135 carrier. But Downeast had beaten the odds and was making money, mainly because its owner was taking a single-minded approach toward profit margin. He routinely pressured pilots to break minimums, fly with overloaded airplanes, and accept mechanical defects in order to raise revenue. According to Nance, the owner "knew all about sea fog and approach minimums, and had scant respect for any pilot of his who would cancel or divert a passenger-carrying, money-making flight because the actual cloud ceiling and visibility were slightly below the legal minimums."[1]

There had been other accidents. On August 19, 1971, the Downeast owner had pressured a pilot into diverting to Augusta—an airport without a precision approach—instead of Portland, because of the financial concerns with busing the passengers all the way back up to Rockland. The captain complied, but after beginning to execute a missed approach at Augusta, he decided to try to implement one of the scud-running techniques that Downeast was becoming famous for. While attempting to establish himself in visual conditions for a return to the airfield, he descended out of the minimum safe altitude of 2000 feet and slammed into a fog-shrouded hill at 520 feet, killing himself and two passengers.

There were two other weather-related accidents over the next few years. In 1976, a pilot clipped a tree while flying well below minimums at Knox County Airport. The minimum altitude for the specific portion of the approach where the accident occurred was 440 feet. The tallest tree in the area was 90 feet. Draw your own conclusions. According to Nance in *Blind Trust*, this accident demonstrated how far Downeast was prepared to go to circumvent the FARs.

> **. . . the Navajo was immediately taxied into the Downeast hangar, the hangar doors locked, and repairs commenced in secret. Even the other pilots (with the company) were not allowed to view the damage the next day. The accident was never legally or formally reported until it was discovered by the NTSB years later.[2]**

The owner made it clear that pilots who could not or would not push through published minimums had no future in his company. He called the safety minded pilots who followed the rules cowards. This attitude went through every level of Downeast operations and created, in essence, a rogue organization. But how can one individual—even if he is the owner—create a rogue organization where everyone facilitates the other's actions?

There was more than supervisory pressure impacting the decisions of the pilots at Downeast, Nance explains:

> **There was a more insidious force that had perpetrated this attitude: peer pressure. When pilots who had no previous airline, commuter, or military flight experience found that they could meet most of the schedules despite the fog (which was notorious**

in the Maine area), by sneaking around the minimums and the rules, they began to develop a sort of perverse pride in their own abilities. A pilot who could fly an overweight airplane, take off in less than legal weather, ignore mechanical problems in order to bring the airplane back to Rockland with revenue passengers . . . was more often than not proud of himself. Any pilot who came on board and couldn't do as well was less of a pilot—less of a man.[3]

It is reported that there was even an informal set of "Downeast minimums," or approach altitudes that were considerably lower than the approach plates stated or allowed. Downeast pilots routinely flew these altitudes. There were stories from passengers who recalled seeing trees brush by only inches below their aircraft, or the night a loud "thump" was heard on the third attempt to get into Rockland. When the aircraft landed at Augusta, a large dent was found on the leading edge of the aircraft's right wing, but the pilot played it off as a "bird strike from a seagull" (the obvious fact that seagulls don't fly in pea-soup fog notwithstanding).

The straw that broke the camel's back for Downeast Airlines came when its chief pilot, Jim Merryman, pushed one limit too many on a foggy night in May 1979. Flying with a weak copilot and a known mechanical defect into weather that was suspected to be below minimums, Merryman crashed the Twin Otter short of the runway, killing all but one on board the aircraft. Even then, the investigation would not have uncovered the multiple organizational problems within the company, had it not been for one dedicated NTSB accident investigator, Dr. Alan Diehl, who stuck to the case for months and finally uncovered the multitude of issues that lay beneath the surface of the Downeast mishap. Diehl's tireless determination uncovered what became the first clearly identified rogue organization.

The sad saga of Downeast Airlines was clearly an extreme case, but it represents the power of a single individual over an organization. Thanks to an improved human factors training, renegade organizations like Downeast have mostly gone the way of the dinosaur. But the drive to "get the job done" still exists today, and many experienced pilots tell stories about subtle organizational pressures that they have encountered. This occurs in all parts of the world, as evidenced by our next study, which has cloak and dagger overtones from the Cold War.

The Rogues That Came in from the Cold War*

In 1986 a Soviet airliner crashed into the Republic of South Africa, killing the President of Mozambique. This was the first head of state to die in an air disaster. The Russian commercial airline crew was supposed to bring him back to the capital, but the giant Tupolev TU-134 flew into a hillside literally dozens of miles off course.

It was not long before I got the call, asking me to report to the State Department. State Department officials explained that they were asking me to go to Africa because of my reputation for unraveling the causes of complex crashes. They then painstakingly briefed me on this incident's potential geopolitical ramifications. Most significant, because the victim was also a famous political figure and former guerrilla leader, some third-world media sources were claiming that this was no accident. These people contended the crash was really an assassination by the South African government, our ally in the region. If true, this would allow terrorist groups to retaliate against other heads of state, including President Reagan.

Furthermore, a variety of officials, some whom were intelligence specialists from another agency, described how the increased Soviet military presence in southern Africa might destabilize this region. These other officials then described the White House's interest in embarrassing the "Evil Empire," as happened after the accidental shoot down of Korean Airlines flight 007 in 1983.

My mysterious briefers then mentioned that my mission might include some personal dangers: one of the air traffic controllers involved had simply "disappeared." Finally, I was told that officially I would be working undercover. This would certainly not be my usual kind of investigation, but as always my goal would be to uncover the truth, and hope the powers that be would do the right thing with this information.

Shortly after arriving, I was warmly received by a group of international aviation safety experts. Looking at the evidence and listening to the cockpit recordings convinced me that this was the worst case of crew error I had ever encountered. It appeared as if the crew was composed entirely of rogues, who willfully broke a myriad of written regu-

* This section was written by Dr. Alan Diehl.

lations and procedures. The five Russian crewmen had made an almost unbelievable series of navigational errors and flew a perfectly good aircraft into the ground, at night, in poor weather. As the flight neared its intended destination, the crew was more concerned about collecting the leftover Cokes and beers from the passenger compartment (apparently to sell for spending money) than in verifying their position or the air traffic controller's intentions. After getting an indication of a failed instrument landing system (ILS) receiver, the crew had difficulty communicating with an air traffic controller, whose English language skills were underdeveloped. This did not help the Russians, who also had difficulty with English, and who constantly switched from Russian to English as they descended off course toward the ground.

The navigator, who turned the aircraft with the autopilot after taking a bearing off a mistuned VOR made the killing error. But the distractions that were present in the cockpit almost defied belief, and pointed clearly to a crew that had become complacent and cared little about procedures or regulatory compliance. The cockpit voice recorder (CVR) indicated that the copilot was listening to a Russian language broadcast of music and news all the way up to impact. The captain was completely engrossed in a discussion about violating fuel reserves on previous flights (apparently an accepted practice with the company), as well as deciding on the allocation of the leftover beer and Coke from the passenger galley. Although all of these leadership and crew coordination errors pointed to a negligent crew, the final mistake drove home the depth of their rogue behavior.

Thirty-nine seconds prior to impact, the ground proximity warning system (GPWS) activated as the aircraft descended over rugged hilly terrain. The only response to this alert was the captain uttering "Damn it!" and continuing his descent. The TU-134A-3 flight manual is clear on the procedure to take when the GPWS goes off.

If the GPWS warning sounds with the aircraft in level or descending flight over hilly or mountainous terrain then the following actions are required by the crew: Pull the aircraft out to climb with a decisive moment of 1.25–1.7 acceleration and maintain the aeroplane in climb for 20–30 seconds with the engines operating at takeoff power.

The crew took none of these actions. Amazingly, in fact, the captain took the ultimate rogue act—*he pushed the nose over, increasing the rate of descent!* The accident board theorized that the captain might have been attempting a classic "duck-under" maneuver, as the crew had been flying over a broken cloud deck for the final 30 minutes of the flight. The accident report stated that "compliance with these instructions, even seconds before impact, would have prevented the aircraft from flying into the ground."

Obviously, the Soviet officials assigned to the inquiry must have seen similar problems before. In fact, the CVR captured discussions of how the company normally and routinely ignored its own safety regulations. But no one outside of their closed society had heard about this philosophy—until now.

It was also interesting to watch the Soviets try to manipulate the facts to minimize their embarrassment. For instance, when it was learned that the crew had landed the aircraft over the allowable weight limits, these officials just increased the maximum legal landing weight, post hoc. The culture of noncompliance here put anything I had witnessed in the United States in the minor leagues of negligence.

There was no evidence of sabotage or hostile action by others. But something was wrong, because the crew had changed the frequency of their navigational radio to an unlisted frequency. I reported this to our consulate in Pretoria. I was told that it was the standard frequency of the Soviet mobile radio beacon, undoubtedly located at or near a newly constructed airfield, whose location was secret.

I offered to try to establish the location of this beacon. Thus, for a few hours I would actually have to become a spy. That weekend I asked to visit Kruger National Park, and suggested that I preferred to ride in the airliner's cockpit, as I normally do back in the States. South African civil aviation agents made the arrangements. As we flew parallel to the Mozambican frontier I asked the crew if I could borrow one of their radio receivers, and quickly dialed into the Soviet mobile frequency. The needle swung to the location of the secret base.

As the investigation was concluding, the Soviets were very embarrassed by the media coverage of their senior airline crew's many mistakes. The Soviets then engaged in a typical face-saving pronouncement. They insisted that their crew was diverted into a South African hillside by a phony radio beacon operating on the same frequency as the one at their intended destination. This seemed ludicrous, because there was no evidence of any radio transmitter around the crash location, but it just might have convinced some third-world terrorist organizations to retaliate.

The endgame of all this cloak and dagger stuff was that, in my professional opinion, there was no politically motivated assassination plot or international intrigue associated with this unfortunate disaster. Rather, a group of crewmembers who were unable to follow company regulations or international approach procedures ran their aircraft into the ground more than 30 miles from its intended destination. The official cause of the accident was listed as follows by the International Civil Aeronautical Organization (ICAO):

> **The cause of the accident was that the flight crew failed to follow procedural requirements for an instrument let-down approach, but continued to descend under visual flight rules in darkness and in some cloud, i.e. without having visual contact with the ground, below minimum safe altitude and minimum assigned altitude, and in addition ignored the ground proximity warning signal alarm.[4]**

Rogue behavior, plain and simple.

OUR NEXT CASE study illustrates an organization that devolved into a rogue organization in a more insidious manner. The results were the same, however, and perhaps it is coincidence that a high-ranking political figure was on board this aircraft as well.

Unforced Errors: A Case Study of Failed Discipline

The case study of the factors leading up to the crash of IFO 21—a U.S. Air Force CT-43—are illustrative and full of examples of failures of discipline at both the organizational and individual levels. Although it is readily apparent that no one individual is responsible for the noncompliance with regulations, over time it became the status quo, resulting in a rogue organization.

Fifteen Seconds to Impact

Captain A. J. Douglas (a pseudonym) must have felt something was wrong. Perhaps it was a glimpse of rising terrain through a break in the cloud cover. Maybe it was just a sense that the crew *must* have overflown the missed approach point, which they were having great difficulty identifying, by now. Or perhaps it was a verbal prod from the copilot, Captain Tim Simmons (a pseudonym)—something like, "Hey pilot, something's not right here, let's go missed approach." Although we will never know what actually occurred in that final 15 seconds, we do know that for some reason, Captain Douglas added power and began a shallow turn to the right. While this intuitive correction was indeed appropriate, it was far too late.

At 2:47 P.M. local time on April 3, 1996, a U.S. Air Force CT-43A—a Boeing 737-200—call sign "IFO 21," slammed into the rocky slope of a mountain nearly two miles north of the intended airport at Dubrovnik, Croatia (Figure 10-1). All aboard were killed, including 6

Figure 10-1.   Crash site. A culture of noncompliance surrounded the pilots of IFO 21—a U.S. Air Force CT-43 (Boeing 737) that crashed into a mountainside near Dubrovnik, Croatia, killing U.S. Secretary of Commerce Ron Brown and 34 others. (*U.S. Air Force photo*)

Air Force crewmembers and 29 passengers—among whom was the U.S. secretary of commerce, the Honorable Ronald H. Brown.

The significance of this accident lies not in the fact that a high-ranking U.S. cabinet member was killed, or that a critical error was made at the moment of truth, although there are lessons for us there as well, but rather in the series of unforced errors—or poor flight discipline—which put the crew in position for the lethal mistake. Only the final error was of the split-second, time-constrained type we train for in our emergency procedure simulators. The remainder of the errors—the ones that built the labyrinth with only one exit—were made out of inattention, complacency, or convenience. In short, they were well-intentioned failures of discipline.

To aid in the analysis of these failures, we must view the event through several lenses, both organizational as well as individual.

Background to a Tragedy

The story of IFO 21 actually begins with a tale of two wars. Following the fall of the Berlin Wall and the end of the Cold War, dozens of airfields suddenly became open to western traffic. Since western aviation personnel had little or no access to these formerly hostile airdromes, there were no instrument approach procedures that had been officially approved by western aviation standards. This led to some confusion as to what requirements had to be met for U.S. aircraft to fly into these newly opened countries and airfields.

The flareup in the former Yugoslavia only made matters worse. As the war raged on, certain pieces of critical terrain changed hands several times. One of these was the Cilipi airport in Dubrovnik, Croatia. It has been common practice for a withdrawing military force to take a few goodies—the "spoils of war"—with it as it occupies or retreats from enemy territories. Such was the case with the precision approach capability at the Cilipi airport, the primary airdrome serving the coastal city of Dubrovnik, through which hundreds of would-be peacemakers and various negotiators entered the still relatively unstable region. During the period of conflict from 1992 to 1995, the instrument landing system (ILS), the very high frequency omnidirectional range (VOR), and a nondirectional beacon (NDB) were all stolen.

The end result of all of this was that the critical crossroads in this hot region was serviced by only one instrument approach procedure, a nondirectional beacon (NDB) approach—the least accurate of instrument approach systems currently in use at major airports. Furthermore, the approach that IFO 21 would be required to execute used *two* different NDBs to complete the approach and the missed approach procedure. An aircraft flying this approach requires *two* automatic direction finding (ADF) receivers to complete both the approach and the missed approach, since regulations prohibit cross-tuning a single receiver after the final approach fix. The CT-43A has only one.

While not exceedingly difficult, NDB approaches require constant attention and good approach planning to fly effectively, and they have a high potential and margin for both pilot and equipment error. Theoretically, adequate crew and staff planning should include a review of the equipment required to fly this approach, which should have quickly identified the CT-43 incompatibility. In this case, it did not. We will look into that failure of discipline more deeply in a moment.

Organizational Failures of Discipline: A Culture of Noncompliance

There were several opportunities at multiple levels of command and supervision to break the chain of events that led to this tragedy. It is appropriate and illuminating to start at the upper echelons of command and work our way down to the aircrew level in this analysis. We will see that a willingness to accept less than full regulatory compliance occurs at all levels, and that an organizational culture of noncompliance may well have set the stage for the crash of IFO 21.

Although the formal investigation of the mishap focused a great deal of attention on the fact that the crew flew an instrument approach that did not meet U.S. Department of Defense standards, there were other factors that may have been equally—if not more—significant. Accidents are seldom this simple, and this one is no exception. We will limit our analysis to two organizational failures at echelons above the airlift wing. The first was a training failure—the failure to implement an effective cockpit/crew resource management (CRM) program as required by a regulation that was nearly two years old at the time of the accident. This was surely a CRM mishap if ever there was one. The second breakdown was one of enforcement, the inability of the command and supervisory positions to enforce orders to aircrews to stop flying to unapproved airfields. It is clear from the investigation that the intent of all echelons above the airlift wing (AW) was for aircrews to stop flying to unapproved fields *immediately* upon notification, yet several months of noncompliance were allowed to occur before the cows came home on April 3.

The remaining organizational and individual breakdowns of discipline will be discussed relative to elements internal to the airlift wing, concluding with the crew of IFO 21. Throughout the process there were opportunities to fix the problems and break the accident chain. Critical organizational decisions were made at each of these junctures, and these decisions turned out to have life and death consequences.

Organizational Failure 1: Failing to Implement the CRM Training Mandate

Cockpit/crew resource management is the flight crew's insurance policy against multiple human failures within the hostile flight environment. It teaches aircrew members to identify, access, and utilize all available resources to safely and effectively complete mission objectives, and has been credited with documented and significant accident reduction wherever it has been thoroughly and systematically implemented. Although regulations requiring aircraft- and mission-specific CRM training for all Air Force crewmembers had been in force for nearly two years, there was no major command CRM program in place at the time of the crash of IFO 21.

This curious disregard for an existing training requirement is only the first verse in a sad song of an organization that appeared to be incapable of fully implementing and enforcing governing regulations and policy. Should it have been a great surprise that subordinate organizations took the same cavalier attitude toward regulatory guidance?

Organizational Failure 2: Failing to Enforce the Prohibition Against Flying Unapproved Instrument Approaches

Pilots do not question the reliability of printed instrument approaches—at least, not until recently. They rely implicitly on the accuracy of the depicted approach plate to provide the required margin of safety above obstacles and terrain. But as discussed earlier, the opening of new airports in previously hostile areas caused the military to question the reliability of these new published approaches and to require a comprehensive safety review. "Air Force Instruction 11-206, paragraph 8.4.1 requires any instrument approach procedure not published in a Department of Defense or National Oceanic Atmospheric Administration flight information publication be reviewed by the major command Terminal Instrument Procedures (TERPS) specialist before it can be flown by Air Force crews"—unless the weather is good enough for a visual approach. These distinctions are made to ensure that approaches developed by sources unfamiliar to the U.S. aircrews meet or surpass western safety requirements. To say that this new restriction would negatively impact on the mission of the 86th Airlift Wing—which provided VIP travel to the entire European region—would be a huge understatement.

Before we go any further into this discussion, the reader needs to know that if this process had been accomplished for the NDB Rwy 12 approach at Cilipi airport in Dubrovnik, Croatia, the TERPS specialist would have found an error of at least 400 feet on the minimum descent altitude (MDA) for the approach (Figure 10-2). If the directives had been followed, either the crew would not have flown the approach at all, or they would have flown it with correct altitudes that guaranteed adequate terrain clearance. In either case, they would be alive today.

The new approach guidance went into effect in November 1995, and a commander in the airlift wing immediately recognized its adverse effect on his units' ability to perform their mission. The CT-43 had historically flown into many airfields where the only published approach was a Jeppesen. "Jeppesen" refers to a company that merely publishes approaches supplied by host nations, and the company is exceedingly clear on this point. In fact, Jeppesen publishes a disclaimer specifically stating that its editors and publishers "*do not review or approve the adequacy, reliability, accuracy or safety of the approach procedures they publish,*" yet there seemed to be some confusion on this point by several organizational supervisors, as the following e-mail from a senior official clearly points out:

the implications ($$ & manpower) of this "new" guidance is significant . . . especially with all the . . . countries opening up!! What's

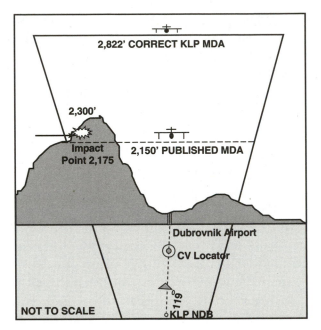

Figure 10-2. This diagram shows a 700-foot difference in minimum descent altitudes (MDAs) after the review that the 86th Airlift Wing couldn't wait for. It is easily seen that IFO 21 would have cleared the mountain if the new MDA had been calculated.

the matter with Jeppesens . . . we've used them for years . . . don't our airline bro's use them all the time?

Obviously, he did not understand—or choose to accept—the concept that Jeppesen was merely a reproducer of approach plates of sometimes dubious reliability. Somehow he equated the term "Jeppesen" with "safe" or "reliable"—a point the company itself goes to great lengths to avoid. Higher headquarters denied several requests for waivers from the airlift wing and made it perfectly clear that the Jeppesen approaches to unapproved airfields were off limits to U.S. aircrews. The airlift wing continued to fly them anyway.

To quote country singer Lorrie Morgan, "What part of *no* don't you understand?" What would prompt professional military officers—especially ones who had shown the mettle to climb through the ranks to command—to ignore clear directives from higher headquarters? In a word, the *mission*. Much like the owner of Downeast Airlines, these guys just wanted to get the job done, and the regulations were starting to get in the way.

However, in the final analysis none of these officers flew the aircraft into the ground, and no number of organizational failures can adequately explain the breakdowns of discipline at the aircrew and individual levels. Yet the multiple breakdowns of the organization surely had some impact on the individual aviators by establishing a climate of noncompliance, and perhaps this begins to explain the apparent disregard of directives which occurred at the aircrew level.

Aircrew Failures of Discipline

From the aircrew perspective, the portrait of the final flight of IFO 21 can be viewed as a collage of external pressures, insufficient crew rest, poor planning, mismanaged resources, violations of regulations, ignored or misapplied checklists and tech order procedures, distractions, lost situational awareness, and extremely poor judgment. For professional pilots, these guys had a real bad day. The accident investigation calls this collection of errors "uncharacteristic mistakes" which included "misplanning the flight . . . flying outside of a protected corridor . . . excessive speed and not having the aircraft configured by the final approach fix . . . beginning the approach without approval (clearance) and without a way to identify the missed approach point."[5] In documenting the crew failures, it is not enough to make a laundry list of errors, or to wag a condescending finger of blame at the dead pilots— who were certainly trying to do their best. We must look into the potential causes of these multiple failures.

External Pressures and Organizational Influences

The flight to Dubrovnik was clearly not a normal mission, but the crew had flown many similar to it. The accident investigation states "external pressures to successfully fly the mission were present, but testimony revealed a crew that would have been resistant to this pressure and would not have allowed it to push them beyond what they believed to be safe limits." What external pressures could have been responsible for such deviations from normal performance?

External Factor 1: High Operations Tempo and Culture of Noncompliance

The 76th Airlift Squadron, and in fact all of USAFE, had been operating at a fever pitch for months, if not years, prior to the mishap. The demands of the mission, coupled with the military drawdown that has impacted negatively on all branches of the service, simply left too few people to do too many things. Like all good soldiers, each echelon from the senior commanders to the lowest ranking of the enlisted forces leaned forward to get the job done. This operations tempo may well have been partially responsible for other accidents and mishaps as well. As we have seen, this combination of high ops tempo and mission-oriented commanders began to create an atmosphere of "can-do at all costs" and caused some to blatantly ignore regulatory guidance in the sacred name of *the mission.*

It is impossible to isolate aircrews from this command atmosphere. In fact, the squadron commander had recently been relieved from command by the airlift wing commander for "a loss of faith in his leadership abilities." The relieved commander felt that he was relieved because "of his concern about flying General Officers and on allowing . . . missions to fly into potentially hostile fire areas." At least one aircrew member was clear in his opinion that the firing of his squadron commander did have an impact on how he approached the mission. "It does force you to find . . . more ways to get a mission done. I don't know if that is good or bad, but it will get you to thinking of how to preclude those problems as quickly as you can." The views of the former squadron commander stressed safety over mission accomplishment, not a popular sentiment at the time.

The wing commander may have felt that such views were interfering too strongly with the ability to accomplish the wing mission. The human factors representative on the accident investigation stated:

> . . . there were indirect messages from the . . . wing that even though safety was properly acknowledged and advocated in the formal sense, mission accomplishment . . . was foremost. Examples include (1) that when there was a safety stand-down day in October 1995, the [squadrons] continued to fly scheduled missions, (2) the day following the mishap, the 76th did not stand

down because missions had to be flown, (3) testimony that there was a constant struggle [with the wing] to lessen the flying per day so that the crews could train or obtain rest for the crews; and (4) they could not have a safety down day because there were too many missions to fly.[6]

Although the accident investigation report stated that "the replacement of the squadron commander and its timing [four days prior to the mishap] were coincidental to this accident," it seems difficult to believe that squadron crewmembers would not perceive the firing of their boss for stressing safety over mission accomplishment as anything but a clear message to get the job done.

External Factor 2: VIP Passengers

Although this unit regularly carried distinguished and high-ranking passengers, the combination of a cabinet member and the flight into a recent combat zone carried certain pressures that were sure to affect the crew. On one previous documented occasion, the Commerce Department party had attempted to pressure a C-20 pilot to take a potentially unsafe course of action when scheduling difficulties were encountered. This may have added to the pressures on the flight crew.

External Factor 3: Multiple Mission Changes

A third external stressor that may have been more important was the many late mission changes to which the aircrew had to respond. Aviators are controllers by nature, and as such they abhor feelings of unpreparedness. It can be stated with some degree of certainty that the crew was agitated—more likely damned mad—about the last-minute changes to the high-profile mission. The accident investigation states "frequent changes to the mission itinerary contributed to the possibility of inadequate mission planning."

Although many, if not most, military missions experience changes prior to and even during the mission, this flight experienced four separate major changes to the original itinerary, the last of which occurred on April 2, the day after the crewmembers had "completed" their official mission planning at Ramstein AFB. This may well have created a situation where the crew had to make difficult planning choices related to adequacy, thoroughness, and even regulatory compliance. In fact, it is quite clear that these multiple changes forced the crew to do some mission planning well into the night prior to a 3:30 A.M. mission show-time on April 3.

Apparently, insufficient crew rest was almost commonplace in the airlift squadron. The accident investigation revealed multiple cases of crews that felt the need to violate crew rest minimums to get the mission accomplished. Although the former squadron commander had tried to discourage this practice, he stated, "Every now and then I hear a trip report come back in and the crew—the aircraft commander will write how they made it happen, four hours away from crew rest. I know some of the guys are still doing that."

In and of themselves, these external factors might not have resulted in the crash of IFO 21, but when coupled with a set of internal factors, the "accident chain"[7] was getting long and heavy.

Internal Factors

While many of the factors that effected the crew of IFO 21 were beyond their control, such as the organizational climate of noncompliance, the potential pressure of flying a cabinet member, and the multiple mission changes, there were also internal factors at play. The internal drive for success often found in high achievers like the aircraft commander can often manifest itself in negative ways. A hesitancy—or even inability—to say no to a task assignment from above is one such hazard. Another possible factor may have been the fact that the pilot was on a rapid career upswing after a less than spectacular start in the airlift squadron. He may have viewed this second chance as something he wasn't about to mess up by failing to accomplish this high-profile mission. As a result of all of these factors, the crew was set up for a common trap called "pressing," which often results in rogue behavior.

Pressing

If the aircraft commander of IFO 21 might have been flying with a partially impaired copilot due to fatigue, he might also have been competing with himself. He had recently seen a rapid upturn in the progress of his flying career, and may well have been trying to demonstrate that he deserved it.

It hadn't always been so. After Captain Douglas's arrival at Ramstein in 1994, the squadron commander had noted that he "did not display adequate procedural knowledge for upgrade to aircraft commander." In fact, the commander did not approve Douglas's upgrade during his entire eight months in command. However, about five months later, in October 1995, the young captain was finally upgraded to aircraft commander. Less than three months following this upgrade, he was granted a waiver and was upgraded to instructor pilot (IP). He completed his instructor checkout on February 15, 1996, and *less than one week later,* the operations group commander approved another waiver of requirements for his upgrade to flight examiner status—the military equivalent of a check airman. So while this aviator had labored in obscurity for nearly 13 months as a copilot, his fortunes had recently changed dramatically. In less than four months, he had been sequentially upgraded to aircraft commander, instructor pilot, and evaluator pilot. Although he may have been a late bloomer, Douglas was on his way now. As the lone evaluator pilot in his squadron, he knew he was viewed as the guy who could get things done. He had come a long way in a short time, perhaps too short.

"Pressing" is defined as an unwarranted—and occasionally obsessive—drive to accomplish flight objectives. It has also been called "get-home-itis," "get-there-itis," or "mission-itis" (see Chapter 9). By any name, it can lead to unsafe conditions associated with poor risk management. When a pilot presses, he or she places more emphasis on mission accomplishment, and less on regulatory compliance and safety. The implications are obvious. But would this scenario drive a normally good pilot into a region of bad judgment, one that could lead to the incredible series of "uncharacteristic mistakes?" Perhaps not on its own, but when coupled with a fatigued copilot, and a few unexpected distractions. . . .

Distraction

One of the greatest enemies of the aviator is *channelized attention,* or the inability to rapidly scan and process multiple inputs, commonly referred to by pilots as "crosscheck." There can be many reasons for channelized attention and lost situational awareness, but the most common is simple distraction—a phenomenon that the crew of IFO 21 was about to deal with in abundance. The accident investigation report explains the source of these distractions:

> **During the flight from Tuzla to Dubrovnik, the mishap crews misplanning of the route caused a fifteen minute delay in the planned arrival time (an unpardonable sin when transporting VIPs). Pressure may have begun to mount for the crew to make the scheduled arrival time, especially because responsibility for the delay now rested with the crew. As IFO 21 neared the final approach fix, there were two additional distractions: a delay in clearance to descend from 10,000 feet and external communication with a Croatian aircraft, 9A CRO.**

Testimony indicates that as IFO 21 approached the final approach fix, the pilot of 9A CRO asked them to switch frequencies and proceeded to explain an "unpublished circling procedure" that he had used to get the U.S. ambassador to Croatia and the prime minister of Croatia on the ground only an hour earlier. It appears that the aircraft commander was hand flying the aircraft (autopilot off) and simultaneously talking to the Croatian pilot. The copilot was talking on the tower frequency and, most likely, running the checklists. Neither was adequately preparing to fly an NDB approach to Cilipi airport.

Final Approach

The post-accident analysis of radar tapes and aircraft wreckage indicates that the following sequence of events took place as IFO 21 passed the final approach fix. The aircraft crossed the final approach fix without clearance and approximately 80 knots above the flight manual final approach airspeed of 133 knots. In addition to being hot, they began tracking approximately nine degrees left of the final approach ground track. The copilot was not backing up the aircraft commander with his navigation instrument settings, and neither pilot had any way of identifying the missed approach point.

At this point, still four minutes from mountain impact, the crew was clearly well behind the aircraft. In addition, the high airspeed was limiting the time available to fix the problems and salvage the approach. A well disciplined and normally functioning aircrew should have realized the danger and executed some version of a missed approach at this time—but the crew of IFO 21 pressed on. Perhaps based on the mission-at-all-costs focus of their parent organization, they felt they had no choice but to "make it work." The crew eventually slowed the aircraft to 150 knots, and descended to the MDA of 2150 feet. But these actions were being taken at the expense of accurate course guidance. The aircraft was still tracking 9 degrees left of course, the weather was poor, and Murphy was waiting patiently on a 2300-foot peak less than 4 miles away at their 12 o'clock position. Simply stated, the crew had broken down as a team entity, and the pilot's individual crosscheck was failing.

The missed approach procedure for Dubrovnik requires a right turn and a climb to 4000 feet, and is identified and executed at the "CV" NDB locator. Post-accident analysis found that the single ADF receiver on board IFO 21 was tuned to the KLP beacon—which was required for course guidance. In the absence of a second ADF receiver, the crew was unable to identify the missed approach point, and as a result overflew it without executing the required procedure. Although there are several *unauthorized* procedures that the crew might have been attempting to use to identify the missed approach point—including timing, inertial navigation system coordinates, cross-tuning the single ADF receiver, and visual identification—whatever procedure they used, if any, failed them. The final failure of discipline had occurred, and the crew impacted the rocky mountainside more than one nautical mile past the published missed approach point, killing all aboard.

An Analysis of Aircrew Actions

The crew of IFO 21 got behind the aircraft and never caught up. A combination of a late descent, poor planning, which added to the pressure of a late arrival, and a relatively difficult approach set the stage for a breakdown of the basic crosscheck and checklist discipline required to fly a safe instrument approach. All of this could have been solved with a single trip around the holding pattern.

The Deadly Chain of Failed Discipline

From the moment that higher headquarters decided they could not find the time to implement the mandated CRM training, they were in effect making a decision to operate outside of regulatory compliance and at a higher than necessary risk level. When the airlift wing decided not to comply with the directive to stop flying Jeppesen approaches that had not been reviewed by DOD instrument specialists, they, too, made a decision which put all of their aircrews in a region of increased risk. The failure of several levels of oversight to ensure compliance on both of these decisions demonstrates that adequate checks were not in place at multiple levels of supervision.

On an individual level, the aircraft commander of IFO 21 allowed his crew to be pushed into a very small corner by accepting mission changes that they did not have time to adequately plan. This resulted in a failure to identify the fact that the CT-43 did not have the required equipment (two ADF receivers) to fly an instrument approach into Dubrovnik. There may have been considerable external and internal pressures at play, but as always in aviation, the buck stops with the pilot in command.

The copilot failed as a team member by not pointing these items out to his aircraft commander, and by violating clearly established crew rest criteria. As a result, he was not as sharp as he needed to be at the moment of truth. He did not adequately back up the aircraft commander on the approach, failed to accomplish required checklists in a timely manner, and failed to advise the aircraft commander to go missed approach as the situation deteriorated and the crew lost situational awareness.

Good Intentions and Rogues

All of these decisions were made with good intentions. At the headquarters level, CRM training was just not a high priority. Staffing was down, operations tempo was up, and there were just too few resources to go around. At the wing level, the mission came first. Each task was important, and the new restrictions got in the way of priority one—getting the job done. The pilots of IFO 21 were clearly aware of the heavy emphasis on the mission, especially in the wake of their squadron commander being relieved of command. They knew the importance of the commerce secretary's mission, and were just trying their best to be "can-do" team players. But good intentions are not sufficient rationale for poor discipline.

The next case study looks at a slightly different situation, one in which noncompliance is built into a system that is not unwilling, but rather is incapable of oversight. One might call it rogue behavior by design.

Systemic Rogues: ValuJet, the NTSB, the FAA, and the Crash of Flight 592

In May 1996, a DC-9 operated as ValuJet Flight 592 left the Miami airport en route to Atlanta with 105 passengers, 2 flightcrew members, and 3 cabin attendants on board. This was a good revenue flight, as most flights were for ValuJet. As the poster child for economy-rate airlines, its business was booming, its overhead was low, its stock was high, and passengers were filling the seats on most routes. But what was the risk of operating a cut-rate airline? At that time, no one was really certain. We still may not be.

Unknown to the pilots, several oxygen generating canisters had been loaded aboard the aircraft in the forward baggage compartment. In addition, the cannisters had been packaged inappropriately, without the yellow caps that would prevent ignition. Worse yet, they had been mislabeled as nonhazardous cargo. These canisters were wrapped in plastic bubble wrap—the perfect fuel for easy combustion and a pure-oxygen fire—and had been placed on top of some tires. As the aircraft lumbered down the runway for takeoff, it is likely that one or more of the canisters fell off the tires, ignited, and started a fire in the forward compartment. The aircraft lifted off at 2:04 P.M. Six minutes later all hell broke loose in the cockpit.

At 2:10:07 P.M. the pilot asked suddenly, "What was that?" Eight seconds later, the first officer replied, "We got some electrical problem ... we're losing everything." Ten seconds later came the words every pilot fears more than any others—"We're on fire."

In less than one minute after initial discovery of the problem, the crew requested immediate vectors back to Miami. At 2:11:12 P.M. the first officer stated that they were "completely on fire." For the next 90 seconds the pilots fought valiantly to regain control of the stricken DC-9, but to no avail. At 2:14 P.M. the aircraft crashed into the Florida Everglades, killing all on board.

Clearly, there was nothing the pilots could have done to save this aircraft. The heat and toxic fumes produced by the oxygen-fed fire led to an uncontrollable aircraft and the deaths of the passengers and crew. Following the crash, ValuJet was square in the crosshairs of the industry, which was looking for an opportunity to dump on the upstart company that many referred to as "Wal-Mart Airlines."

Rigid Cost Cutting

William Langewiesche, a writer for the *Atlantic Monthly*, paints a picture of the cost-cutting measures taken by ValuJet as part of its business equation:

> **ValuJet pilots were non-unionized . . . the company required them to pay for their own training . . . [the captain] earned what the free market said she was worth—about $43,000 per year. . . . Pilots were not the only low-paid employees at ValuJet—flight attendants, ramp agents, and mechanics made a lot less than they would have a more traditional airline.[8]**

There were other cost-cutting measures as well. The company parceled out every possible tasking to subcontractors, to the point that many experts in the industry referred to ValuJet as a "virtual airline" with few employees of its own. One of these subcontractors was Sabretech, a contract maintenance company whose employees inadvertently made the critical packaging and mislabeling errors.

Gene Nelson, Ph.D., is an expert on the interface between science and public policy who has written extensively on the ValuJet disaster. He sums up the problem of putting profit margin ahead of safety by quoting Michael Crichton's novel *Airframe*. The following quote comes from a fictional industry expert to reporter Jack Rogers:

> **. . . by the time the bodies start piling up, as you know they will, you've made your fortune off the stock, and can afford the best**

counsel. That's the genius of deregulation, Jack. When the bill comes, nobody pays. Except the passengers.[9]

Before we move on to the oversight role of the government agencies, it is important to understand that some economy airlines, such as People's Express and Southwest Airlines, had historically excellent safety records, a point missed by many amidst the frenzy of ValuJet bashing. So economy does not necessarily or automatically equal reduced safety. However, ValuJet had a poor safety record even before the crash of Flight 592, which may have been indicative that they had gone too far in their cost cutting, or perhaps it was other organizational issues unrelated to profit margin. Once again, Nelson addresses the complexity of the oversight issue, and points to both corporate and governmental responsibility for safe operations:

In early 1992 to mid 1993, Timothy Flynn, Maurice Gallagher, Robert Priddy, and Lewis Jordan each invest $1 million to get ValuJet off the ground. Lewis Jordan said "We were interested in being the Wal-Mart of the airline business." Quoting further from the Miami Herald, May 4, 1997. . . . The problem: Wal-Mart does not conduct business at 35,000 feet above the ground. . . . These people were supposed to be safeguarded by an aggressive, interlocking net of governmental and corporate checks and balances. It was an illusion. The net had holes large enough for a jetliner to fall through.[10]

So where were these holes in the governmental safety net?

A Rogue System

Following the crash of ValuJet Flight 592, many voices from inside and outside the industry began to analyze not only the failures of corporate oversight, but also the failures of government. One of the most outspoken critics was Rodney Stich, a former FAA inspector and the author of *Unfriendly Skies*, an expose of dirty politics in air safety. According to Stich, the primary reason that the ValuJet plane crashed was because FAA officials in the western region had eliminated the need for fire detectors and fire extinguishers in certain types of cargo compartments.

He provides the listing of factors for consideration in an online open letter he calls "Those Actually at Fault for the ValuJet Crash." The following are quotes from his letter.

- **Hazardous cargo will always be accidentally put into aircraft cargo compartments, as well as approved hazardous cargo accidentally placed there, occasionally improperly packed.**
- **On a worldwide basis fires are routinely occurring in such compartments (many of which are controlled or extinguished by the very detection and extinguishing system unmandated by the FAA.)**
- **Those who were involved in aircraft being delivered without fire detectors and extinguishers knew about these consequences.**
- **As I [Stich] have frequently seen as an FAA air carrier operations inspector, FAA management, involved in the "revolving door syndrome," seek to ingratiate themselves with industry as they seek a high-paying job with a major carrier. [Stich is apparently strongly hinting that FAA inspectors will side with cost saving measures from an airline in order to curry favor for future employment.]**
- **Others at fault included the aircraft manufacturers who knew the dangers and who presented the aircraft without safeguards of the fire detectors/extinguishers for the cargo compartments, as well as the initial buyers of the aircraft who also knew these dangers.**
- **The NTSB, who knew of the dangers and did nothing.**
- **The Airline Pilot Association, who knew of the dangers and said nothing.**[11]

The picture painted is an ugly one. Stich maintains that while ValuJet and Sabretech were responsible for accidentally making an error which resulted in hazardous cargo being placed in the cargo compartment of Flight 592, far more responsibility for the disaster should go to those responsible for the absence of safeguards, specifically the fire detectors and extinguishers for the cargo compartments. He further maintains that the reason the safeguards were not in place was due to an unholy relationship between the FAA, the NTSB, and the air carriers. For a 40-year detailed and documented history of the nasty politics of air safety, read the third edition of *Unfriendly Skies.*[12]

Death by Design?

Are there systems that actually precipitate rogue behaviors? In this case, apparently so. But it takes an insider to see the flaws, and they are often ostracized long before they can make their cases known, often in the name of profit.

There have been recent challenges from insiders to the military safety system as well. Dr. Alan Diehl, a lifetime accident investigator with both the NTSB and the U.S. Air Force Safety Center, maintains that the military system is seriously flawed and is incapable of investigating itself. After making these challenges he was removed from his position in the Safety Center, but he continues his battle to correct the allegedly flawed system.

Anywhere money, power, and prestige are involved, truthful and thorough inspection will be extremely difficult. In the absence of these things, the public is endangered by the potential for rogue behaviors on the ground and in the air.

A Final Perspective on Rogue Organizations: The Tough Questions

If Downeast Airlines had not suffered those mishaps, if Secretary Brown had been delivered in one piece, if ValuJet Flight 592 had not crashed and set off the media frenzy that followed—would we still view these events as cases of rogue organizations, or as positive demonstrations of a "can-do" attitude? Would all have been forgiven and forgotten if they had hacked the mission? Simply put, does the *result* of a decision—or string of decisions—determine the legitimacy of the process used to get there? Have we reached the point in our aviation decision making where the end truly justifies any means of achievement? Has the unwritten motto in aviation become "*Don't get caught*"? It has in rogue organizations.

We have walked a long trail to get to this point. We have seen what constitutes rogue behavior and have seen that it is not unique to any location, to any type of flying, or even to flying in general. We now know that both internal and external factors can take a normally good pilot into regions of bad judgment, often with lethal consequences. It is time to ask the question, "What can be done?" Our final chapter addresses this challenge.

CHAPTER ELEVEN

What to Do About the Rogue

IN A VERY UNSCIENTIFIC opinion poll conducted by *CNN Interactive*, an online news website, the question was posed, "Do you worry about flight safety?" Of the 1110 respondents, nearly 40 percent responded that they *often* worry about their safety in commercial air travel. Another 43 percent said they *sometimes* worry. Only 18 percent said they felt comfortable and never worried about air safety when they traveled. I found this somewhat surprising, since aviation is still statistically safer than most all other forms of transportation. Perhaps a part of this fear is rooted in the fact that rogues still remain among us, and when they strike, the media is quick to publicize their failings as individuals—and our collective failure to remove them from our midst. Perhaps a story about an even less scientific survey sheds more light on the rogue phenomenon.

Methuselah

The story goes that a particular aviation researcher was desperately searching for a reliable source of data to determine the greatest threat to aviation safety. In the course of his wanderings, he found himself in a small smoke-filled pub called the Hangar, located just outside of a well-used airstrip. As his eyes adjusted to the hazy darkness, the researcher saw what he was looking for. Leaned against the bar, in a leather bomber jacket with more patches sewn to it than Rags the clown, was the epitome of the pilot sage. His rugged complexion was tanned and wrinkled from thousands of hours under the ultraviolet rays of high altitude. Various navigational charts stuck out of his threadbare flight suit, a cigar hung from his lips, and his throttle hand was wrapped around a longneck Sam Adams. The call sign on his name tag read "Methuselah." Yes, surely this was the source of *the answer.*

As our intrepid researcher engaged the old pilot in conversation, he found that he had found the right man to ask. Methuselah had over 25,000 hours of flying time. He flew professionally for a major international carrier, owned a Pitts Special for fun on the weekends when he wasn't flying fighters for the local Air National Guard, and was a member of the Civil Air Patrol. "*Perfect,*" thought the researcher, "I have general aviation, sport, commercial, and military flying experience all rolled up in one man. Surely he can answer my question. If anyone knows the greatest danger to aviation, it must be the man here on the barstool next to me."

After carefully establishing rapport with the sage by buying him another half-dozen Sams, the researcher got up enough nerve to ask the question he had been planning for almost a decade. Through years of painstaking research, he had isolated three possible problems relating to aircraft accidents, which he had so insightfully identified in his doctoral thesis at the university back east. Now he had found just the right man to ask the postdoctoral question. He could finally identify the greatest threat to air safety.

The researcher didn't want to mess this up, so he slipped his hand in his flight jacket and clicked on the small tape recorder he always carried with him for just this moment. "Sir," he asked clearly, "I need to ask you just one question. What do you see as the greatest threat to aviation safety, *ignorance*, *apathy*, or *isolation?*"

Methuselah thought reflectively for a moment, blew out a cloud of blue smoke, drained the last half of his beer, and turned and fixed the researcher with eyes the color of polished steel. The researcher held his breath. He would finally have his answer. The pilot spoke. "I don't know. I don't care. Leave me alone."

Slaying the Three Dragons

The point to the story, obviously, is that all three factors—ignorance, apathy, and isolation—inhibit professionalism and facilitate rogue behavior. There is also a fourth factor—*contempt*—which we will deal with separately. These factors can be viewed on three levels. As a military historian, I often look at things in military terms, and it works well in this instance. Ignorance can be looked at as a *strategic*-level challenge, meaning that there is a big need for a universally shared understanding of what it means—and what it does *not* mean—to be an expert pilot. Apathy must be handled at a lower level, within organizations such as companies, clubs, military structures, and so on. This would be considered the *operational*—or middle—level in warfare. The challenge of isolation—the failure of the message to get to *all* aviators—must be undertaken at the lowest of all levels. *Tactical* warfare must be waged by each of us individual pilots to reach outward to others, and inward to ourselves, to drive rogue behaviors out of our midst. Let's begin at the top, with the strategic challenge of defining common standards of aviation excellence—the first step toward reducing rogue behavior.

Strategic War: Redefining Airmanship

There is a saying that "Idle hands are the devil's tools." I believe the same applies to our minds. Three of the greatest strategic thinkers of our time have reached the same fundamental conclusion. Tom Peters, the author of the culture-changing best-seller *In Search of Excellence*, points to the need for every organization to define a shared set of standards to pursue. Edward Demming, the father of *Total Quality Management*, says it is not enough just to define and pursue standards, but rather we must have a process of continuous improvement to reach the highest levels of performance. Peter Senge, the Director of the Center for Organizational Learning at MIT and the author of the best seller *The Fifth Discipline*, points out the need for a holistic view of complex phenomena. Airmanship certainly fits in this category. The search for a strategy to pursue excellence in airmanship stood on the shoulders of all three of these giants.

Several years ago I was given the task of attempting to define universal standards of excellence in aviation, to provide a common direction for training and education. I was amazed to find out that there were nearly as many definitions of "airmanship" as there were pilots. The research journals were of little help. Everything seemed too specialized for a layman aviator to use for personal improvement. General John Shaud, former commander of the USAF Air Training Command, put the dilemma in perspective in the foreword of my earlier book *Redefining Airmanship:*

> **Outstanding airmanship has been called by many names over the years, from "Sierra Hotel" to the "Right Stuff." However, the complexity of modern flight operations has added new dimensions to airmanship, and a shared meaning of airmanship may have been lost. Perhaps we are all a little at fault. In our zeal to improve operations and safety, we have studied the flight crew, aircraft, and mission from literally hundreds of angles. In the process, we have dissected flying operations almost beyond recognition. While the tacticians, social scientists, and engineers have added greatly to the sum of our knowledge on a variety of important and relevant subjects, the flyer's ability to merge all of this knowledge into a complete picture of airmanship has greatly suffered. Meanwhile, high technology has increased the air machine's capabilities by an order of magnitude. This may have created apathy in our young flyers, who gradually became more of an interested passenger than a committed pilot, and because of technology, they get away with it—most of the time. This is inappropriate for our high-risk operation.**
>
> **While we should continue to debate such things as tactics and techniques, the fundamental essence of *who we are*, and *what we stand for*, should be universally understood. Airmanship is far too important for relativistic interpretation. There is a very real need in aviation to put it all back together.[1]**

Five years of historical research into what is present when good things happen in aviation led me to some inescapable conclusions as to what makes an expert pilot.

The Airmanship Model

To discover the essence of airmanship, one must begin by asking the questions "What is airmanship?" and "How do we develop it?" The answer to these questions can be found by looking back at the history of manned flight in and out of combat, as well as forward to the likely demands of future technologies and conflicts. Interestingly, both lenses produce similar views of airmanship. Historically, great aviators tend to possess certain common qualities and characteristics, and a glimpse into the crystal ball of future technology or potential enemies suggests little change. The changes that *have* occurred over time appear to be changes of degree only, and not fundamental shifts in the nature of what constitutes superior airmanship. This analysis reveals three fundamental principles of expert airmanship, regardless of the time frame analyzed: *skill*, *proficiency*, and the *discipline* to apply them in a safe and efficient manner. Beyond these basic principles, five areas of knowledge were identified as common among expert airmen. Expert airmen have a thorough understanding of (1) their aircraft, (2) their team, (3) their environment, (4) the risks, and (5) themselves. When all of these elements are in place, the superior aviator exercises consistently good judgment and maintains a high state of situational awareness.

An expert aviator combines many factors into a comprehensive whole, and further understands that all of these factors are *dynamic*—requiring constant and calculated attention. A flyer with the right stuff understands the capabilities and limitations of himself or herself, the team, the aircraft, the physical, regulatory, and organizational environment, and the multiple risks associated with the flight. An expert flyer builds upon a bedrock of flight discipline, skills, and proficiency. No single-focus flyer approaches excellence. An expert in regulatory knowledge who can't fly the aircraft effectively due to lack of proficiency is an incomplete aviator. Conversely, a golden-hands pilot who doesn't understand the rules can do tremendous damage with a single error.

But the combination of knowledge and technical expertise is still not enough. Even if an aviator understands the risks associated with the flight environment and can outfly everybody in the squadron, that aviator is ineffective if he or she cannot integrate with the crew, or the joint team of air traffic controllers and other aircraft. This requires a special set of skills that have come to be known as *human factors*. Total airmanship blends technical and tactical expertise, proficiency, and a variety of human factors to smoothly and effectively integrate the capabilities of the human and the machine. Total airmanship leads to improved situational awareness, fewer mistakes, increased operational effectiveness, improved training, and safer flying operations. By eliminating gaps in airmanship, a flyer is better able to handle the rapidly changing and

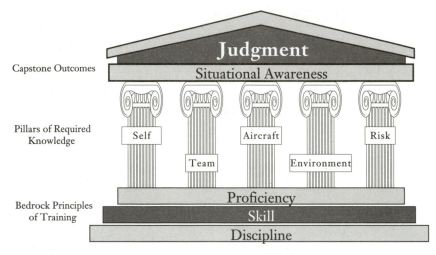

Capstone Outcomes

Pillars of Required Knowledge

Bedrock Principles of Training

Airmanship: The consistent use of good judgment and well developed skills to accomplish mission objectives. This consistency is founded on a cornerstone of uncompromising flight discipline and developed through systematic skill acquisition and proficiency. A high state of situational awareness completes the airmanship picture and is obtained through knowledge of one's self, team, aircraft, environment, and enemy.

Figure 11-1. The Kern Airmanship model leaves no room for rogue behavior, and provides pilots and other aviators with a picture of expertise for self-assessment and personal improvement.

dynamic environment of flight. True airmanship does not allow for rogue behavior (Figure 11-1).

The identification and communication of a shared ideal of what it means to be an expert pilot is the first big step towards eliminating rogue behavior. No longer will the rogue be able to sit behind a fuzzy interpretation of what constitutes a good pilot. With a shared set of standards, we will have made a major leap in conquering the strategic challenge of ignorance. The following synopsis of the historical model of good airmanship leaves no room for the rogue pilot or rogue behavior.

Ten Principles of Airmanship[2]

Airmen need more than regulatory guidance, procedures, and word of mouth techniques to define—and become—an expert. We need the same type of guiding principles that other fields enjoy to measure our progress on the road to airmanship excellence. The following principles are proposed as signposts and standards of airmanship development. Each principle of airmanship is followed by a standard by which to judge development. These standards are not quantifiable in the traditional sense (i.e., ±10 knots), but rather are qualitative measuring sticks for use in determining personal levels of airmanship. It is hoped that flyers who now understand the nature of good airmanship can conquer rogue behaviors and will use these principles as tools to take the next step—personal action. In any case, knowledge of what it means to be a superior airman will unmask the rogue in others and in ourselves. This in and of itself makes the study of airmanship worthwhile.

Principle 1: Airmanship Must Be Viewed as a Whole

All aspects of airmanship play upon each other. Failure to understand the interrelated nature of each part weakens the entire structure. Historically, aviators have tended to identify with single-trait flyers who perform great feats—the miracle recovery, the lowest pass, the tightest traffic pattern, the smoothest landings. Some see the systems expert or the tactics aficionado as their role model. Both of these approaches are flawed, unless they are accompanied by a holistic view of what complete airmanship means: discipline, skill, proficiency, and knowledge of self, aircraft, team, environment, and risk. Airmanship means situational awareness and good judgment based upon these attributes. Missing pieces of the airmanship structure signify either a lack of understanding or an apathetic attitude toward airmanship. It always signifies the potential for rogue behavior and disaster.

The Standard: Multidisciplinary Competence

Airmanship encompasses physical, mental, and emotional skills, or as the educational psychologists like to say, the psychomotor, cognitive, and affective domains. Airmanship means riding all three of these horses simultaneously and consistently well. Obviously this is not an easy task, and some will balk at the attempt to achieve such competence. But a golden-hands pilot who can't control his or her emotions in flight is not exhibiting good airmanship. Nor is the calm and cool systems expert who can't land in a crosswind. True airmanship requires physical, mental, and emotional competence.

Principle 2: Airmanship Demands Consistency

Expertise demands consistency. The demands of flying operations are constantly changing, like the lights on a stereo equalizer that move up and down depending on the nature of the music. One part of a flight may require concentrated risk analysis, as you are faced with a hazardous weather front, while the next mission segment may require close teamwork or a decision based upon personal capabilities and limitations. Because we seldom know where or when the next airborne challenge will arise, we must be consistently prepared in all areas. Our actions should be congruent with our personal assessment of our aircraft, our team, and ourselves. This is not to say that we can't have a bad day. Even the best professionals on the Pro Bass Tour don't catch fish every day on the lake. But an expert rides out the rough days with an expectation of success the next time out. This confidence is built upon real skill and knowledge, and leads to consistency of action and well-deserved success.

The Standard: Predictability

"Surprise" is a bad word in aviation. Unfortunately, it can't always be avoided when it comes from an outside source, but we should never surprise ourselves. Consistency means avoiding surprises by approaching each situation with a confidence born of preparation. Given a common set of circumstances, your approach to the situation should be nearly the same each time. You should not be surprised when you succeed at something you are prepared for. Likewise, when you operate near the margins of your performance capabilities, you should not be surprised with less than perfect results. If you surprise yourself on a regular basis, you likely are lacking consistency or are unable to make accurate self-assessments. Rogues are full of surprises.

Principle 3: Airmanship Requires Balance

No single-focus flyer can approach airmanship excellence. A natural consequence of taking a holistic viewpoint towards airmanship is to ensure that your airmanship structure is in balance. This means making a conscious effort to advance airmanship along two fronts—maintenance and development. We all have strengths and weaknesses, and our natural tendency is to let our attention gravitate to our areas of strength. We like to be good at things, so we do the things we are good at. However, this is only appropriate after we have achieved competence in *all* areas of airmanship, which means addressing our weak areas first, no matter how uncomfortable it makes us. While we are shaping our weaknesses into strengths, we must not completely neglect our strengths. This maintenance function is often a tricky proposition, because only you know when your proficiency is beginning to deteriorate. Try to give your strong areas enough attention so that they are maintained as strengths.

The Standard: No Weak Areas

The ability to shift our education and training focus to areas of need while simultaneously maintaining areas of strength and specialization is one of the clear indicators of a mature aviator. The standard is competence across the board. Rogues will always have at least one weak area, but it will likely be well hidden.

Principle 4: Specialization Occurs Only After Balance Is Achieved

All of us are eager to be the best at something—a recognized expert. Some of us are drawn to tactics, others to instrument procedures, aerodynamics, flight characteristics, or systems knowledge. But whatever your area of interest, specialization first requires balanced competence and readiness. A firm grasp of all areas of airmanship imparts credibility and relevance to the area of specialization. Remember, nothing in airmanship exists in isolation, so a solid grounding in all areas is required to fully appreciate and develop any selected area of specialization.

The Standard: Broad-Based Competence

Much like the principle of balance, specialization demands readiness, and readiness means that your airmanship is fully up to speed. Seek first to be a competent airman—then to be a specialist. Many rogues are one-trick ponies.

Principle 5: Airmanship Is Uncompromising Flight Discipline

This principle needs little explanation. There is no room in good airmanship for intentional deviations from accepted regulations, procedures, or common sense. Violations of flight discipline create a slippery downhill path toward habitual noncompliance. Once you take that first step in this direction with a willing and intentional deviation, you are far more likely to do it again. Good airmanship is not compatible with flight discipline violations of any kind or of any magnitude.

The Standard: Zero Violations—Zero Tolerance

It is not enough to practice good flight discipline, you must also make it clear that you do not tolerate poor flight discipline in others with whom you fly. This may initially be difficult, as many feel uncomfortable confronting others and value loyalty to friends above safety. Real loyalty speaks out against unsafe practices and makes it clear that poor flight discipline by anyone is unacceptable. Aviators share a moral obligation to each other to maintain safe operating conditions. Keep in mind that we all share the same sky, and innocent people live below.

Principle 6: There Is No Substitute for Flying Skill

Good aviators fly well. They also understand that flying skills are perishable, and that constant vigilance must be maintained if they are to be preserved. Unless we are in a formal training setting, this vigilance will take the form of mature self-assessment. An aviator must have or develop the kind of maturity that allows weaknesses to be recognized—and then we must have the discipline to work on these areas, even though we would much rather be practicing on areas of personal proficiency which we feel much better about. Airmanship goes beyond merely stick-and-rudder skills. It means honing and refining procedures and techniques to such a personal level of excellence that a missed checklist step or botched radio communication just doesn't happen anymore. Error-free flying—as well as "good hands"—is the mark of an aviator.

The Standard: Stick-and-Rudder Proficiency in All Areas of Flight and Procedural Perfection

Note the three parts of this standard. First, accurate and mature self-assessment must become part of your post-flight routine. Only you know whether that crosswind caught you by surprise, or if your stomach tightened up in knots when the controller changed the runway on you. No instructor can ever be as effective at pinpointing your weak areas as you are. Use this gift. Second, seek to achieve procedural perfection. This is one area where there are really no shades of gray. There are a finite number of checklist items and associated procedures. Learn them all and practice until you don't make omissions. This requires personal discipline and habituation, but it is well worth the effort. Finally, continuously hone your flying skills. Start with your weak areas, and when you get them up to speed, improve your strengths. Rogues will seldom admit a weakness.

Principle 7: Airmanship Requires Multiple Knowledge Bases

Throughout history, superior aviators have drawn from deep pools of knowledge in several areas. We cannot hope to reach our potential without following the path they have established. Begin with the five pillars of knowledge identified by researchers as essential to good airmanship, and then add what you feel are relevant to your personal flying. Expert flyers possess knowledge of themselves, their aircraft, their team, the physical, regulatory, and organizational environments, and the risk. Work these areas systematically until you reach a comfortable level in each, and then establish a procedure for periodic review.

The Standard: Instant Recall of Critical Items, and Sufficient Knowledge of Self, Aircraft, Team, Environment, and Risk to Maximize Performance

There is an old joke that asks, "What are the three things considered most useless to a pilot?" The standard answer is "Runway left behind, altitude left above, and . . . (fill in the blank)." My blank filler would be "inert knowledge," that useless book learning that can be recalled at ground speed zero for test purposes but is not known well enough to be recalled when your life is on the line. Throughout this book we have seen examples of aviators who were unable to recall important information when it was needed, who often paid the ultimate price for their lack of preparation. The only solution to inert knowledge is deeper study and drill, so that critical knowledge recall becomes a subconscious event and knowledge leaps to the surface effortlessly when needed. The second half of this standard is knowing where to find other information if required—not only for use in flight, but to develop your knowledge across the breadth of airmanship. Topics like cockpit/crew resource management (CRM), situational awareness, weather, and others should all be readily available to deepen your understanding in these important areas. Rogues are seldom interested in this type of broad-based improvement effort.

Principle 8: Airmanship Is Maximizing Situational Awareness (SA)

No one maintains perfect situational awareness (SA) at all times, yet a consistently high state of SA is another mark of a superior aviator. Situational awareness is directly correlated to an aviator's attention, or lack thereof. Each of us have only a certain amount of attention to spread around all of our flight tasks, so development and expertise in the lower parts of the airmanship model free up more attention for SA. For example, a disciplined, proficient, and knowledgeable pilot does not have to give much conscious thought to the procedures and skills required to fly an instrument approach; his or her preparation makes it almost second nature. If a sudden distraction occurs, like a runway change or some unexpected weather, this pilot is usually quite capable of recognizing and reacting to the change in a safe manner. In contrast, a pilot who is less prepared, and is struggling just to fly the approach, is far less likely to handle the distraction and simultaneously complete a safe approach. The point is that each has an attention saturation point, beyond which we lose SA. Airmanship is preparing ourselves through discipline, skill, and knowledge to have the maximum amount of attention left over to handle the unexpected distraction. But since any of us can become overloaded, we must also be able to recognize the symptoms of lost SA, and we must have the critical actions for recovery "hardwired" to prevent disaster.

Three Standards of SA

The three standards of SA are as follows:

1. Understand components of preparation for maintaining SA.
2. Recognize lost SA in yourself and others when it occurs.
3. Know immediate action steps for recovery from lost SA.

Maintaining SA requires a solid underpinning of airmanship, with all that that necessitates. Recognition techniques are important to develop the ability to recognize lost SA in others, as well as in yourself. Perhaps the most important aspect of understanding situational awareness—and the one that should be committed to memory first—is the list of steps to take to safely return home in the event of an episode of lost SA:

1. Get away from danger.
2. Stabilize conditions.
3. Give your mind a chance to get caught up.
4. Once on the ground, analyze the situation that led to the loss of SA, so that it doesn't happen again.

Principle 9: Solid Airmanship Leads to Good Judgment

Judgment has taken on an almost mystical quality among aviators, yet it is really quite simple. Once all of the prerequisites are in place, good judgment becomes a natural and automatic consequence of airmanship preparation. You show me an example of poor judgment, and I'll show you poor preparation. In nearly every case of poor judgment, you will find a problem with discipline, skill, or knowledge that existed prior to the episode of poor judgment. There is an old adage in aviation that "You can't teach judgment." Like many dangerous misconceptions, this is partially true. Judgment cannot be taught as an independent objective, but it can certainly be accomplished by learning the fundamentals of airmanship. This is achievable and relatively uncomplicated. Yet the myths that judgment is either something you have or you don't, or that it can only be obtained through experience, are simply wrong. Those who have not taken the time to understand airmanship have accepted these myths for decades. In fact, teaching judgment to ourselves is really quite uncomplicated, although certainly not effortless. All we must do is build a solid and complete airmanship structure, and good judgment will naturally flow from it. Nothing of value comes easy. You can't win judgment in the lottery or wake up with it one morning. You can't learn it from Chuck Yeager, your instructor, or from me. It is a personal journey through airmanship, based upon individual strengths, weaknesses, and desires. The trip itself is enlightening and enjoyable, and the destination is well worth the price of the ticket.

The Standard: Consistently Sound Decision Making

Good judgment is the ultimate measuring stick of a superior aviator. Nothing makes aviators feel better than to have someone tell them that they exercised good judgment in a tough situation. But even poor aviators can make good decisions, and the true standard of judgment is consistency. Whoever coined the adage that "Superior airmen use their superior judgment to stay out of situations where they must use their superior skills" was right on target. The inverse is also true. Superior skills, discipline, and knowledge create conditions (i.e., stability, SA, etc.) where good judgment is easy to apply. These attributes of airmanship also create consistency in decision making—the mark of a superior aviator and the antithesis of the rogue.

Principle 10: Good Airmanship Is Contagious

Airmanship excellence is self-sustaining and contagious. The pursuit of excellence is exciting, fun, and infectious. When others sense your enthusiasm with the journey, they too will begin to take a closer look at their own levels and approaches to airmanship. Share your efforts with them. Peer review is one of the most effective and efficient forms of improvement known. Its utility is no secret in the business world, or in the Israeli Air Force, where it is formalized and mandated for combat pilots. Share your discoveries, resources, and insights. Find a partner or build a team.

The Standard: Sharing What You've Learned with Peers

Although the pursuit of airmanship excellence is by definition an individual project, there are great personal and organizational advantages to sharing your efforts with other aviators. First, it is likely that you share local airspace with your colleagues. Their predictability and airmanship directly benefits you, as well as all others who share the same sky. Second, it is always easier to stick with an improvement plan if you know that you are not alone in the effort. Finally, we have a moral obligation to share what works in a high-risk endeavor like flying. The little bit of information that you pass along may be what saves a colleague's life—or yours, someday.

The 10 principles of airmanship are not designed to be all-inclusive, or to be a magic panacea for poor airmanship or for all rogue behavior. They are offered in the hope that they will reinforce the material contained in the preceding chapters, and remind us of the essentials as we pursue personal excellence. The traps of early specialization and gaps in knowledge are all too frequent in many of today's flyers, who then fail to understand why they occasionally get in over their heads and make poor decisions. By keeping the principles in mind, it forces us back to the work to be done—building and refining the entire airmanship package.

As you can see, rogue behavior and airmanship are incompatible. But simply painting a picture of ideal airmanship will not stop rogue behavior. We must also convince aviators who feel they are already practicing good airmanship to look at—and act upon—the new model. This requires that the battle against apathy be fought on lower levels as well.

Operational War: Combating Apathy

Rogue pilots are an unhappy fact of our existence as a community of aviators. Documented evidence shows that they are lethal both to other aviators and to the public at large. They give the typically good reputation of aviation a black eye, and cast all of us in a negative light each and every time they do another stupid thing. Certainly something must be done to bring these noncompliant aviators back into the fold, or to eliminate them from our midst. But how should we respond? What options are available? What if, in those immortal words, "We have found the enemy and he is us?" Obviously, the first step toward defeating the rogue on an organizational or individual level must be an admission that a problem exists.

Overcoming Denial

The reality of the rogue is being denied. This is occurring on at least two levels—individual and organizational. As we have seen throughout the course of this book, often the "can-do" attitude coupled with an "I'm in charge" mentality can lead a normally reliable pilot into rogue behaviors. In the following case study, both the organization and the individual fail to overcome denial.

A Failing Aviator in Denial

On December 1, 1993, Captain Marvin Falitz had a decision to make. The Northwest Airlink pilot was en route from Minneapolis-St. Paul to Hibbing, Minnesota, in a Jetstream BA-3100 with 18 passengers on board. He was cruising above icing conditions, and was concerned about the descent through the ice into the Hibbing airport. The Jetstream has a reputation for poor handling during icing conditions and Falitz made the call to descend rapidly through the icing conditions. Perhaps the term *rapidly* is an understatement, as NTSB investigators later determined that the aircraft was descending at an average of 2225 feet per minute, more than twice the rate allowed by the flight manual.

As the captain started his descent for Hibbing, First Officer Chad Erickson was busy. He had been directed to ensure that the radio-activated lighting system at Hibbing was correctly configured, and was struggling with this task as the captain began his nosedive into the clouds. Perhaps because he was task saturated, or perhaps because Falitz was known as very difficult to work with, the first officer failed to make required callouts of the plane's altitude during the approach to Hibbing. The safety board found that Erickson "was distracted from his duties [to monitor the descent] . . . as a result of poorly planned instructions from the Captain." Safety board member John Lauber went a bit further in his analysis of the breakdown in crew coordination, stating "At critical times, the Captain couldn't resist piling the workload on this guy."

In addition to the peer pressure applied by the captain, which prevented the first officer from accomplishing his monitoring duties, there were equipment considerations. The aircraft was not equipped with the modern ground proximity warning system (GPWS), which would have warned the crew that they were diving into terrain several miles short of their intended point of landing. Flight 5719 never did level off at the minimum descent altitude, and the 2 crew members and 18 passengers impacted the ground in a steep descent approximately 3 miles short of the Hibbing airport. Was this simply a case of task saturation, or was there more involved here?

A Rogue in Waiting

A closer look into the captain's background provides evidence of an aggressive and often abusive crewmember. An article by Steven Thomma in the *Minneapolis Star-Tribune* claimed that the captain had once punched a fellow crewmember and on another occasion walked out of the cockpit, claiming that his colleague "made him sick." He had been called "headstrong, argumentative, and extremely overbearing," and had been accused of intentionally "jostling the flight controls to give passengers a rough ride out of contempt for the airline."[3] Clearly, this troubled captain made crew coordination difficult, if not impossible. A brief look at the captain's training history shows a rogue in the making from an early stage.

According to the accident report, the captain had failed three proficiency checks, and in all three his judgment had been assessed as "unsatisfactory." In two of the three flights, "crew coordination" had also been graded as "unsatisfactory." A previous training captain had said that Falitz had been receptive to crew coordination training, but that it might have been a "cooperate and graduate" approach apparent only during the course itself. Certainly, there were many indicators of a potential rogue in denial.

Many who were interviewed by the company stated that Falitz had been angry with the company he worked for. Perhaps this was due in part to his having to give up a captain's position on the larger SF-340— and 12 percent of his salary—in order to remain in Minneapolis. Most described him as "highly intelligent" but *prone to violate rules he thought to be beneath him.* For example, his personnel file showed violations of company policy regarding sexual harassment, sleeping in flight, and flying with mechanical irregularities. The safety board was on solid ground when it found that the Captain's "poor attitude and lack of adherence to standard operating procedures were major factors in the cause of the accident."[4]

What Could Have Been Done?

The captain's poor interpersonal skills were evident from his earliest days with the company, and his recent anger with the company had led to a situation where he felt "targeted" by various parts of the organization. This feeling of persecution is classic *transference*, a situation in which an individual feels the need to blame others for his or her own predicament. The evaluation and training team had done its part by identifying the problem through check flights, and there was adequate documentation in the captain's personnel file. What else could the company have done?

Short of removal, which is legally very difficult, the company had done an admirable job of identifying the potential problem. Adequate follow-up training might have driven the crew coordination message a bit deeper into the captain's head, but what was really lacking in the company—as in most aviation organizations—was a culture which will not accept or tolerate such self-serving behavior. Five of six first officers who were interviewed by the accident board claimed to be "intimidated" when they flew with this captain. Many pointed out that Falitz was constantly telling them how to do their jobs. The CVR from the accident bears this out. Even as the aircraft was impacting the trees, the captain was telling the first officer how to turn on the runway lights, a task the FO certainly knew how to accomplish. Often the organization provides the umbrella for denial.

Institutional Denial

The second level of denial occurs within an organization, which is motivated to downplay the possibility of rogue behavior by profit, survival, and public affairs concerns. In an industry that survives on the perception of the public, to be associated with rogue behavior is a very bad thing. This is especially true in passenger operations, where companies that have a bad safety record are likely to end up in bankruptcy. In the military, senior officers see a bad safety record as a blot on their records, with serious implications for promotion to the next rank.

Therefore, the tendency to close ranks is almost automatic. Let's take a look at the example of the U.S. Marine Corps EA-6 mishap that killed 20 skiers in the Dolomite Mountains in Italy. The evidence of rogue behavior was rather overwhelming. An aviator (actually, a crew of four aviators) was flying more than 700 feet below the established minimum altitude. This in and of itself is a rogue act, but when combined with the fact that the pilot had not flown a real "visual contour" low-level flight in nearly seven months, and never on this particular route, it becomes obvious that extremely poor judgment was in play. Add to this data the fact that the aircraft was operated well above the recommended speed and was established to have been below the minimum altitudes on more than one leg of the flight, and you have a pretty good picture of an aviator who was intentionally violating regulations. The Marine Corps investigation of the event was quick to point out that this type of flying—affectionately dubbed "flat-hatting" in the Marine Corps—is strictly prohibited. Curiously, no one who was interviewed by the accident investigation board had ever known the pilot to flat-hat. Further, the report stated that no one interviewed had ever known of *anyone* who flat-hatted. Even an unsophisticated aviation reporter from a major magazine picked up on the obvious: "It is interesting that the Marine Corps has a special name for something no one has ever seen." As the investigation into this tragedy progressed, the focus shifted from individual accountability to one of "organizational breakdown" or "information dissemination issues," perhaps another attempt to distance the organization from the rogue.

What can an organization do to short-circuit rogue behaviors?

Top-Down Commitment: The First Key

First and foremost, the value of personal and organizational commitment must be communicated—clearly. Perhaps the finest example of this type of no-nonsense approach I have ever seen was written by General Thomas M. Ryan, the commander of the U.S. Air Force Air Training Command (ATC) in the early 1980s. It came about as a result of—you guessed it—a rash of flight discipline incidents and accidents.

It is simple and direct, precisely the type of communication required to effectively communicate with a rogue.

A VIEW FROM THE TOP

I am extremely concerned about the recent increase in the Air Force aircraft accident rate. The number of accidents attributed to breakdowns in aircrew discipline is most distressing. Such breakdowns cause mishaps and fatalities—losses of lives, hardware and combat capability that we cannot replace.

ATC, as the first command, has a special responsibility to set the standard. ATC instructors build attitudes, professionalism, and flying skills, and I am convinced we are building a solid foundation. I am proud that I see you teaching by example in the air and on the ground.

When there is a breakdown in discipline, the first impulse is to make the rules more restrictive; however, this is seldom the right action. The small number of deviations indicates the problem is generally with the individual and not the system. More specifically, there are two distinct problems. One is the individual who does not follow the rules. The other is the individual who does not know the rules.

I am confident that the majority of our people know the rules, follow the directives, and make proper decisions—and I don't want to unduly restrict them to control the individuals who can't or won't meet our standards. Instead I expect all flying supervisors to follow three guidelines. First, recognize, encourage and reward the people who are accomplishing the mission. Second, identify and motivate the people who have not learned our rules. Third, act decisively to ensure that those who choose not to follow our standards do not fly our aircraft.

This letter stands as a clear policy statement in its own right, but what really makes it effective is the guidance it provides for "all flying supervisors," encouraging them to follow up with their own policy statements. The following is a subset of guidelines developed by Colonel John Block, the wing commander at Mather Air Force Base, who served under Ryan in 1982.

THE THREE TRUTHS

- **Truth 1—Existence:** There exist many rules and regulations that govern flying. The proof of this fact can be found in any pilot's briefcase or bookcase. Dash-Ones, Basic Flight Rules, Instrument Flying procedures, local area procedures, how-to-fly-this-jet manuals, in-flight guides, checklists, flight crew information files (FCIF) . . . they all exist and every pilot has copies of the ones that pertain to his or her aircraft.
- **Truth 2—Responsibility:** It is the responsibility of every pilot, student pilot, copilot, first pilot, aircraft commander, instructor pilot, flight examiner—to know the rules and regulations and to apply them to every flight. Following the rules is not an optional event. It is a critical aspect of the aviation business.
- **Truth 3—Accountability:** Straightforward and simple—those who cannot, and particularly, those who *will not* follow the rules and regulations will not fly our aircraft.

Cascading Policy

This form of "cascading policy" is powerful. It communicates far more than the obvious "I support the boss" approach taken by many midlevel supervisors, who will post—and not amplify—guidance that comes down from above. Colonel Block wanted every aviator in his organization to understand that he was taking an *active role.*

Rogues tend to view passive acceptance of a policy or procedure much differently than active participation. Organizations should make initial statements broad enough to allow subordinate levels to amplify or expand their own positions and gain greater commitment to the cause.

This can be viewed as the antithesis to the culture of noncompliance we have seen in several case studies. By taking action at every level, a culture of compliance is established, and rogues will find few sympathetic souls in these organizations. Persistence is the key to success because rogue pilots have thick skulls. The message of flight discipline must be driven home loudly, clearly, and often.

The organization must also enforce these standards once they are communicated. The words of Richard Thornburgh, the former governor of Pennsylvania, echo these concerns and speak to leaders from all levels of the aviation hierarchy:

> **Subordinates cannot be allowed to speculate as to the values of the organization. Top leadership must give forth clear and explicit signals, lest any confusion or uncertainty exist over what is and what is not permissible conduct. To do otherwise allows informal, and potentially subversive, "codes of conduct" to be transmitted with a wink and a nod, and encourages an inferior ethical system.**

Do you suppose Governor Thornburgh ever ran into a rogue? I'd bet my next six months flight pay that he had.

The final level of warfare that must be waged is on the level of the individual, because there are always those few people who just don't get the word.

Tactical War: Overcoming Individualism and Isolation

Perhaps the most important—and the most difficult—obstacle to overcoming rogue behavior is to reach into the hearts and minds of each and every aviator with the message. There are two problems here. The first is simply getting the word out—one of the primary purposes of this book. The second is to convince those who resist the message that rogues will no longer be tolerated among us.

The "10 Percenter"[5]

"Don't take the machine into the air unless you are satisfied it will fly. . . . Never leave the ground with the motor leaking. . . . Pilots should carry hankies in a handy position to wipe off goggles. . . . Before you begin a landing glide see that no machines are under you. . . . Don't attempt to force machines onto the ground with more than flying speed. The result is bouncing and ricocheting."

The preceding directives are extracted from flying regulations dated January 1920. Ever since the beginning of military aviation, we have been writing regulations and procedures to improve mission effectiveness and safety. For just as long, commanders and supervisors have been plagued with the problem of the *10 percenter*—that minority that never gets the word. They have devised methods, ways, and systems; they have written standard operating procedures (SOPs) all aimed at insuring that *all* crewmembers would know *all* they need to know in order to accomplish the mission safely and efficiently. Yet for some reason, some remain uninformed, and the seeds of the rogue are often sown in this 10 percent.

Without organization and constant follow-up, this education process can be a hopeless venture resulting in duplication of effort, overemphasis in some areas, lack of adequate emphasis in others, conflicting information, and lack of standardization. Too often the operations staff establishes a procedure by covering it in a pilot's meeting, by writing an unnumbered letter to the subordinate parts of the organization, or by calling the chief of training on the phone to pass the word.

Without follow-up by a written directive, these methods are often ineffective. The person who passed the information out has a clear conscience; he or she feels that the job has been done. The procedure itself, however, seldom becomes firm. The spoken word is soon forgotten and often is received only at second, third, or fourth hand; in the process it is usually hung on the bulletin board or filed in the pilot information file or some such place, and there it stays long after the specific procedures it established are changed or rescinded. The 10 percent never get the word.

Of course, it is the responsibility of each individual to seek all current information, but we all know how busy life is these days. Therefore, it becomes vitally important to have a reliable system for disseminating aircrew information. Every flying organization is faced with the task of developing effective and safe procedures and making these procedures known to crewmembers. We simply can't allow the potential rogue the excuse of the 10 percenter.

Once armed with the shared vision of airmanship, and informed with the latest information, the final layer of defense lies with each individual.

The Need for a Personal Code

A safety expert from Down Under argues for the presence of an individualized code, which is the only one, he says, that really works for everyone. Doug Edwards, an Australian safety expert, believes that at least part of the answer to the rogue pilot lies in a move towards greater professionalism. One of the classic markers of a true profession, Edwards argues, is that there exists "a voluntary code, written and maintained by the practitioners themselves." This code is constantly invoked across all levels of training, inspection, and evaluation on both the formal and informal levels. "Professions are self-regulating," states Edwards. He further argues that flying has not yet reached that stage, nor do we appear to be moving in that direction:

> . . . flying ought to be a profession, up there with doctors and engineers. (I know people think it is, but it's not.) Here's the argument: The community expects safe air travel. Passengers entrust their lives to pilots. This is the highest level to which vicarious responsibility can be taken.[6]

The definition of a profession, Edwards points out, must include a self-defined code of ethics, a code which "lays down the things that are simply not done."

The fact is that a good number of pilots—especially rogues—take a perverse pride in disrespecting authority. For many pilots, the FAA, NTSB, or other regulating authorities are the targets of scorn and disrespect. Edwards says that this mindset "legitimizes disobedience" in the mind of the rogue. This brings us to our final aspect of rogue behavior—contempt for authority and others.

Combating Contempt

Perhaps the toughest nut to crack is the flyer who knows what good airmanship is, who is in possession of all of the latest regulatory information, and who still takes unnecessary risks just for the hell of it. This is the subset of the rogue that the aviation community must identify—and then remove. This can be a difficult task.

There are three keys to this process. First, supervisors and fellow aviators must be able to identify rogue behaviors. Hopefully, this book will aid in that process. Second, the same group must have the moral courage to report the behaviors to those in a position to do something about it. Finally, once informed, these leaders must act. Looking back to our study of the quintessential rogue Bob Hammond, the leaders were aware of the problem for over three years, but for some reason were unable to act. This, in turn, caused other aviators to lose faith in the leadership and develop a twisted view of airmanship. Rogues beget rogues.

The ability to remove rogues is tied directly to the ability to effectively document their actions. In many cases, it can be a very legalistic, and often painful, process. This is because rogues are often popular, and there will nearly always be a group of flyers that will testify that the rogue is the epitome of the great pilot. Understanding airmanship—true airmanship—will be key in these cases. The difficult process is made much easier when you look upon the myriad of tragedies that rogues have visited upon innocent bystanders in the past. When you are forced to remove a contemptuous rogue, realize that you are on the side of the angels.

The Last Word on Rogues?

It has been the stated purpose of this book to further the debate on aviation misfits. To that end, I hope it has been successful. It is not—repeat, *not*—the last word on rogue pilots. Further research and discussion is needed into the breadth and depth of the problem. How many rogues are there? In what situations are they most likely to emerge? Why do good pilots go bad? What are the most effective methods for dealing with a rogue? Is the effort to rehabilitate a rogue worth the cost? Do we have the systems in place to track rogue pilots if they switch companies or change aviation fields?

These and many other questions need to be addressed before we will be able to eliminate rogue behavior. Until then, we fight the battle against the rogue one pilot at a time, beginning with the one in the mirror.

Acknowledgments

"NO MAN IS AN ISLAND." The words of John Donne were true when he wrote them in the sixteenth century, and they certainly apply to this project. I began my quest to describe the rogue several years ago, and these pages are filled with the contributions of dozens of friends, colleagues, and, in a few cases, complete strangers. To protect their anonymity, I shall not name them here, but you know who you are, and I sincerely thank all who provided the vignettes, documents, interviews, and leads on the rogues described herein.

In addition, I would like to thank the U.S. Air Force; the Dean of the Faculty at the Air Force Academy, Brigadier General Dave Wagie; and the head of the USAF Academy Department of History, Colonel Carl Reddel. Their support was essential in making my job flexible enough to pursue aviation safety and pilot performance—two topics not in my job description as a history professor, but clearly a moral responsibility that ties in closely to the core values of the Air Force and the Academy: *Integrity first—Service before self—Excellence in all that we do.*

Once again, a special thanks to Shelly Carr, the greatest acquisitions editor in the business, and to everyone else at McGraw-Hill, as well as to my father-in-law Hosia Blankenship, who provided essential technical computer support at a critical juncture in this project, and to my son Jacob, for proofreading my manuscript.

A loving thank-you to my beautiful wife Shari and my high-energy sons Trent and Jacob for their support and assistance in keeping me focused on what is really important in life. A long-overdue thank-you to

June and Joe Kern, my Mom and Dad, and my brothers Mike and Joe, who all contributed to my sense of priorities, values, and service.

Finally, and most important, none of this would be possible without the undeserved gifts and saving grace given to me from my Lord Jesus. As in all things, I thank Him first and last.

Notes

Introduction

1. P. Shenon, "Defense Department 'Cannot Dispute' Recklessness in Italy Jet Accident," *New York Times*, February 5, 1998, p. 1.
2. C. S. Lewis, *Mere Christianity*, New York: Macmillan, 1943, p. 113.

Chapter 1

1. The KC-135 is a Boeing 707 four-engine jet used as an air refueler for other Air Force aircraft.
2. The bomber pilot's fond euphemism for air refueling pilots. Tanker toads called their bomber brethren "bomber pukes."
3. Reprinted in part with permission from *Flying Safety* magazine. Michael Fagan, "The Best Pilot in the Squadron," March 1982.

Chapter 2

1. Pseudonyms used throughout. All quotations come directly from the official U.S. Air Force accident investigation report approved for public release or from personal interviews by the author.

Chapter 3

1. This historical material is taken from *The Origin of Air Warfare*, published by the historical office of the Italian Air Force, 1961, and translated by Renato D'Orlandi.
2. Information taken from Babette Andre's excellent article in the online newsletter *General Aviation News and Flyer*, December 20, 1996.

Chapter 7

1.   Reprinted with permission from *Flying Safety* magazine. Wing Commander Graeme R. Peel, RAAF, "The Failing Aviator," August 1992.

Chapter 8

1.   This information is taken primarily from the U.S. government report on the Blackhawk shootdown.
2.   Michael G. McConnell, *AFR 110-14 USAF Accident Investigation Report*, vol. 1, 1994, p. 7.
3.   The reader may recall that after less than one week of air combat during Desert Storm, Saddam chose to fly all his remaining combat aircraft into Iran, rather than lose them to the United States.
4.   Identification Friend or Foe (IFF) is the primary means for identification beyond visual range in a hostile area. There are four modes that can be interrogated, and in this case, the helicopters had not changed over from the "outside the area" to the "inside the area" codes on Mode 1.
5.   This was certainly a weak defense, inasmuch as the wingman would fire a heat-seeking missile into the second Black Hawk less than a minute later.
6.   National Transportation Safety Board, *In-Flight Loss of Control and Subsequent Collision with Terrain, Cessna 175B, N35207, Cheyenne, WY*, Report PB97-910402 NTSB/AAR-97-02 SEA96FA079, Washington, DC: NTSB, 1996.

Chapter 9

1.   Neil Williams, *Aerobatics*, Shrewbury, England: Airlife Publishing, 1991.

Chapter 10

1.   John J. Nance, *Blind Trust: How Deregulation Has Jeopardized Airline Safety and What You Can Do About It*, New York: William Morrow, 1986.
2.   Nance, *Blind Trust*, p. 21.
3.   Nance, *Blind Trust*, p. 38.
4.   C. H. Coolidge, Jr., *AFI 51-503 Report of Aircraft Accident Investigation on USAF CT-43 73-1149*, U.S. Air Force, 1996, p. 60.
5.   Coolidge, *AFI 51-503 Report*, p. 60.
6.   Coolidge, *AFI 51-503 Report*, TAB EE-1/10.
7.   "Accident chain" refers to a series and sequence of events that lead to a mishap, any one of which if avoided would have theoretically "broken" the chain.
8.   William Langewiesche, "The Lessons of ValuJet 592," *The Atlantic Monthly Unbound*, March 1998, p. 6. Internet: www.theatlantic.com/issues/98mar/valujet1.htm.
9.   Michael Crichton, *Airframe*, New York: Alfred A. Knopf, 1996, p. 107.

10. *Miami Herald*, May 4, 1997, p. 1.
11. Rodney Stich, "Those Actually at Fault for the ValuJet Crash: An Open Letter," Internet: www.flight592.com/flight592discussion/_disc5/0000003b.htm.
12. Rodney Stich, *Unfriendly Skies*, 3d ed., Albuquerque, N. Mex.: Diablo Western Press, 1990.

Chapter 11

1. Foreword by John Shaud in Tony Kern, *Redefining Airmanship*, New York: McGraw-Hill, 1997.
2. For the complete discussion of airmanship, including detailed chapters on each element of the model, see Kern, *Redefining Airmanship*, from which this section was adapted.
3. Steven Thomma, "Pilot in Crash Near Hibbing Had Checkered Flight Record," *Minneapolis Star-Tribune*, December 17, 1993, p. B-1.
4. John J. Osland and J. Christensen, "Hibbing Air Crash Blamed on Captain," *Minneapolis Star-Tribune*, May 25, 1994, p. 12A.
5. Paraphrased and reprinted with permission of *Flying Safety* magazine.
6. Doug Edwards, personal correspondence, 1997.

Bibliography

AeroKnowledge ASRS (CD-ROM) accession no. 81432, Aeroknowledge, Trenton, N.J., 1995.

Aircraft Accident Investigation Board Report: *U.S. Army UH-60 Black Hawk Helicopters 87-26000 and 88-26060*, vol. 2, 1994.

Aircraft Accident Investigation Board Report: *U.S. Army UH-60 Black Hawk Helicopters 87-26000 and 88-26060*, vol. 12, 1994.

Alter, Jonathan: "National Affairs: Maiden Flight," *Newsweek*, April 22, 1996.

André, Babette: "Captain Jepp, the Gentle Air-Mapping Pioneer, Passes Away," Internet: General Aviation News and Flyer at http://www1.drive.net/evird.acgi$pass*222 . . . /ganflyer/dec20-1996/capt._jepp_dies.html15, 1996.

ASRS Directline No. 8, Internet: http://www-afo.arc.nasa.gov/ASRS/dl8, 1995.

Aviation Monthly Safety Summary and Report, "Accident Statistics," April, 1996.

Baidukov, Georgiy: *Russian Lindbergh: The Life of Valery Chkalov*, trans. Peter Belov, Smithsonian Institute Press, Washington, D.C., 1991.

Baron, R. A., and D. Byrne: *Social Psychology: Understanding Human Interaction*, 7th ed., Allyn and Bacon, Boston, 1994.

Beaty, David: *The Naked Pilot: The Human Factor in Aircraft Accidents*. Airlife Publishing, Shrewsbury, U.K., 1995.

Block, John: Personal correspondence, April 1998.

Brannigan, M.: "Captain WOW: When Is Mental State of a Pilot Grounds for Grounding Him?," *The Wall Street Journal*, New York, March 7, 1996.

Bringle, Donald: "The topgun mentality," *Proceedings*, April, 1996. pp. 8–9.

Crichton, Michael: *Airframe*, Alfred A. Knopf, New York, 1996.

Coolidge, C. H., Jr.: *AFI 51-503 Report of Aircraft Accident Investigation on USAF CT-43 73-1149*, vol. 1, U.S. Air Force, 1996.

Degani, A., and E. Wiener: "Philosophy, Policies, Procedures and Practices: The Four 'P's of Flight Deck Operations," *Aviation Psychology in Practice*, 1994, pp. 45–67.

Deitz, Shelia R., and William E. Thoms (eds.): *Pilots, Personality, and Performance: Human Behavior and Stress in the Skies*, Quorum Books, New York, 1991.

Department of Transport and Regional Development Bureau of Air Safety Investigation (Australia): *De Havilland Canada Dash 8 VH-JSI, Broome, Western Australia*, May 17, 1996.

Dernovoy, Vladimir: "The Russian Wings," *PENC UN* (in-flight magazine), June, 1998.

D'Orlandi, Renato (trans.): *The Origins of Air Warfare*, 2d ed., Historical Office of the Italian Air Force, Rome, 1961.

Edens, E.: "Individual differences underlying cockpit error," unpublished doctoral dissertation, National Technical Information Service, Springfield, Va., 1991.

Edwards, Doug: 1997. *Fit to Fly*, CopyRight Publishing, Brisbane, Australia.

Fagan, Michael: "The Best Pilot in the Squadron," *Flying Safety*, March 1982.

Fry, G. E., and R. F. Reinhardt: "Personality Characteristics of Jet Pilots as Measured by the Edwards Personal Preference Schedule," *Aerospace Medicine*, **40:**484–486 (1969).

Gregorich, S., Robert L. Helmreich, John A. Wilhelm, and Thomas Chidester: "Personality Based Clusters as Predictors of Aviator Attitudes and Performance," in R. S. Jensen (ed.), *Proceedings of the 5th International Symposium on Aviation Psychology*, vol. II, Columbus, Ohio, 1989. pp. 686–691.

Harris, Sherwood: *The First to Fly: Aviation's Pioneer Days*, Simon and Schuster, New York, 1970.

Hawkins, F. H.: *Human Factors in Flight*, 2d ed., Ashgate Publishers, Brookfield, Vt., 1987.

Inkso, C. A., R. H. Hoyle, R. L. Pinkley, G. Y. Hong, R. M. Slim, B. Dalton, Y. H. Lin, P. P. Ruffin, G. J. Dardis, P. R. Brenthal, and J. Schloper: "Individual-Group Discontinuity: The Role of a Consensus Rule," *Journal of Experimental Social Psychology*, **24:**505–519 (1988).

Jensen, R. S.: *Pilot Judgment and Crew Resource Management*, Avebury Aviation Publishers, Aldershot, U.K., 1995.

Kelly, Bill: "NDB's High Margin of Error," *Aviation Safety*, June 15, 1996.

————: "Regulations Are Made to Be Broken, Right?" USAF Flying Safety Magazine, November, 1994, pp. 17–18.

Kern, T.: *Flight Discipline*, New York, McGraw-Hill, 1998.

————: "A Historical Analysis of US Air Force Tactical Aircrew Error in Operations Desert Shield/Storm, U.S. Army Command and General Staff College monograph, Fort Leavenworth, Kans., 1995.

————: The Human Factor Newsletter. U.S. Air Force Air Education and Training Command, Randolph AFB, Tex., 1994.

————: *Redefining Airmanship*, New York, McGraw-Hill, 1997.

Kitfield, James: "Crisis of Conscience," *Government Executive*, October, 1995.

Langewiesche, William: "The Lessons of ValuJet 592," *The Atlantic Monthly Unbound*, March, 1998. Internet: www.theatlantic.com/issues/98mar/valujet1.htm.

Lewis, C. S.: *Mere Christianity*, Macmillan, New York, 1943.

————: *The Screwtape Letters*. New York, Touchstone, 1961.

Lienhard, John H.: "The First Daredevil," *Engines of Our Ingenuity*, no. 1225, Internet: http://www.uh.edu/admin/engines/epil225.htm.

McConnell, Michael G.: *AFR 110-14 USAF Accident Investigation Report*, vol. 1, June 1994.

Merrero, Frank: *Lincoln Beachey: The Man Who Owned the Sky*, Scotwall Associates, San Francisco, 1997.

Monan, W. P.: "Distraction—A Human Factor in Air Carrier Hazard Events, *NASA Aviation Safety Reporting System: Ninth Quarterly Report*, National Aeronautics and Space Administration, Moffett Field, Ca., 1978, pp. 2–23.

Nance, John J.: *Blind Trust: How Deregulation Has Jeopardized Airline Safety and What You Can Do About It*, William Morrow, New York, 1986.

National Transportation Safety Board: *In-Flight Loss of Control and Subsequent Collision with Terrain, Cessna 177B, N35207, Cheyenne, WY*, Report No. PB97-910402 NTSB/AAR-97-02 SEA96FA079, Washington, D.C., 1996.

National Transportation Safety Board: *A Review of Flightcrew-Involved, Major Accidents of U.S. Air Carriers, 1978 Through 1990. Safety Study*, Report No. PB94-917001 NTSB/SS-94-01, Washington, D.C., 1994.

Novello, J. R., and Z. I. Youssef: "Psycho-Social Studies in General Aviation: Personality Profiles of Male Pilots," *Aerospace Medicine*, **45**:185–188 (1974).

Olcott, J.: "Complacency: The Silent Killer," *National Business Pilots Association Magazine*, June, 1996.

Osland, John J., and J. Christensen: "Hibbing Air Crash Blamed on Captain," *Minneapolis Star-Tribune*, May 25, 1994.

Parasuraman, R., R. Molly, and I. Singh: "Performance Consequences of Automation-Induced Complacency," *International Journal of Aviation Psychology*, **3**(1):1–23 (1993).

Peel, Graeme R.: "The Failing Aviator," *Flying Safety*, August, 1992.

Phillips, R. J.: *A Principle Within: Ethical Military Leadership*, presented at the Joint Services Conference on Professional Ethics XVII, Washington, D.C., January 25–26, 1996.

Rawnsley, Judith H.: *Total Risk: Nick Leeson and the Fall of Barings Bank*, HarperCollins, New York, 1995.

Reed, Robert C.: *Train Wrecks: A Pictorial History of Accidents on the Main Line*, Bonanza Books, New York, 1968.

Reinhardt, Richard: "Day of the Daredevil," *Invention & Technology*, Fall 1995.

Rippon, T. S., and E. G. Manuel: "The Characteristics of Successful and Unsuccessful Aviators, with Special Reference to Temperament," *The Lancet* (London), September 28, 1918, pp. 411–415.

Roseberry, C. R.: *The Challenging Skies: The Colorful Story of Aviation's Most Exciting Years*, Doubleday, Garden City, New York, 1966.

Sheehan, Neil: *The Arnheiter Affair*, Random House, New York, 1971.

Shennon, P.: "Defense Department 'Cannot Dispute' Recklessness in Italy Jet Accident," *New York Times*, February 5, 1998, p. 1.

Smith, Perry M.: *Taking Charge: A Practical Guide for Leaders*, National Defense University Press, Washington, D.C., 1986.

Stich, Rodney: "Those Actually at Fault for the ValuJet Crash," Internet: www.flight592.com/flight592discussion/_disc5/0000003b.htm.

———: *Unfriendly Skies*, 3d ed., Diablo Western Press, Albuquerque, N. Mex., 1990.

Sumwalt, R. L., and A. W. Watson: "What ASRS Incident Data Tell About Flight Crew Performance During Aircraft Malfunctions, *The Ohio State University Eighth International Symposium on Aviation Psychology*, Ohio State University, Columbus, Ohio, 1995, pp. 758–764.

Thomma, Steven: "Pilot in Crash Near Hibbing Had Checkered Flight Record," *Minneapolis Star-Tribune*, December 17, 1993, p. B-1.

Treadwell, Terry C., and Alan C. Wood: *German Knights of the Air 1914–1918*, Brassey's, Herndon, Va., 1997.

U.S. Air Force: *Aircrew Awareness and Attention Management Workbook*, Langley AFB, Va., 1994.

Wiener, E. L.: "Complacency: Is the Term Useful for Air Safety?," *Proceedings of the 26th Corporate Aviation Safety Seminar*, Flight Safety Foundation, Denver, Colo., 1981, pp. 116–125.

Williams, Neil: *Aerobatics*, Airlife Publishing, Shrewsbury, U.K., 1991.

Wolfe, Sidney, Mary Gabay, et al.: *Questionable Doctors: Disciplined by the States or the Federal Government*, Public Citizen Health Research Group, Washington, D.C., 1996.

Index

Note: Boldface numbers indicate illustrations.

About the Author

LIEUTENANT COLONEL TONY KERN has flown various types of military aircraft throughout his 18 years in the Air Force, including service as a B-1B bomber instructor pilot and flight examiner. He is one of the Air Force's leading experts on aviation safety and crew resource management (CRM). Colonel Kern has been instrumental in institutionalizing human factors into the military environment, having held key leadership and staff positions at the Air Education and Training Command. He holds advanced degrees in political science and military history, as well as a doctorate in higher education, specializing in aviation training system design. He has published several papers and articles on education and training, leadership, safety, and aviation human factors. His first book, *Redefining Airmanship*, was a major work detailing the historical essence of successful flight operations and established clear benchmarks for airmanship excellence. His second book, *Flight Discipline*, further defined this critical cornerstone of professionalism. He lives with his wife and two sons in Monument, Colorado, and teaches flying and history at the U.S. Air Force Academy.